"From the very beginning of her recording career, Jewel's lyrics reflected the America she lived in, with her conversational poetic touch. My friend Ben Keith brought her to my ranch to record, collecting our favorite musicians together for her early songs. The result, the enduring *Pieces of You*, was a great record. Jewel's lyrics resonated with the times. In this, her first memoir, she has a lot to reflect on and the touch to tell her story well."

—Neil Young

"Jewel's life in *Never Broken* reminded me so much of my own. But if we hadn't come from hardship and nothing, we wouldn't have made something out of ourselves. Her life is in her songs and in her voice, and after knowing her, I know it's her soul. She is honest and tender yet has a backbone and a fire that only comes from her roots. In her stories about her childhood I can't help but see so much of my own. The good, the bad, the love, the heartbreak. It's all there, and it's all Jewel."

—Loretta Lynn

"Jewel is a truth-teller. *Never Broken* occupies that sacred space of soulful storytelling, hard-earned wisdom, and beautiful writing. I couldn't put it down, and I can't stop thinking about it. This is a book that lingers in your heart."

—Brené Brown, PhD, author of *Rising Strong*

"*Never Broken* reads like one of Jewel's songs—it's vulnerable, passionate, and forthright. And it tells a compelling story, in this case, one about a young, gifted woman's journey to becoming an adult and an artist. Her writing, too, is like her voice, which, bolstered by sturdy melodies, rings with honesty and clarity. This book is filled with deep, rewarding pleasures."

—Anthony DeCurtis, contributing editor, *Rolling Stone*

"Though I first came to know Jewel by listening to her music and pretending we were friends, our relationship evolved into a real one when we met and recognized a kindred spirit in each other. No one has given Jewel anything she didn't work hard for. *Never Broken* is her story of survival—part memoir, part wisdom, and wholly appealing to everyone."

—Nia Vardalos

"Jewel's *Never Broken* is the perfect celebrity memoir. . . . *Never Broken* wants to be the story of a young woman from the hinterlands who stumbles into various experiences and reacts just the way her reader would. But her knowledge keeps sneaking through."

—Daniel D'Addario, *Time*

"Jewel renders an intimate portrait of a young woman who, although immensely talented, has spent her life 'surviving and recovering and problem solving since being a toddler.' [*Never Broken*] is lushly descriptive, chronicling the author's earliest days on the old 'homestead,' singing in saloons, busking in Mexico, and later living out of broken-down automobiles while trying to make a living in the music business. The author mines her psyche for the benefit of both herself and anyone else embroiled in profound emotional crisis. . . . A moving musical essay that should strike all the right notes with a wide selection of readers."   —*Kirkus Reviews*

"Jewel's evocative and captivating how-to for living a full and creative life. . . . Jewel's writing is conversational poetry, filled with rich details, as she explores her heritage or explains what she taught herself about music, art, and the music business. . . . Her book will delight her fans [and] reach beyond that base to those intrigued by what it takes to be successful after years of plugging away. Jewel's lyrics, generously included throughout, reflect her authenticity and generosity."
—*Publishers Weekly*

"Singer and poet Jewel has lived a famous rags-to-riches story and now tells all the painful details of her turbulent life in this appealing memoir. . . . Fans will be impressed by the singer's tenacity and most likely shocked [as] she chronicles her struggle to earn a living, regain control of her finances, and maintain her marriage. . . . Her determination to carve out a happy life in the midst of so much conflict is admirable, and her honesty is both bracing and appreciated. . . . Her story is sure to inspire."   —*Booklist* (starred review)

"A deeply personal memoir [that] reveals a cycle of struggles and abuse that, until now, she had kept private. . . . Jewel reflects on an abusive upbringing and the highs and lows of her professional career, including discovering that she was broke at what should have been the pinnacle of success."   —*The Tennessean*

"Jewel's intuitive insights into her life are gifts that must be opened, shared, and experienced. Courageous and inspiring, *Never Broken* is the story in all of us dying to be told, deserving to breathe, and taking us home to our authentic selves."
—Miles Adcox, CEO, OnSite Workshops

jewel
never broken

songs are only half the story

BLUE RIDER PRESS
New York

blue
rider
press

An imprint of Penguin Random House LLC
375 Hudson Street
New York, New York 10014

Blue Rider Press is a registered trademark and its colophon
is a trademark of Penguin Random House LLC

Pages 385–86 constitute an extension of this copyright page.

Library of Congress Cataloging-in-Publication Data

Jewel, date.
Never broken : songs are only half the story / Jewel.
p.   cm.
ISBN 978-0-399-17433-9 (hardcover)
1. Jewel, date.   2. Singers—United States—Biography.   I. Title.
ML420J38A3   2015   2015024911
728.42164092—dc23
[B]
ISBN 978-0-399-18572-4 (paperback)

Printed in the United States of America
3   5   7   9   10   8   6   4

Book design by Meighan Cavanaugh

Penguin is committed to publishing works of quality and integrity.
In that spirit, we are proud to offer this book to our readers;
however, the story, the experiences, and the words
are the author's alone.

I dedicate this book to

anyone who is struggling in darkness,

seeking to know their light.

The privilege of a lifetime is being who you are.

—*Joseph Campbell*

be ground
be crumbled
so wildflowers will come up where you are

—*Rumi*

MY NEW SHAPE

40
40 years old
when did this happen

blonde
but gray sneaks in
I'm sure
though I would never know
because I lose myself in
the (hair color) bottle

I am fit enough
maybe more fit
than when I was 20

I have less hair
thanks to an underactive
thyroid
stress induced they say

. . .

I use Latisse to make
my eyelashes grow

I text 50 times a day

I have a scar
above my pubic bone
from a C-section
when they lifted my
sweet boy
from my abdomen

I am newly separated
from my husband
shocking
would have lost the ranch
on that bet

. . .

actually, I did . . .

basically
I am a blank canvas
well not blank maybe—
an unwritten chapter
is perhaps the better metaphor

sure I have a history
a hell of one, actually
I am dinged-up
and weary and my heart
is sore
but really
in the most essential way
I am as new as I ever have been
the best is not behind me
damnit
it's ahead of me
for the first time

I never stood a chance before
because
I was a slave to what I could not see
a puppet to past patterns
but I have taken a knife
and carved myself free
it cost me dearly
but what I gained is myself

the truest treasure is
a soul who believes
in its own existence—
and I believe!
I am here!
I am showing up!
I have to go slowly
so I don't skip by
what this moment is

divorce

D
I
V
O
R
C
E

this is the best
worst time
of my life

it is a death
a tragedy
a sad and fiery end
to a dream I desperately wanted
the loss of innocence for my son
and God how this breaks my
    heart

. . .

but it is also a second chance
and I can't let sorrow
or self-loathing
or reproach
rob me
of the gift

from fire comes
a stark silence
as flame drives
what is most essential
deep inside

all else burned away

I let all else leave me

I keep only what is most truly me
thank God
for this fire
bless this fire

bless this new shape

I am sexual
I am spiritual
I am mother
I am playful child

I am
unapologetic

U
N
A
P
O
L
O
G
E
T
I
C

it took me
40 years
but I'm here
finally
it has been
hard-won
and you can bet
I'm not giving it up
for anyone
no more submissive posture
no more tentative shape
no more body
bent like a question mark

. . .

I know what's best for me
above all others

finally
I reserve the sacred right
to redefine myself at will

I can stand in my own power
and not make myself small
for anyone
to make them feel safe

I will shrink myself
no longer
to make
any human feel
secure

I spent a lifetime being small
for those closest to me
but this is not the woman
my son will know

my son will see my new shape
my intuition speaking loudly

he will see a woman integrated
a businesswoman
an artist
a nerd
an intellect
a heart
for I am all things

I am woman

W
O
M
A
N

and

W
H
O
L
E

human.

Dear reader,

I have been overwhelmed with the warm response to this book, and I want to take a moment not only to express my gratitude but to acknowledge the feedback I have received.

I have been asked by journalists why I chose to write this book and share so much. My answer has been that while I am aware the details of my life are unique to me, the themes of struggle, hardship, and heartbreak are not unique to any life story. If we don't share the truths in our lives—the bad along with the good—then we miss out on knowing we are not alone, and even more important, that there is hope for us. So many of you have shared with me your stories of struggle and of your own triumphs, and it has touched me deeply.

I have been asked by readers whether there were any exercises or things I did to overcome the challenges in my life and retrain myself to build healthier habits and behaviors. In fact I did practice many over the years. So I have built a website where they can live, in hopes that the tools that created change in my life and helped retrain me to make better decisions for myself might benefit any of you seeking to be not merely a passenger in life but the driver.

At the end of this book there are twenty principles that each helped me to avoid repeating the patterns of abuse I was raised with. On my website, www.jewelneverbroken.com, I have expanded them into easy-to-navigate exercises that I still use for strengthening my sense of inner peace and resiliency. They are simple practices and easy to use in your daily life. I have also created a community board for individuals seeking other like-minded people, in hopes that visitors can reach out for support from kind people who also want to be the best versions of themselves.

The website will continue to evolve so that more experts in the fields of personal growth may connect with an audience seeking a deeper sense of purpose. I believe that no matter your background or resources, we all deserve to be the architects of our lives, to add meaning and intention into everything we do for ourselves and our families.

Hope to see you on the site, and until then, sending love to you on your journey, wherever it finds you.

Jewel

foreword

I should probably not be here today. I should probably not even be alive. Being alive, I should have become an addict, knocked up as a teenager, or stuck romantically in a cycle of abuse. If you look at my life at any stage you might've said, *This girl will never make it*, and you probably would've been right. What I had going for me, however, was that at a fairly young age I figured out what I wanted. Happiness. You have to know what you want to ever be able to have it.

Here are the broad strokes: My two brothers and I were raised by a musical family, and I spent my early childhood performing with my parents in Anchorage for tourists. When I was eight, my mother left and my dad moved us to the family homestead in rural Alaska, a log cabin with creek water to drink, no plumbing or most modern conveniences. My dad did the best he could, but handled the stress of being a single parent by drinking and perpetuating the only parenting style he knew—the one he was raised with—which was creative at its best, and abusive at its worst.

At age fifteen I was finally fed up, depressed, and worried that if I didn't make a break for it I would lose myself entirely. I decided to move out. Aware that by doing so, the probability of me becoming just another statistic was high. Kids like me end up doing the same thing we saw while being raised . . . there are rarely happy endings. I wanted to beat those odds, and I knew that to do so I would have to use all my logic, heart, wit, and talent to end up differently. To be different, I had to act different. Which left me with a problem: how do you act differently than the way you are taught? This question set me on a journey to learn a new way of being, so I could create a life with a different outcome, rather than just feel fated to repeat the cycles and patterns I was familiar with. I vowed to study myself and my life like a scientist, to see what did and didn't work—how to get what I lacked and so desperately wanted: happiness.

So at fifteen I moved out on my own and paid my own rent on a one-room cabin by working several jobs. I got a scholarship to a private school at sixteen. I put myself through high school and graduated. I became homeless later that year. I was discovered by record labels at nineteen. I became a worldwide phenomenon at twenty-one, traveling the globe nonstop. I fell in love at twenty-five. At thirty, I found out that not only was all my money gone, but I was several million dollars in debt. The same year I came to feel that my mom, who was also my manager, was not the person I believed she was. And here I am today. Forty years old, newly divorced. I earned back a fortune, I'm discovering new ways to do business. Finally, there is my greatest success: I am lucky enough to be a mother. And I'm still continuing the journey, relearning how to be truly safe in the world, and it isn't what I thought. It's not by avoiding pain in life—that's impossible—it's by knowing that safety is in vulnerability, not in armor. It sounds counterintuitive but it's true. Life takes each of us to the anvil, shapes us with fire and hammer, and some of us break while some of us become stronger, more able to face the day. Even happy.

The great myth is that you need money, time, love, education, expensive therapy, a house, a fill-in-the-blank to get the happiness you want. I am here to tell you, *you need nothing other than what is in your heart*. How much do you believe that you deserve something, and how willing are you to do whatever it takes to achieve it? Personal growth, fulfillment, success, and even happiness—be it personal or professional—are not for the lazy, for the faint of heart, for the victim, for the one who passes the buck. Change is for the warrior. If you look in the mirror and say, *I am willing to be the one who is accountable and take responsibility for my own happiness and the shape of my own life*, then I welcome you as a friend on this journey. I believe in you. I believe we are whole, intact, and capable of claiming the quality of life we all deserve. This I know: our essential self cannot be erased no matter what we endure.

The truth is that no one can keep you captive. No one can keep you unhappy. No one can keep you abused. Our lives rise to the level we accept. I do believe we can rise from the screaming blood of our losses, of extreme pain, physically debilitating emotion, psychological neglect, and apathy, and not merely survive, but thrive. We do not need to let our histories or our losses define us except in the way we choose. We can use them as fuel to create real depth, beauty, connectedness, and compassion in our lives. Our stories can make us exceptional people, not damaged ones. If we choose to be truthful with ourselves. And if we choose to digest and release the pain rather than try to avoid it. This is how pain accumulates and creates more pain, leading to neurosis, pathology, and brittleness of spirit.

We cannot always control or avoid what happens to us, but we can control what it does to our spirit. And the quality of our spirit becomes the filter through which we see life. And as the philosophers say, reality is our perception of it. I believe those words. Our reality is what we believe it to be. What we believe informs our thoughts. Our thoughts inform our actions. Our actions build our lives.

My own life has been an exercise in challenging my beliefs so that I could reimagine my future. So that I could avoid becoming the statistic and instead become the architect who tried to consciously draw the lines of her own life, free of the heartbreak that birthed me.

When I first left home, I got a few jobs, singing locally and giving horse rides to tourists, and at night I would get out my notepad and pen to write. I called my journal "the happiness project," and I had no idea that it would lead me not only on a journey of deep personal discovery, but would also lead me from the fishing village of Homer, Alaska, to songwriting, to the White House, to the Vatican, to the cover of *Time* magazine, and beyond. Most important, the exercise of writing and looking inward led me to myself, and to discovering my own definition of happiness. It is a journey I am still on today. But I get ahead of myself. Let's start at the beginning.

pioneer spirit

My name is Jewel Kilcher and I am an Alaskan. My grandparents on both sides helped to settle the state in the late 1940s, when it was a territory still. When my grandparents settled in Homer, it was a frontier town, a small fishing village with very few modern conveniences. It might as well have been the 1840s. My dad rode in a horse and wagon to town when the tide was low enough to give passage below the steep cliffs of Kachemak Bay. Living was hard, and those who were drawn to Alaska in these early days, before its statehood, were self-sufficient and idealistic, wanting to carve out a new existence in an untamed land. The women were incredibly strong, often raising kids and also running homesteads while the men were out hunting and on adventures. This meant killing and canning food, keeping livestock, shoeing horses, felling trees, haul-ing water, making jams, fishing, drying salmon, and keeping the precious sourdough starter alive and well in an icebox. Beheading and boiling chickens, preserving cooking fat in lard cans . . . the list goes on.

I have heard stories of the larger city of Anchorage during this time, when women and young girls and boys were not allowed on the streets after 9 p.m. for fear of rape. The streets were mud, and citizens carried firearms openly. It felt as lawless as the much older Wild West depicted in the movies. The people were spirited, with flint in their eyes and dreams in their hearts, looking for gold claims or just an escape from the rest of the world to live the way they wanted to live.

I owe much of my success to the pioneer women of Alaska. Today they are still strong and self-sufficient, not wilting flowers waiting for a man to help. They shoe their own horses and peel logs and build homes and get anything done that needs doing. They are feminine and wild as a mountain meadow. I owe a tremendous debt to the women I was raised amid. My paternal grandmother, Ruth, was a supreme example, and she and her husband, Yule, taught each of their eight children everything that was necessary to survive. While women in Alaska certainly knew they were physically weaker than most men, it never meant they weren't clever enough to find a way to get the job done. My aunts used chain saws and axes like an artist's chisel to build furniture and cut lumber. They operate their own businesses, travel the world, run cattle, and are Marine Corps colonels and chefs. I was so lucky to be raised believing in some part of myself—believing that if I put my mind to something, I should be able to figure it out. My parents did not coddle me, and I was allowed to explore my mind. I read books by great authors and never assumed my mind had a sex, much less a weaker one. It wasn't until years later, as I traveled the rest of the world, that I realized this was something unique. This is not a message many young girls hear during their childhood, and we do them a great disservice. I was not a child who had a lot of self-esteem, and had little else working in my favor. Often I felt broken and insecure, ugly and odd, but this one core belief was a tremendous blessing that gave me the courage to face my life and take it on my own terms. The fabric of my very being would become so threadbare, but when push came to shove, this belief was enough at times to pull me through. It is at the core of my character, and something I can take no credit for.

I also owe much of my adventurous spirit to the spirit of Alaska. It is a big, untamed country that has much to offer for those willing to fight for it. The land provided for us, but it was never a simple give. The rivers are cold and strong, full of glacial silt that will fill your boots and drown you. The bay is full of fish, but the weather can turn quickly and a mere five minutes of exposure to that gray, cold water is enough for hypothermia to set in. The mountains are full of glaciers, fresh water, game, and berries, but navigating them is exacting and they demand grit and respect. The summers are full of daylight—the sun never sets at the peak of summer solstice—providing a short but productive growing season for those willing to weed gardens and fields of potatoes. The soil is black and rich, full of minerals from glacial runoff. The grass is stout and keeps livestock in good flesh. I remember riding my horse all day at the head of Kachemak Bay, where the three glacial rivers meet and where we would graze our cattle for the summer. It was open-range grazing, no fences, and it was a truly beautiful sight to see cattle and horses roaming free in the large grass valley, the Sheep, Fox, and Swift Rivers cutting like silver blades through the thick green. I would spend my days alone up there on my horse, chasing eagles on the beach. I would climb cottonwood trees to see if I could peek inside their nests. One evening, when I was about fourteen, I remember returning home as the sun was just turning golden, and I was unfathomably starved. I looked at the clock in the cabin to see it was 2 a.m.—I had been out all day and most of the night, my biological clock fooled by the long hours of daylight.

Jasper Jewel Carroll, my maternal grandfather, was the thirteenth child of coal miners, and his mother, knowing he would be her last, decided to name him after all the precious stones that line the path to the gates of heaven. Everyone called him Jay. My maternal grandmother's name was Arva. They were among Alaska's first settlers, living in a log cabin with a dirt floor in the beginning. They were Mormon, dating way back, and had six children. Their eldest daughter, Nedra Jewel Carroll, is my mother.

Jay was a bright young man and good with mechanics. He built a snowmobile out of spare parts before anyone had seen one around that part of the woods. He built his own plane and then taught himself to fly it, eventually becoming a legendary bush pilot. He was known for treacherous landings in remote mountain regions, to find game for hunters or to take adventurous souls to untamed land. He was also something of a drunk, which is how he lost his left leg. He was flying half-lit in a blizzard with a client, who was also half-lit, I can only imagine, and they crashed into a mountain. They hiked to a small cabin and were rescued eventually, but not before severe frostbite and gangrene set in.

I knew my grandfather only years later. He was sober by this time, and had yellowing gray hair that was slicked back with thick pomade, the way I imagined sailors wore it in the '50s. He chain-smoked wherever he was, indoors or out. He wore thick glasses and polyester pants. I remember watching with great curiosity as he sat down each morning in his La-Z-Boy recliner to put on his socks. He had a large, hard, round belly that protruded like a melon from under his wool flannel shirt, and he had to strain to bend around the thing to reach the socks to his toes. His prosthetic leg was smooth flesh-colored plastic and disappeared quickly beneath the sock. He hardly ever said five words, and those words were usually commands. "Jewel, hand me that remote." "Arva, 'bout time for lunch." "I'm headed out for a drive."

Grandpa Jay had a routine everyone in town set their clocks by. Ham steak and eggs for breakfast, then a drive out to the gas station in his black El Camino, with a red firebird brazenly painted on the hood. He owned the station and his son Jay Jay helped him run it. Then home for lunch, that El Camino crawling at 45 miles an hour back to the house. Lunch. Nap. Drive out to the Spit (a large tongue of land that juts into the water, a famed attraction of Homer), the horses under the hood never given a chance to let loose. He was such a famously slow driver that folks in town could be heard saying, "Well, it's two o'clock, better get on the road before we get stuck behind Jay."

Jay died of a perforated ulcer. He collapsed in the bathroom at home, blood spilling everywhere. At the hospital, after they announced he'd passed, the nurse came out with a ziplock bag that held a neat roll of two thousand dollars cash. She handed it to my grandmother, saying they had found it in his hollow leg.

For years after Grandpa died, I could not keep my mind from wandering morbidly when I went into that bathroom. I would stare down at the linoleum flooring and imagine my poor grandmother, dutifully cleaning all that blood from the very spot.

My grandmother Arva was the quintessential doting grandma. In a world where nothing was stable or kind or sweet, she was its counterpoint. She was affectionate and warm. She gave me Twinkies and doted on me and I knew she loved me. I stayed with her often, and had a small room that was sort of mine. I watched her, ever the subservient housewife and slave in the kitchen, serve Grandpa. But with me, she was funny, and opinionated even, though always in her kind way. She took me to church with her and always made sure I had a nice little dress to wear.

I got the feeling she had lived her life for everyone else and she was just waiting for the chance to be free. Once, when I was a teenager, she said to me, "I sure hope your granddad dies soon so I can go live a little." This floored me, as she never said a cross word otherwise, much less such a shocking confession. We were in the car, and I remember the soft, round outline of her cheek, her smooth nose in profile, as she paused a bit too long, as if contemplating the one stop sign in town.

After Grandpa died she got a new hip and an RV and hit the road, visiting relations all over the Lower 48 (what we Alaskans call the continental U.S.). I was happy for her.

MY PATERNAL GRANDPARENTS were Ruth and Yule Farnorth Kilcher, a middle name my grandfather invented for himself. They had come to Alaska from Switzerland. Well, actually they were living in Germany at the time, just before World War II. My grandfather told me that they were part of a group of young idealists from various disciplines—painters, singers, filmmakers, philosophers—determined to leave Europe before the war. They had heard that the Territory of Alaska was giving away homesteads, free land to anyone willing to settle the wild country. They sent a scout, Yule, a dashing and charismatic philosopher, musician, chess player, and linguist, to go ahead and secure the place. Reportedly, he stowed away on a ship and was discovered by the crew. When he was brought before the Italian captain, he recognized the officer's dialect and guessed the town in Italy where he was from. Yule guessed correctly, and followed up the trick by singing folk songs particular to that region. The captain was suitably impressed, and I like to imagine my grandfather and that captain, drunk from wine, singing songs as they sailed through the dark night. Yule eventually made his way to the New World. He hiked over the Harding Icefield with a ladder on his back, and when he came to a crevasse in the ice, he would lay the ladder over it, walk across it, return the ladder to his back, and keep going. It took him two years, but he finally arrived in Homer and secured a homestead free of charge, a gift from the government. He sent word to his comrades, telling them to come on over: he had found a beautiful place, and they could create their Utopia. But everyone had moved on with their lives. Everyone but Ruth. Ruth was an aspiring opera singer, and she decided to leave her dreams of singing, her loved ones, and everything she knew, to marry a man she hardly knew, because she felt that if she was ever going to have children, they must be raised in a free country. With the war imminent, she left a modern Europe for a new and unsettled land to become a pioneer woman. No electricity, no water, no market. Just mountains and a fertile but unforgiving land. They built a cabin from trees they felled. They took a horse and wagon to town on the beach at low tide. She learned to hunt, can, and cut hay by hand.

Ruth had eight children, six girls and two boys—Mairiis (who we called Mossy), Wurtila Dora, Linda Fay, Attila Kuno, Sunrise Diana Irene, Edwin Otto, Stellavera Septima, Catkin Melody—and taught them all how to sing. The family sang folk music from the old country instead of saying prayers before each meal, and music was passed down to generations in our family like antiques or heirlooms are in others. Songs are my history—the story of us. Where there was pain in our family there was also song not far behind, and healing.

My dad is Attila Kuno Kilcher. We call him Atz. He was the fourth child and eldest son, born in Switzerland while his parents were there visiting relatives. Atz's childhood was a mix of tremendously hard work and also creativity and freedom that his parents fostered in living generally by the principles of the philosopher Rudolf Steiner.

When I was young, I would hitchhike to town, and once my rides found out I was a Kilcher, they would say, "My, how lucky you are!" But they did not live with my grandfather. I would quip in the glib tone of a teenager that "Yule was a man loved dearly by all but those who knew him well." A cynical thing for a teenager to say, but I was trying to get at a point that was hard to speak about—the gap that often lies between a person's higher self and their struggles with the darker self. Yule was enigmatic and brilliant, but like many early settlers of the West, he had a hell of a hard streak. You had to, I imagine, to tame wild land. To build rafts of raw timber and sail across uncharted Alaskan waters. He also had an abusive streak, physically and psychologically, and Ruth and many of his children suffered dearly when his moods turned dark.

Yule was a state senator for one term, and upon hearing he'd lost the reelection, my dad offered his condolences while they were driving together somewhere. Yule was so angry and embarrassed by the defeat that he accused my dad of being happy about the loss. He screamed repeatedly, "You're glad your old man has lost! I know what you're thinking!" until my dad began to doubt what he had actually thought in the first place. It is the first memory my dad has of his own psychological suffering. Physically, Yule hit my dad often, backhanding him head over heels or striking him with a tool that Yule deemed had been fetched too slowly. When Yule found out my dad had been smoking, he made my dad strip down naked and then walked around him and whipped his whole body. Yule built many layers of shame and cruelty into his abuse and punishments, in both mind and body. My dad suffered a lot of trauma in his childhood, and then went off to Vietnam and sustained more.

My dad never heard the words "I love you" from his father until Yule was on his deathbed. In his final hours a miracle occurred. Yule softened and looked at my dad and said he was sorry, that he loved Atz and was proud of him. That moment changed my dad's life. It gave him something he had needed so desperately. Many stories like my dad's end without hearing those words. Many stories like mine end without a parent making amends, or achieving a loving, honest relationship. Mine did, because of my dad's willingness, and my own, to do the hard work it takes to learn a new emotional language. He and I share a common goal: to be accountable, fulfilled human beings. I have a relationship now with my dad that I cherish.

As for Yule, I loved and feared him. He was one of the brightest men

I have ever known, and when he gave you his attention, you felt like the sun was shining on you alone. He spoke many languages and knew the root words that unified them. He was forever espousing philosophy. His temper was quick, though, and his sharp mind could turn on you, leaving you bare. He would walk into the barn where we lived, unannounced, and begin to read our mail. He had a thick Swiss accent and wore a beret over his thinning brown hair. He smelled of stout sourdough bread and garlic. He was not overly tall, but was lean and powerfully built, with chiseled features.

Ruth was the perfect counterpoint. Her Swiss accent was gentle, lilting, musical. She was every bit the poet and artist. She had high cheekbones and wore her long hair in a simple but elegant fashion. She wrote and won awards for her column in the Anchorage paper.

Yule helped draft the Alaska Constitution. After they'd signed it, the jade chandelier that was hanging overhead broke, and each man took several pieces. I remember my grandmother telling me the story, pressing a cool shard of that jade into my young hand.

As Yule became political and went on to be elected as a Democratic senator for one term, it was up to Ruth to run the homestead along with her children. As the years turned to decades, the abuse and long winters finally wore her down, and she took twelve-year-old Catkin, her youngest, gave up her stake in the homestead, and went to the Lower 48. She married a Marine and lived out the rest of her days in Knoxville, Tennessee. Years later I went to visit her there, and she gave me a self-published book of her poetry. It was called *Voice of the Initiate*. She told me of her youth in Switzerland, her dreams for the artistic colony in Alaska, how she gave up her dreams of singing to have kids in that beautiful wild country. How she taught singing to all her children. She had tears in her eyes as she pulled a file from a box near her bed. Inside it were press clippings of mine. She said it had been worth giving up her dreams to see them come true for me.

I honor and respect the generations who have come before me, and I wrote them a song about this unpayable debt of gratitude. I was privileged to perform it as a duet with Dolly Parton on my newest album.

My Father's Daughter

She stepped off of the boat to see flowers in his hand
The man she would marry was as hard as the mountains
She had his children in a log cabin
Soon I'd be another star in this family's constellation
In the land of the midnight sun
Searching for gold

I am my father's daughter
He has his mother's eyes
I am the product of her sacrifice
I am the accumulation of the dreams of generations
And their stories live in me like holy water
I am my father's daughter

My father raised me in an old log cabin
And he sang for me the songs his mother sang to him
In honkey-tonks and empty bars,
Just me and him and that old guitar
He passed on a legacy wrapped up in a melody
And I carry on
Searching for gold

I am my father's daughter
I have his eyes
I am the product of his sacrifice
I am the accumulation of the dreams of generations
And their stories live in me like holy water
I am my father's daughter

Every time I step onstage
And the music finds me
I don't need gold to remind me

I am my father's daughter
I have my Grandma's eyes
I am the product of such sacrifice
I am the accumulation of the dreams of generations
And their stories live in me like holy water
I am my father's daughter
Oh
I am my father's daughter

two

broken harmonies

But we did not always live on the homestead. We started out in Anchorage. We started out as a family, with a mom and everything.

My father was the first one of his family to carry music from a passion into a profession, and began writing his own songs when he was a teenager, eventually making a living at it. He took his guitar to Vietnam, where music helped him to assuage the trauma of his childhood and the effects of war. When he met my mother, he found a new family in her religion that felt safe to him. He converted and they were married in the Mormon Church. At first they lived in a remote cabin at the head of Kachemak Bay. They had their first child, my older brother Shane, in 1971. Their second son, Vance, was born in September of 1972. He died suddenly, before he was a year old.

My dad decided to pursue academics, and they moved to Utah, where he got his master's degree in social work at Brigham Young University, becoming the first college graduate in his family. I was born there in 1974 while my dad was attending school. When he graduated, we moved back to Anchorage, where he worked with troubled youth. We lived in an apartment until my dad had the money to build us a larger house. Only a few memories stand out for me. I remember feeling safer by making myself a pallet of blankets by the bedroom door, choosing to sleep there instead of in my bed. I remember a giant rotating Big Boy sign across the street. I remember a small kitchen window where sunlight streamed in. When we moved to a larger house shortly after, I got my own room and was allowed to pick my own carpet—pink shag. My younger brother, Atz Lee, was born in 1976.

Around this time my parents began to sing together, first doing dinner shows at hotels for tourists. Their act evolved into a variety show that consisted of some original songs (my dad singing lead, my mom harmony), a segment where they showed a 16-millimeter film that documented Dad's family pioneering and settling the state, and a few skits with him dressed as a sourdough (local vernacular for an original Alaskan settler: part gold miner, part hillbilly, part frontiersman) and my mom as a can-can saloon girl with a feather boa and long, curled rooster feathers in her hair.

Music was the happy part of our lives. The sound of my parents practicing during the day, melody and harmony wafting through the house like the smell of baking pie, but for the ears and for the heart. Warm, sweet. Me, wandering around the house till I found them, engrossed and focused. I loved that focus. Even more than the singing, I loved the feeling of being so overtaken by something. At a very young age I fell in love with the puzzle of harmonizing and learning melody and vocal control. I became fascinated with the effort of learning, so consuming that everything else left your mind. The time travel of losing yourself in practice. Even when there was fighting in the house, even when practicing with them was hard, I loved the puzzle of trying to get better. No matter how much my dad yelled or how impatient and angry he was to work with, I hung in there. Shane and Atz Lee were part of the act at first but could not tolerate the heated and often agonizing practice sessions with my dad. I practiced all the time. In my room. At school. Learning to yodel is probably the reason I had no friends in kindergarten. It's just not a pretty thing to learn. My brothers teased me, saying that I sounded like a cross between a dying seal and a cow in labor. But I was determined to learn because my dad had told me I was too young to. What an insult! Too young? I took it as a challenge and became obsessed with disciplining the crack in my voice. Teaching my tongue to obey the tongue twister of *yodel-ay-ee yodel-oh-oo yodel-oh-oo yodel-ay-ee* over and over until I had it mastered. My gratification was in practicing, and when my dad said with delight that I was ready for the stage, I had an unfamiliar sinking feeling.

I was five when I first went onstage, my handmade Swiss outfit awkward and itchy. I was so nervous that I got the hiccups, though luckily no one could tell because yodeling sounds like hiccupping anyway. The crowd of hundreds clapped with thundering enthusiasm, but I was too embarrassed to stay and I bolted offstage. I was not a ham or an outgoing child, but what hooked me was feeling like I had done something—I'd won a battle I wasn't supposed to have won. I YODELED! Hear me roar! Soon my dad was using me during the daytime as a tease for the nightly show. I got into my little outfit proudly, stood in a hotel lobby near the check-in desk, and I yodeled my little heart out as boatloads of Japanese tourists snapped pictures of the cute blonde American girl, while my dad sold tickets to that evening's performance.

Before shows, I played in the elevators while Shane, all of eight years old, set up the lights and learned to run the sound equipment (he was running all the gear for the show by the time he was nine). During breakdown afterward, I blew out all the candles on the tables, dipping my fingers in the cooling wax to create casts of each digit. Endless fun. In the off-season we toured native villages, singing for Inuit (we don't call them Eskimo—it's a derogatory term). I have dreamy memories of my parents and me being dropped off in an ice field at midnight in broad daylight, as the sun never sets up there, and being picked up by natives on dog-sleds and taken to a host's house. Being presented with a whole moose leg, longer than my body, for dinner, with salty homemade bacon and a concoction of seal oil, sugar, and snow that they passed off as ice cream.

We sang in village after village, my parents and I. My dad and I developed a bit where we selected an audience member to compete for a prize. My dad would teach them to yodel on the spot, then they would go head-to-head with the six-year-old, and the winner got a bottle of wine. We always let the audience member win. Alcohol was illegal in the villages, so we used sparkling apple cider for a prize, which still almost caused a riot. Just the sight of that champagne-shaped bottle nearly got us trampled. I remember the natives being warm and reciprocating. After our show, they entertained us. I remember seal mittens and polar bear boots and beautiful woven fans and the smiling beautiful brown faces dancing with stories about hunts and love and death and birth.

At this point my music education was mostly homespun, composed of my dad's songwriting and our family singing. I was not raised watching a lot of TV or listening to the radio or popular music. Once my dad saw I was serious about yodeling, he began teaching me about harmonies and exploring vocal control, but as much as anything, I was learning to be a professional. If I wanted to sing in the show, I knew I was expected to behave. No whining backstage. No pouting onstage. I was expected to smile and be polite, because this was our living and it deserved respect.

We were in some ways the ideal Mormon family, with family dinners and church, complete with a family act. But a different type of family act was playing out offstage. My parents fought a lot, their strained voices escalating to full-blown yelling behind closed doors and thin walls. And when they were not fighting, I often had the sense they were playacting. They seemed disconnected, hollow somehow, deeply withdrawn. There were hugs given to each other, and to their children, but tension crackled like a live wire until they announced their divorce.

I was eight. My brothers and I found ourselves enrolled in therapy classes that taught us about the finer points of divorce. We were talked to about why it was not our fault, and also clued in to different tactics parents might employ during this new phase of our lives. For instance, the Disneyland effect meant one parent might spoil the children to gain their favor. I didn't think there would be any risk of that here. Onstage, my brothers and I were learning the nuanced art of performing, while offstage we were receiving an adult-level education about divorce before we'd ever had a chance to learn about love or marriage.

I have no idea why it was my mom who stayed in the big house by herself, with all our empty rooms collecting dust, while my dad moved my brothers and me into a single spare room at a friend's house for a short stint. We lived like this until the contract for the dinner show was up at the Hilton in Anchorage.

The night I realized our family was to be forever broken is permanently emblazoned in my mind. It was around 11 at night. We had just completed our last set as a family at the hotel and were loaded up in our station wagon, which was packed full of all our belongings. My brothers and I sat in the very back, on blankets my dad had spread out with pillows to serve as a makeshift bed while he drove us six hours through the mountains to Homer, where we relocated that night. I remember a new strong emotion nearly suffocating me as I watched my mom through the rear window. She was still in her show clothes. Ruffled maroon shirt. A thick denim skirt. A long, curved rooster tail feather in her hair, lit by a single streetlamp that cast a sickly green hue. Her hand waving goodbye until she was out of sight.

My throat ached as I choked back tears. Shane mercifully told a joke, a dumb one, but we all used it as an excuse to laugh while tears ran down our faces. All of us laughing, grief masked by twisted smiles in the back, while my dad drove. I will always love Shane for giving us permission to cry the only way he knew how.

My dad suddenly found himself a single father of three. No wife to help. We moved into a one-room house behind my uncle Otto's machine shop. I remember the smell of spark and metal and grease. My room was a narrow hallway closet. Dad built a narrow loft bed, complete with a ladder for me to climb, and my few clothes hung from the coat bar beneath it. I left the sliding accordion doors open when I slept, but enjoyed closing them during the day, making a neat fort of my closet-room. Dad built oddly shaped bunk beds in the triangular water closet for my brothers, with holes strategically placed so the water pipes could grow through the beds like metal trees. The first time my dad hit me was in this house. It felt like suddenly my whole life was submerged and I was living underwater. All his values seemed to change overnight. His actions ran in stark contrast to the sober Mormon family man I knew, and went against every tenet of our faith. We went from being a happy churchgoing Mormon family to being the estranged kids of an absent mother and a dad who was a drinking, smoking ladies' man.

Dad began dating another woman, and when she became pregnant, the church excommunicated him for having a child out of wedlock. They were on-again-off-again, but when they were on, we often stayed in her two-room trailer. I got the couch. They tried to make a go of it, and made it through the pregnancy. My dad was most nervous about how I would accept my new little brother, but he didn't need to be. I loved him instantly. He was like my own baby. I held him, dressed him, and loved him dearly. My dad sent me to a therapist again at this point to help me deal with any feelings I might have about it. I felt he should be in therapy, not me. I remember sitting on a brightly colored pillow across from the brightly dressed therapist with the brightly painted smile and telling her so. I said, "My dad is doing this to our life. I'm not. Why am I here?" Soon after Nikos's birth there was a bitter breakup, and I only got to see him rarely. I was able to maintain some contact with him for a few years and babysat him several times, but he eventually moved to Oregon, and I didn't see him again until I was twenty-one. I mourned the loss of my little brother and eventually wrote him a song called "Nikos." In later years, and after much healing for everyone involved, our families have had the opportunity to be close again.

three

you don't outrun pain

My dad had left behind his social work, and now we supported ourselves on music alone. I took my mom's place in the act, but we no
longer performed in fancy hotels, singing instead in honky-tonks, juke
joints, restaurants, lumberjack haunts, and veterans' bars. There was no
more variety show for tourists; in these places we were required to do
five-hour sets of covers and my dad's originals, supplying the background
music while people ate and drank. I was probably the only fourth grader
who went from elementary school straight to the bar. I was still adjusting
to a new school on weekdays, and on weekends I transformed into a bar-
room curiosity. School politics and social graces were confusing, but onstage I was confident and secure—look at that cute girl yodel! Most gigs
were local, but eventually we toured across the state, sometimes with a
band, but mostly it was just my dad on guitar singing lead, me doing harmony. My dad was a great entertainer, personable and professional, and
could not only play and sing thousands of cover songs but wrote originals
as well.

I was learning harmonies to the classic songs and popular covers my dad included in our set lists. "Brown-Eyed Girl," "Heartbreak Hotel," "Free Fallin'," "Hotel California," "The Circle Game." I had never heard the Rolling Stones sing "Wild Horses" or the Beatles sing "Yesterday," only dad's acoustic interpretations. For the most part my musical influences were songs, not the artists. Singing five-hour sets every night of all the best songs ever written taught me about storytelling. I didn't see the cult of personality attached to the songs, only the pure power of the words and stories. I never heard Elvis sing until I was in my late teens. I never heard Jim Croce sing . . . it goes on. I didn't have access to much pop culture. I do remember Odetta, Maria Callas, and *Ella Fitzgerald Sings the Cole Porter Songbook*. As I grew older and MTV was all powerful, I knew of Cyndi Lauper, although I didn't gravitate toward Madonna when she first came out. She was too far from my world. Nor did I get the Beatles at the time. It took me years to appreciate pop music. My dad was my biggest musical influence, and then as I grew up, I listened to old folk songs from Ireland and England. I listened to old blues artists—some obscure and some more well-known. My lack of music history has vexed me for much of my life. At the same time, I think having the silence in which to develop my own sound was priceless.

To develop my singing I spent hours alone. I wouldn't call it practicing as much as I would exploring. Experimenting and getting to know my voice and its limits, and how to push them. Later I learned more about tone and breath by listening to great singers. I was a good mimic and learned a lot by studying artists with specific colors. Nanci Griffith for her bright sweet ironic tone. Ella was an endless teacher for me, and still is. Sarah Vaughan is one of the finest voices in history—her tone almost operatic, and her breath control staggering.

I had no tape player or cassette tapes until I was a teenager, and TV and radio were just not habits we seemed to be into. I wrote my first song after learning about Martin Luther King Jr. in fourth grade. I was so touched by his life story it inspired me to write the lyrics for "I Have a Dream." It was not a long or lyrically complex song, though it had some interesting melodic choices for an eight-year-old.

I have a dream that people can be free
I have a dream that people can be friends
Ever since I was a little boy
I wished I could be free

Singing two nights a week and having a front-row view of the mating rituals of drunks and barmaids was another adult education in more ways than one. I have always had a poet's heart, and I felt honored somehow to watch unnoticed as people lived such raw lives in front of me. I memorized faces and characters that would fill short stories and songs for decades to come. There was one couple who were bitter drunks and fought all the time. I would sidle up to the bar once sparks started flying and eat maraschino cherries and eavesdrop as innocuously as I could. The man noticed me listening one evening, and said, "Making up is the best part, kid." The look on her face betrayed the fact that she did not agree. In her I saw anger, hurt. Her youth lost in a blur of drink and cigarette smoke. Deep wrinkles like road maps of heartbreak carved into her skin. Her face stuck with me for years and I finally wrote "Rosey and Mick," which ended up on my album *Perfectly Clear.*

So many characters and faces that will forever be engrained in my mind. The smell of stale beer and vomit as we did our sound checks before the doors opened. As I got older, my favorite places to sing were biker bars. The bikers were always protective and sweet toward me.

When I was about twelve, playing at the Trade Winds biker bar in Anchorage, a man was outside foaming at the mouth, overdosing on PCP. Angel dust, I remember a woman whispering to me. When I saw the red lights flashing through the window, I set my mic down silently mid-song and walked from the stage to the bathroom so I wouldn't get kicked out for singing in there underage. I knew the routine. A couple of the biker men saw me do this and nodded to their women, who silently followed me to keep me company. The bathroom was long and narrow, and I remember the women coming in, drink making them warm and wordy. We sat on the toilets, the doors all flung open, and two sat on the sink counters, all of us looking at each other in the long mirror above the sinks. The stalls on each side of me were occupied by women weathered and road weary, bleached blondes, brunettes, and one redhead, all wearing acid-washed jeans, tank tops, and leather jackets. Slight variances on the same theme. My stall in the middle, startling in contrast. A twelve-year-old wearing a long-sleeved shirt buttoned up to the very top button, showcasing a whimsical and heartbreakingly sweet pattern of kitty paw prints in beige. Long honey blonde hair straight as sticks tucked behind my ears, posture erect as I visited with the ladies, glad for their company.

The brunette on the sink wore fringed boots that hung off the edge of the counter. "You sing real nice, kid. Real nice."

"Thanks," I said, enjoying the compliment.

"You know, my old man is finally gonna make an honest woman of me. The son of a bitch," she said, to several chuckles from the other stalls before she continued. "You guys should sing at our wedding."

I knew not to accept gigs on my own, and so I said, "My dad handles all of our bookings, but I'm sure we would love to sing at your wedding." In most bars I felt invisible, but it was always the bikers who kept an eye on me, sensing my vulnerability the way only other outcasts can. Bikers had their own code of ethics, which was palpable to me even at that age.

With time I learned to be street-smart and to trust my instincts elsewhere in barrooms. I had to. When I was about nine, a man in Alice's Champagne Palace placed a dime in my hand, folding my small fingers around the cool silver, and said, "Call me when you're sixteen." Another time I was walking to the bathroom, and as a man passing by caught a quick glance of me, he said casually, "You're going to be a great fuck when you're older." I learned to let my energy expand only on stage. Offstage and between sets I stayed small and drew little attention to myself. My dad made rounds and visited with patrons, and I would entertain myself by looking in a Michelob beer mirror, learning how to move each muscle in my face. In fifth-grade science class we were told about involuntary muscles, and how we couldn't move them, so I set out to prove that wrong, starting with my lower eyelids. I mastered moving my ears in all directions, isolating my lower eyelids and each nostril separately, and each quarter of each lip independently.

I loved to observe people. I watched love and life play out in a million ways, but one of the best things I learned was this: You don't outrun pain. I saw men and women in those barrooms all trying to outrun something, some pain in their life—and man, they had pain. Vets broken and drifting, abused women, abused boys who had grown up to be emotionally crippled men. I saw them all trying to bury that pain in booze, sex, drugs, anger, and I saw it all before I was able to indulge in many of those behaviors myself. I saw that no one outran their suffering; they only piled new pain upon their original pain. I saw the pain pile up into insurmountable mountains, and I saw the price people paid who buried all that pain, and along with it their hope, joy, and chance at happiness. All because they were trying to outrun the pain rather than walk through it and heal. I knew I was young, and that I'd already had more than my fair share of confusion and pain. I resolved at that time to never drink or do drugs, to try to find the courage to face myself as honestly as I could. I was keenly aware that numbing my feelings and instincts meant cutting myself off from the only real safety net I had. I knew I was vulnerable, I knew there were predators around me, and I also knew that my body came equipped with the most exquisite alarm system in the world—emotions and instincts—and that, for the most part, mine worked beautifully. I could tell in a second who felt safe and who did not. I learned to read people instantly.

At home my feelings were alive and well, if not always pleasant. I could tell that being hit did not feel good, and because I was emotionally alive, I could tell it was not my fault. But as any child who has suffered this way knows, the unpredictability and randomness of even infrequent rages can be excruciating. I could tell I was scared, and being able to tell that meant I could tell when I wasn't. If I cut myself off from my only alarm system by numbing my feelings, I would be defenseless. Not having access to my senses could lead to disaster, and so instead of turning away from my feelings, I turned toward them. I studied them. I turned to writing rather than to drugs to take the edge off. I vowed to try to tell the truth about myself when I wrote—not the version of myself I had to learn to be in order to keep my dad's temper from flaring, nor the version I had to be in bars to stay unseen, nor the persona I was onstage. At school, at home, in bars, I was an emotional contortionist, alternating between awkward self-aggrandizing and trying to win favor so as to fit in. When I wrote, I let myself be dead honest, flaws and all. But I was myself, I felt real. I went inside myself when a pen was in my hand and enjoyed that space in there. When I went in deeply to myself and my creativity, I was amazed at what I knew and saw. I had answers to things I did not otherwise have access to. I was able to see patterns in places that had confused me before. I wrote about the way my dad treated me. The way he made me feel that so many things at such a young age were my fault, and I was able to untangle the web of his projection and separate myself from him. At times I was too young to make sense of it all, but I vowed to come back later when I had better skills to deal with it. Until then, I told myself I could not control the pain or my situation, but I could control the pain I inflicted on myself. I was confused, scared, hurt, but I was alive in there. At least I had that. Maybe if I didn't let it go, maybe if I used words like Hansel and Gretel used breadcrumbs, I could find my way out of the woods and avoid being eaten by the witch and the wolves. Maybe.

four

emotional english

In fifth grade we moved from my uncle's machine shop to the saddle barn on the homestead where my dad was raised. The barn was situated about a hundred yards from the cabin where my dad had grown up and where my grandpa Yule still lived. One large room downstairs housed the kitchen, living room, and dining area with a view of green meadow, gray waters of the bay, blue mountains, and white glaciers. A metal oil drum that had been welded into a coal-burning stove sat in the middle of the floor, radiating heat, its rusted pipe climbing through the ceiling to lend warmth to the upstairs, where I shared a room with my brothers. There was a small room, partitioned off, which was Dad's. Countless times he must have gone into that saddle barn as a young man for cinch or rasp. No wonder he seemed disoriented all the time now that it was so completely repurposed.

Winter was the price you paid for the unearthly Alaskan summers, dark and cold in a way you could not shake off or dress for. It *is* possible to dress for, but our hand-me-downs and secondhand clothing always left me with a chill. Alaska's famed midnight sun eventually gave way to the winter solstice, its stingy grip allowing only the faintest dusk to slip through its fingers for a few hours a day. The coal stove would go out in the middle of the night, and I remember waking with frost on the tips of my eyelashes, making it nearly impossible to get out of the cozy nest of feather blankets in my bed. We would wake to inky blackness, and I would cook breakfast while Shane did the lion's share of chores, milking the cow and feeding the horses while Atz Lee got dressed and ready for school. My dad was usually asleep still, often hungover in those years. We did the dishes and then walked two miles in darkness on the dirt road to the bus stop. Sometimes the ice would be so bad we could not walk a couple of steps without falling, so we devised homemade snow cleats by taking the removable soles out of our shoes, poking screws through the rubber bottoms, and then replacing the padded sole. It was a bit uncomfortable, as the screws always tried to push back up, but the thick padding kept them from poking us too badly.

At school, recess was taken in a twilight state, that weak light lasting only a few hours, darkness descending again by the time we rode back to the bus stop. I remember looking down and not being able to see my feet. My eyes would strain to see the outline of the dirt road in front of me, but often it felt like we walked back and forth by braille on those days with no moon.

At home in the evening, Shane again did the chores, Atz Lee got coal for the stove, and I would either milk the cow or help start dinner. My dad was a great cook, a skill required of him in Vietnam. His creativity shined in the kitchen; he loved to bake breads from scratch and make Swiss-style apple tarts. Our food was what we raised with our own hands, and the flavors of my childhood stay with me still. Fresh butter that I would make in the morning before school, squeezing out the buttermilk with a spatula. Fresh raw whole milk. Meat from our own cattle that we bled and butchered each fall. Fresh vegetables from our garden that we canned in the winter. Water from the creek. Sourdough bread from a starter that was older than I was. Alaskans can be quite proud of their sourdough starter. It is a living thing that must be fed and nurtured in the fridge. When you take some out, you add a few more ingredients back in so that its flavor keeps maturing. We got our starter from Yule, and he'd inherited his decades earlier.

I was proud to live on the homestead and to live off the land. I knew the sound of porcupines climbing the trees in winter, and could track the cattle in the snow back to where the water was. Wolves sang me to sleep at night across the canyon, and the winds whistled, exciting my imagination. Alaska is a land of extremes, with mountains climbing out of the ocean and glaciers that reach down into the sea like great white limbs, impossibly slow. Too much food in the summer, and too little in the winter. It is a place that requires great preparation for a human to have any sort of consistent sustenance. It requires a hardy, practical, and energetic approach to life, one that served me well on the long and winding road I've taken since then.

Extreme characters also seem to be drawn to Alaska, especially the smaller towns. Extreme political views, from hippie communes (there were a few rather famous ones that settled near the head of the bay in the '70s, including the Love Family and the Barefooters), left-wingers, expats, outlaws, and mountain men who felt they needed to get just that much farther from the government. On East End Road lived a female belly dancer with a full beard. There was Stinky, who lived in an underground shelter he'd dug in an old junkyard—a refrigerator lying on its back served as a door, and it would hinge open, coffinlike, and up Stinky would emerge from his underground dwelling, still convinced a Cold War was possible. There were immigrants like my family, and fishermen, lumberjacks, and Russian Orthodox in their brightly colored traditional clothes. All of us living separate lives on the same peninsula. The rule was that everyone had the right to be themselves and pursue liberty how they saw fit. At night when we sang, I was always amused to see such a collection of hippies, hillbillies, and rednecks all sitting at the same bar.

One of my favorite things about Alaska is that people are not jaded or too touched by pop culture. There is a tangible optimism that comes from making a living with your own hands. It's honest and grounded and down-to-earth, qualities that served me well in a business that was anything but.

Our own home reflected the extremes of the land. My dad's drinking continued. I remember him being so "sleepy" on the drive home after gigs that he would ask me to help keep the wheel steady. There was lots of yelling, rage, outbursts, though not always when he was drunk. The abuse escalated in the drinking years though. It was random and I could never predict what would spark my dad's temper, and it began a lifetime of walking on eggshells for me, trying to read the signs and check moods. I think he hit the boys occasionally as well, but I felt he had a particular problem with me for whatever reason. Maybe it was female need. Maybe I reminded him of my mom. Maybe. All I knew is we fought a lot.

In some families this brings siblings closer together, but it seemed to splinter us. Shane handled it by being the responsible older brother, reliable and true, who would escape into fantasy books. Atz Lee was the favorite, and quite a rascal, defiant in his right to play and goof off. He could take hours just to fill a bucket of coal, the fire long out while we were waiting for him. I handled the stress by trying to be the best at singing and horse riding, and by trying to eliminate the competition. I didn't understand that it was not my brother's fault he was the favorite, and I resented him badly for it. I had a sharp tongue and I used my intuition like a weapon; whatever insecurity and weakness I sensed in him, I exploited. I tried to make him feel as badly about himself as my dad made me feel about myself. My need to be loved was so strong that it took several years for my writing to expose the real issue, and for my conscience to get a foothold and defend my younger brother. To this day I am deeply regretful and sorry that I was not mature enough to see he was not an enemy but a victim in the same war. It took years of reflection to see that being the favorite can be a worse trap, as it leaves no door to exit by; loyalty to the love one receives, dysfunctional as it may be, is sometimes too strong a force to break free from. I had no idea what a gift it was that at least I knew I wanted out.

Something my life has taught me is not to see things in black and white. People are neither all good nor all bad. Hurt people can become hurtful, and my father's own actions reflected this.

The worst incident I can recall involved Atz Lee and I both one morning as we got ready for school while my dad slept, hungover. As usual we were careful not to wake him for fear of his temper. Atz Lee and I got to fighting, as we often did, but it had to be done silently. Nothing in particular got us going, just some squabble that escalated, and we began to brawl with the mute button on. Kicks and punches and bites delivered in comic quiet. He would push me so hard it would knock me over, but he would break my fall at the last minute, offering me an extended arm, which I'd take so as not to land with a crash. I would bite him, then cover his mouth as we both stopped long enough to ensure he did not scream too vociferously. It was like a silent and brutal ballet, both of us having a go at each other and yet protecting ourselves from our father. This time, however, we woke him. We both froze as we heard his voice erupt like a cannon, calling us up to his room.

Atz Lee and I went from being mortal enemies to being children unified in fear in the blink of an eye. He was seven, me nine. I remember climbing the wooden stairs, each saying we loved the other as we clung together, arm locked in arm. We reached his door and he was standing naked but for his underwear, his spine bent with rage. The room was tiny, just enough space for a twin bed against the wall that adjoined ours. We stepped inside, our backs to the window. I remember being vaguely aware of a willow bassinet that lay at our feet. It had been the bassinet that my grandmother carried my father in, made of willow roots. My father began screaming, I don't care to recall what exactly, and it snowballed from there. I do remember his face being distorted with rage, barking at us like a drill sergeant. I remember veins bulging and a redness that can be achieved only by going genuinely apeshit. He hit my brother upside the face. I was next. It knocked me into the cradle. But I did not cry. I decided to deprive him of that satisfaction. I stood up and stared at him with a smirk on my face. He knocked me down again, incensed, and then dragged me to the bed. The next thing I knew, Atz Lee was there next to me, my dad straddling us both, shaking us, our heads knocking together. He kept yelling, spittle flying in my face. I thought I was going to die.

I don't remember leaving his room. I do remember climbing down the stairs weakly, in utter shock. In the absence of sanity, our bodies took over instinctively, and as if on autopilot my brother and I gathered our things to walk to school, my nose still bleeding. We had no idea what to do with ourselves. The episode took long enough that we knew we had missed the bus, and so we walked the eight miles to school, our faces red and stinging. I was in fifth grade, Atz Lee in third. We felt so much older, but must have looked impossibly small with our thumbs stuck out trying to catch a ride, part of us hoping a car would not come for a long while, to give our faces and our crying time to return to normal. And yet another part of us fantasized about everyone seeing what our dad had done to us. That feeling vanished as quickly as the marks did, though, as it does for any animal that senses survival is the enemy you know.

I remember the day being dreamlike. It was so strange to witness how life just went on. Kids made jokes, kids laughed as usual. Teachers taught, recess happened, and kids played. It all just seemed like time should have stopped and some protective force in the universe should have risen from the ocean and said, *Anoint these children with love! Take a moment not to pity, but to see them so they may know they are deeply worthy of tenderness!* This did not happen though.

At midday, my dad came to the school with our bagged lunches. In the scramble I had forgotten to make them. He was sheepish, this time his spine bent with shame and regret. I wanted so badly to be mad at him, but the child in me could not withstand the sad and broken form he now took, and I thanked him as I took the crumpled paper bag from his hand.

I was so alarmed by what was happening at the time, by my father's sudden behavior, that a knowing part of me thought, naively, that I could have a talk with him and that I would somehow be able to resolve this and I would stop being hit. I saw that my dad was afraid and I think that having a nine-year-old explain that you're afraid and acting poorly by lashing out must have enraged him. I do know that my father was gripped with terror, a deep feeling of inadequacy because of the way he was raised, and I think he reacted in the most protective way he could, which was to say that I was the problem and he wasn't. I remember the lights inside going out a little bit for me then. I remember my mind being torn down by his mind, his logic, his adult reasoning enough to confuse me into wondering if I really was the problem. And I began to really doubt myself.

I cry now as I write this. So lasting are the scars of the child who never feels worthy of love. So many cycles in my life of having to learn that I am indeed worthy of tenderness. The lessons I learned from my dad, that he learned from his, would take me many years to unlearn.

My dad was seldom this violent. It was typically a lot of rage and yelling. The more I learned in later years about his own childhood, the more amazed I am that he did as well as he did with us. He was far less violent than his own father.

As children, we are taught what I call Emotional English. This is an emotional language we are taught in our homes, and just like our spoken language, the emotional language we speak most fluently as adults is the one we learned as children. What we are taught about interacting emotionally with each other and the world is modeled for us by our families, and is what we will grow up doing. No matter how frustrating, damaging, and frightening it is, we will perpetuate the examples of our parents and family—unless we can learn new ones. The tricky thing is that a person can go to school to learn a new language, we can find classes anywhere, in any town, but how do we learn a new emotional way of relating to our lives, loved ones, and most important, to ourselves?

I have so much compassion for my dad. He endured so much as a child, and then he was shipped off to war. He had suffered from PTSD and it was triggered by the divorce and raising us kids and living in the barn. I'm amazed he held it together as well as he did. While he and I did not speak for most of my early career, we have a healthy and loving relationship now. Through a combination of therapy and self-examination, he has fought hard for the happiness he has, and has not only made amends to me, but allows me to feel a lot of safety and emotional maturity when we're together. I love my family, and I love my dad—there were lots of good times and they were enigmatic brilliant pioneers who settled a new wild country. It took extreme personalities to carve a living from these extreme environments.

Back then, when I looked at my family's emotional dynamic and projected it into my future, it looked bleak. Having studied PTSD and the effects of its trauma on the brain, I've learned to see this incident in a new light. There is nothing that makes what happened okay, but what happened does have a cause. It is common for people like my dad to self-medicate with alcohol or other things. When triggered, their first reaction is one of fight or flight, and blood stops flowing to the part of the brain that handles logic, redirecting it to the left hemisphere. You can see it in real-time studies done on the brain. A person consumed with irrational rage is literally out of their mind. Later I learned that there are two kinds of trauma: "Little t," which includes issues of prolonged abuse, neglect, and alcoholism, and "Big T," which encompasses war, rape, and near-fatal accidents. My father was the victim of both.

But at least our dad was ours. He stayed with us and fought it out. My mother was absent, except for eccentric and happy notes I might receive on holidays. I never valued what a stand-up guy my dad was to keep us, despite his terror and inadequacy. He did not abandon us. It wasn't until much later that I was able to appreciate this. At the time, being mad at him was easy. He was there every day. Learning to be mad at and fear my mom would take a lot longer.

five

a breadcrumb trail

My dad never said a bad word about my mom, and it wasn't until I was in my thirties that I asked about it. He said that when I was eight, she had told him that she needed a break from being a mom and that she wanted to explore her life without us. Rather than try to convince a woman to take kids she did not want, he took us, ill equipped as he was.

After the divorce, I missed my mother terribly. I even named a white teddy bear Nedra so that I could snuggle with my mom each night. As is the way with small kids, I never asked why we lived with my dad and not my mom. I never asked why Mom didn't come to see us. It just was. My heart ached for her so, and in years to come I made desperate attempts to see her, going so far as to hitch rides to Anchorage. I would show up on the doorstep wherever she was house-sitting (our house had been sold at some point). My mother often cried and seemed sad. She dated a man who made it clear he did not like children, though that didn't keep me from liking him. He was into gourmet food and art and talked to me like an adult the few times I was around him.

To me, my mother seemed magical. She was always quick with a mystical story and seemed shamanistic and powerful. She was an artist and full of expansive ideas. She worked in stained glass and etching and won competitions for her work in local galleries. She made anything seem possible, exuding passion without anger or violence, a seemingly calm and nurturing reprieve from my dad, who felt tightly wound, dangerous and angry all the time. I had such a child's need to believe she wanted me and loved me, that when she insinuated to me at one point that my dad had blackmailed her so he could keep us from her after the divorce, I ate it up. She was fuzzy on the details, and had I been able to reflect a bit more clearly at the time, or had I cared to see through my love to find the truth, I would have seen holes in this concept, if for no other reason than the fact that my dad did not act like he wanted us.

When I was in fifth grade, I think, I remember that I was very homesick for her but had no way to get to Anchorage. I guess my dad could not take me, and she would not come get me. In Homer you could call the local radio station if you wanted a ride somewhere. You offered to split gas and said where you were going and what date you needed to be there. So I put an ad on the "ride line," saying I would split gas (with money saved from babysitting, I believe) and that I wanted to go to Anchorage. The person who answered my ad was a man who had taken some photos of me a couple of months earlier. He had seen me in a grocery store with my father and was taken with me, offering to shoot my pictures for free. He was a professional photographer, he explained, and would be happy to let us keep some of the photos to advertise our show. He would even take some of my dad and me for posters if he could use the photos in his portfolio. My dad was flattered and wanted some headshots for our shows at the Homestead Tavern, the restaurant-bar we sang in at the time, so I got dressed up in the prettiest dress I owned, but it had been bought for me before the divorce and it didn't fit well, in any sense of the word. It was a bit small and a bit frilly. My dad brushed my hair and we went to this small trailer. The photographer was warm and enthusiastic, and inexplicably made me so uncomfortable that I could barely sit still. I wanted to crawl out of my skin being around this man. My dad was oblivious, he was so flattered, and both men were telling me how to pose against a marbled blue pleather backdrop. Meanwhile, I couldn't even elicit a smile. My father was baffled. I didn't smile in one picture. He was very disappointed in me. When we left I said, "That man made me very uncomfortable," and my father chastised me, saying, "You know, that man was doing a very nice favor for us and you really should have been more polite." We did get the photos eventually and I looked very uptight—stern and perturbed. I still have them. When I look back at the photos, I actually laugh.

Fast-forward several months. Jewel Kilcher is looking for ride to Anchorage, will split gas. The photographer was my only answer. I was very apprehensive, though he never made any obscene gestures; he never gave me any reason to mistrust him other than creeping me out. I questioned myself—why am I so uncomfortable? Just take the ride. I missed my mom so badly I decided to go ahead with it. I think my dad dropped me off at the gas station in town, but I can't remember. I had my money in my pocket and offered it to the photographer for gas. He wouldn't take it. He was very nice and said he had an extra sandwich in case I was hungry on the five-hour drive. I had packed my own.

I remember that he was very proud of his sports car, and I also remember that I kept my hand on the passenger-door handle so I that could fling myself into the road at any moment. My internal alarm was really going off. I had a small pocketknife in my jeans pocket. When I asked him what took him to Anchorage, he told me that he really had no purpose for going—he simply was going so I could have a ride. I think he felt this would have a positive effect on me, but it just creeped me out further.

Alaska is full of these long, desolate stretches of road where there are no towns and no civilization. I had to use the restroom at one point, and normally I would not think twice about peeing alfresco, but I knew my only option was waiting for the mountain rest area at the halfway point. I waited to say something until we got near, and he pulled over. There was no traffic, no one there. I was so frightened to go into the bathroom by myself that I waited until finally another car pulled up and a woman went into the restroom, so I could go in with her. I don't know why I thought that would keep me any safer. I let the photographer know when he dropped me off at my mom's house that I did not need a ride back.

I made it to Anchorage and to my mother's doorstep safely. Looking back, I think my mother was less than thrilled to see me. She would leave me alone, but not before telling me amazing stories about the power of our minds, one example being that one could turn lightbulbs on and off with enough concentration. I would stare at a lightbulb for hours, convinced I could turn that damn thing off if I focused hard enough. Sadly she failed to tell me about brownouts, and when the lights dimmed occasionally, I really felt I was getting somewhere! My mom would be so proud! When I couldn't get them to turn off completely, she told me not to worry; if I focused hard, anything was possible.

To avoid riding home with the photographer, I took a "fisherman's ride" back to Homer. It was a cheap service for fishermen who had been out at sea, a dirty van that piled everyone in and then stopped in towns along the way. Homer was the end of the road, the last stop, and so the return trip took twice as long easily, because the towns are so spread out. The men reeked of fish, but it was better than being in that sports car.

Sometime after that my father appeared in front of me as I was sitting on my bed, with tears in his eyes. He held an article in his hands that he had cut out from the paper. It said that the photographer had been arrested on suspicion of child pornography and molestation. Apparently he had also been taking nude photographs of children. My dad said that from now on he would always trust my instincts, that he would never doubt me again. To his credit, he kept his word, in a way. He always trusted me to take care of myself when it came to men in the bars where we sang, though I wouldn't have needed to if he'd done his part in scaring the guys off.

By fourteen I was considered fair game in that town, and the attention was flattering but a lot to handle. It did teach me to be very clear with my own sexual energy, to never be ambiguous, and to shut down advances in a way that kept the man's ego (and temper) intact. Again, a skill that would serve me greatly in my future work in the music business.

My dad and I bumbled our way through my youth. On one hand, I was a very precocious, self-sufficient young woman; and on the other, when it came to my most intimate relationships, my parents' influence made me doubt my instincts and myself. It wasn't something they set out to do. It was collateral damage.

I remember being alarmed and scared because a sense of fullness and a sense of peace in my life began to really be lost. I was deeply unhappy. A wet and heavy fog settled over me that I could not shake. The joy was seeping out of life. And I began to show troubling behavior. I began to steal in fifth grade. Small things—a Popsicle from the cafeteria. I was trying to fill something inside, trying to find power in my powerless life. I also began to try to build myself up by exaggerating. I tried to make myself seem better than I was to people around me. Whatever I had actually done was not good enough—it had to be fantastic. If I was so lovable, then why did those closest to me seem to see fit to treat me so badly? I didn't consciously draw these conclusions—it's just the way a child internalizes abuse. I felt like the colors in my cathedral were fading. I felt lost. Like my compass was disappearing. In trying to regain that compass, I made a pact with myself when I was about nine that I would always tell the truth when I wrote in my journal, because I had begun lying to other people. I began to split in two at that time in my life, and I didn't know how to stop it. But thankfully, some part of me was wise enough to create a safe and sacred place, which became my writing. I allowed it to always be an honest reflection of myself, flaws and all. So while I was lying and exaggerating and shoplifting, I was at least able to watch myself do these things. That may not sound like a great gift, but it kept the lights from going out completely. And it allowed me to witness myself, to have an experience of myself outside of my bad behavior. Even though I was frightened and confused and sad and lonely and behaving in ways I wasn't proud of, I could see myself do it. And if you can see yourself do something, if you can witness your behavior, that means you are something *other* than your behavior. And if you can see your behavior, there is hope for change. We can't fix what we aren't willing to see. I had no idea how to change. I didn't even understand what was happening to me. For now all I could do was be willing to see.

I made another pact with myself around this time to abstain from drink and drugs, and in fact never touched alcohol until my mid-thirties. I was aware from watching drunks in barrooms that drinking further numbed and detached you from yourself, and I knew that if I tuned out my fear completely I would be in great peril, and that I couldn't afford to put myself any more in harm's way. These pacts didn't keep me entirely safe. They didn't keep me from making mistakes. They didn't protect me from tremendous trauma and turmoil in my life, but they kept me alive inside. They gave me a breadcrumb trail back to my most authentic and whole self.

I wrote a line in a song once: "We are never broken." I believe that truly. It is a hard-earned belief, and rose out of many years of experiencing the opposite. I believe we forget who we are over time, and in our state of forgetfulness we struggle and employ all kinds of learned behaviors that don't necessarily help us or bring us happiness. Each of us has a self that exists undamaged and whole, from the moment we are born, waiting to be reclaimed. My life has not been about fixing what is broken. It has been about engaging in a loving and tender archaeological dig back to my true self. It is a process I unknowingly engaged in when I sensed I was getting buried alive in my life all those years ago. And it is something I continue to do to this day.

What is a spirit? Is it a thing, like a glass that can crack or a cord of wood that can be split? There is no real explanation for what a spirit is, just a sense of it, but I know that a spirit cannot be broken any more than water can be broken, or any more than air can be split apart. It can only be perceived as broken. And believing that we are broken is the same as being broken. It means we experience ourselves that way. That perception shapes our reality. It is an illusion we must strive to avoid, as great misery comes from such a belief.

hard wood grows slowly

In spite of the turmoil, moving to the homestead was a dream come true for me. The land is priceless. Our outhouse had a better view than any mansion I have visited. My grandfather put the land in a trust, with guidelines for how the property was to be preserved into perpetuity. It can never be sold off or split up, though he allocated five-acre plots to each of his children on the homestead. All eight of them still sit on a family board and run the homestead as a group.

I felt blessed to have the serenity and beauty of the homestead to counter the darkness in my home life. Green meadows ripe with timothy bluegrass that gently rolled into the glassy gray waters of Kachemak Bay. Mountains like the Alps that climbed from the water right into the heavens just six miles across the bay, and glaciers that crashed back into their liquid self. Nature became my church, and as oppressive and tangled as life was inside the four walls of the saddle barn, nature was ever more expansive, pristine, and nurturing. Nature was the bosom that held me, gave me a safe place and received my tears. She heard my laughter and my cry. My horse and I could escape that dark house and we would run so fast I felt drunk beneath the midnight sun, sleeping in the mountains by a stream until my heart mended enough to go back home. Nature was also my greatest teacher. To this day I calibrate my inner life to what I have observed in nature, and one of the most significant lessons it has taught me is that hard wood grows slowly. I know, not the flashiest phrase, but a profound one. I watched soft wooded trees shoot up in the spring and rot only a few years later. The harder woods became friends of mine. I played in their branches, told them my secrets, and confessed my sins to them for years.

There was a lone spruce tree, enormous, that we called the Pegas Tree. The family fable was that my grandmother Ruth had left her true love Pegas behind in Europe because he could not procure the visa he needed for life in a new land. My grandmother felt so strongly about escaping the war and having kids in a free country that she decided to leave and marry Yule and start a new life. Pegas came to visit, and the family story goes that they spent hours sitting beneath that idyllic tree. I have no idea if it's true, but it was romantic to think about, although my main reason for being there was the fact that it was beautiful. I would daydream for hours, staring up through those thick branches, the weak sun sifting through in a kaleidoscope of yellow, blue, green, and white. I felt like a princess in a tower overlooking the most beautiful of kingdoms. I would lay on my back and give all my tears to the earth and let myself be held by her. Being starved for love, I played a game where I visualized love pouring out of every rock, I imagined love streaming into my heart from every leaf of every tree, I imagined the oxygen that left the branch of each tree entering the branches of my lungs, and then my breath leaving my body and entering the trees again. I imagined love from every salt cell in the sea, and from the glaciers with their heavy slow bodies, and from the birds that cried in the distance. And I felt truly loved there. I felt nurtured. I told nature all my secrets and all my dreams and I let the hard stone support me like a father and the soft soil nurture me like a mother. I wanted to be like that tree. I didn't want to grow more brittle with time, like my dad seemed to be doing. I wanted to become . . . what was the opposite of brittle? Strong? Not exactly. Big? No, that wasn't quite it. As I looked at the roots digging deeply, spreading out, forming an interconnected base, I saw the hard wood as dense fiber, woven tightly, and that's when it struck me: the strongest things bend. The opposite of brittle was bending.

Great survivors have the ability to yield, adapt, give. This stopped me in my tracks. My life was not teaching me to yield, it was teaching me to cover up, protect, harden. I felt a panic. Hardening was the opposite of yielding. I walked home deep in thought and wrote in my book, *things that don't bend break.* This lyric has stayed with me my whole life, reincarnated in many songs. It made such an impression on my soul. Once I began to be punished for seemingly being alive, I knew it was no longer safe to be honest about who I was with the people closest to me. I showed the world and my family one face. Outwardly, I made myself as small and dull as possible. But inwardly, I was limitless and expansive, and my words on paper became the rings of my inner tree. The rings of stress and distress were there in black and white, but a feeling of calm came over me when I wrote about what I was learning from studying nature. Slow growth meant thoughtful growth. Thoughtful growth meant conscious choices. It was a ladder of thought that pulled me up over the years until I arrived at one of the mottos I try to live by: hard wood grows slowly.

If I wanted to grow strong and last, and not be brittle or broken easily, I had a duty to make decisions that were not just good in the moment but good for long-term growth. I would not let myself drink or do drugs because that was a quick fix to escape an uncomfortable feeling. The better thing was to get to the root of what I was feeling. It meant solutions had to be the right ones for long-term happiness—there were no shortcuts. I could not use drugs to numb, I could not use anorexia or bulimia to lose weight, and it also meant not using cynicism to cover my real feelings of anxiety or vulnerability. In a world of cool, casual, hip, and snarky, I knew if I indulged in these feelings, I would sink to the bottom of my life like a stone. I had to respond to my life with vulnerability, sensitivity, and honesty, because they were my only real defenses in this dangerous endeavor called surviving life. I vowed to try to remember to take the time to grow slowly. To take the time to make notes and study. To stay in my body even when I was in pain. I have summoned this motto repeatedly in my life—later, it helped me handle my agoraphobia, crippling fear, and anxiety while I was homeless. It helped me have the courage to lose weight the right way even when the press dubbed me "the fat Renée Zellweger" at age twenty-two, and with countless other decisions that shaped not just the kind of artist but, more important, the kind of human I would become, as well as the kind of longevity I would have. It helped give me permission to discover and actively create who I was, not who I felt pressured to be.

seven

calm within chaos

When I was in sixth grade, my dad moved us back to Anchorage so he could go back to school to get his teaching degree. We lived on the university property in campus housing. The house was dark and small, but I enjoyed having my own bedroom again. The backyard was also small, nothing like having the freedom of a horse and thousands of wild acres to escape into.

It was a new urban experience, and I had trouble fitting in with the city kids. Most of my clothes were bought secondhand, and I recall my snowsuit had "Roberts" written in bold black Sharpie down the arm, clearly the surname of the previous owner. I knew I was low on the totem pole when the nerdiest and greasiest kid in class began to tease me for smelling like horse poop. Someone had found out I lived on a homestead with an outhouse and that was enough to unify the group decidedly not in my favor. Every social group needs a common enemy to rally against. Every group needs to identify an "other" to define and unify their own identity, and I appeared to be it. The amazing thing was that I knew for certain I did not smell like horse poop. I smelled like Irish Spring. All the time. That was the year of the Great Soap Decision.

Money was always tight, but perhaps tighter now that we did not have our own vegetable garden and beef we raised. We had to buy all our groceries now, and the strain in the house was obvious. I remember a tooth rotting, and one day it just crumbled into tiny shards in my mouth. I knew we didn't have the money to fix it and worried about telling my dad. We did get it fixed, though I'm not sure how he was able to swing it. My dad came up with some ways to cut costs elsewhere. He announced that we were going to pick one soap for the house. All soaps and detergents were basically the same, he said, so why waste money on five different kinds? It was our decision, he said, empowering us with the mission. My brothers and I weighed our options. We could use shampoo for dishes and laundry. We could use laundry soap for dishes and hair and washing our bodies. *Or* we could use dish soap for everything, or a bar of soap. Bar soap it was. For whatever reason we settled on Irish Spring. Dad bought a pack of fifty bars the next day at Costco. I remember the first time I washed my hair with it, rubbing that bar into my long hair and making a foamy green lather that reeked of musky, manly scent. The result was clean hair, though the texture felt more like something one feeds to barnyard animals than the luscious locks my burgeoning preteen womanhood had hoped for. A bar was ever present by the sink for hand washing, and also to be soaked in a sink of hot water until it was potent enough to cut the grease on the dishes. Laundry was a bit trickier. We would cut flakes with a sharp knife, the soap peeling in buttery layers, and drop them in the washing machine. I got to where I hated the smell of that soap. And the teasing at school I seemed helpless to stop.

Luckily for me, a popular, pretty girl named Diane took me under her wing. Maybe she felt sorry for me. Maybe she liked me. I have no idea. I liked her. She was confident and had a cool perm that she wore in a short modern style and had the latest in clothing and jewelry. She was like a walking Jordache poster. Pastel Esprit shirts with the collars turned up, blue eyeliner, black spandex with turquoise leopard-print slouchy sweaters, acid-washed denim—she was the culmination of the best the '80s had to offer, and I wanted to be her badly. I also thought she was rich, which, looking back, is funny, because I realize now that she lived in a large cluster of low-rent apartments. But her mom was nice and her dad was a pilot and they had clean white carpets and she had things . . . lots of things. A boom box and mother-of-pearl earrings and Popsicles. And she *shaved*. No one had explained to me that women shave their legs. I hadn't been around many women in a setting to see their legs. It was an entirely new idea to me that year. A light dusting of feather-fine blonde hair had cropped up on my shins just months before, and after seeing Diane's perfectly smooth, lotioned limbs, I resolved I better follow suit.

One night I crept into the bathroom and got Dad's razor. I went back to my room like some refugee and locked the door. I turned out the lights, so my brothers wouldn't see them on and come knocking as I struggled to figure out this strange ritual I knew nothing about. Not knowing was deeply shameful. I know. Common sense should have informed me otherwise, but it was foregone in favor of secrecy and shame, both powerful blinders.

Using one hand to guide the other, I began to apply the dry razor to dry skin, only to realize in short order that some water might help things along. I rolled my pants legs down, went to the kitchen as nonchalantly as possible, and filled a glass. My dad and brothers were in the living room watching TV, none the wiser. I went back to my room and got the job done, occasionally swishing the razor in the cup of water as quietly as possible. When I finished, I turned on the light to admire my handiwork, only to see by the cuts and nicks along my shinbone and ankle area that I would need some tissue. And more practice. And light.

The next day I ill-advisedly wore a skirt, and my dad, noticing the telltale cuts, took me aside that evening and said calmly, "Jewel, I am going to ask your mom to come by tomorrow. Maybe it's time she takes you bra shopping."

Just hearing my dad utter the word "bra" in the same breath as my own name made me want to crawl under a table. I thought we had an unspoken agreement not to discuss these things. He wasn't prudish or shy, and in fact he was the one who explained to me how babies are made when I was quite young. He had a book with pictures and handled it with a social worker's discipline. No shame, no awkwardness, just the facts. But that was before the divorce, before he had a string of girlfriends coming and going, strange women sitting with mixed feelings at our breakfast table while I made them oatmeal and my dad slept upstairs. And it was before I had figured out I was fantastically modest. Back on the homestead, I was the only one within a twenty-mile radius who did not take part in the group saunas on Sunday nights. No one in our area had a shower, so Sunday was basically a potluck and bath night. My grandfather would build a fire in the sauna and anyone who came by would get naked and pile in the small hot wooden room together to bathe and scrub and sweat. The brave would jump into the ice-cold pool outside the sauna door, which was basically a five-foot hole in the earth with visqueen to cover it and keep water in. Then folks would get dressed and share food.

I have vivid memories of all shapes and shades of body hair. You saw it all in that sauna. Chubby with bush. Cherubic with no bush. Thin with gray hair, the occasional exotic redhead. All the kids stripped down as well and everyone drank fresh birch-sap water we collected in jugs. I hated it though. I was the only one who wore a bathing suit in the sauna, waiting it out until everyone left to strip down and scrub up with fresh creek water and a cloth I brought from the house. My understanding of women and sexuality was from barrooms: that women gave themselves away and that men were perverts. I saw firsthand what a woman was willing to do for a compliment, and that men made chauvinistic and creepy comments with no idea any line had been crossed. At home there was little privacy to be found, and so I took it where I could get it.

As much as I hated to admit it, and as much as I hated the situation, the fact was I did need a training bra. All the girls had them, and while I can't say I was developed enough to have earned one, I hated to be left out of the teasing and bra-snapping going on at school, as the boys learned this new trick and the girls feigned it annoyed them when really they were proud their new accessories were noticed. The only cheeks burning with shame there belonged to the girls with no bra straps to show.

"Okay," I answered my dad, and like that, the topic was changed.

I hadn't seen my mom much, even though she still lived in Anchorage. I wish I could go back in time and tell my twelve-year-old self to ask why the hell not. I instinctively knew not to. She picked me up the next day and drove me to a mall, and as she guided me through the maze of racks of strange-looking contraptions, I tried my best to hide the fact that I was absolutely dying inside. When she involved a store clerk in our mission, I almost lost all composure. I stood mutely and imagined myself running from the building into the street to let the cold air hit me. I hid my embarrassment and went into the dressing room to try a few on, while my mom and the clerk waited outside the thin curtain, mere inches away, for my verdict.

"Is the fit all right, honey?" the store clerk said.

"Yeah," I answered meekly. I had no idea what a good fit was from a bad one.

"Let's see," my mom said. I stepped out to be examined. Four eyes focused directly on my nonexistent bosom, the cotton triangles of fabric so white the outline could be clearly seen through my shirt.

"Oh, that looks great, don't you agree?" the clerk said.

"Is it comfortable, Jewel? You don't want it to feel too tight."

"It's good," I said shyly. "Let's go home."

In the car on the way back my mom talked about how my feminine issues were nothing like hers had been. Her mom was scared of talking about such things. One day Arva had flung open my mom's bedroom door, thrown a sanitary belt and napkin into the room, and shut the door as quickly as it had been opened.

In reality my mom did not know how it happened for me. When womanhood arrived a few years later, she was gone, and I was alone in a house with some strangers she was staying with, and when I saw the blood, I wrapped my underwear in toilet paper, walked out the door, got a city bus to the grocery store, and stood dumbfounded in the feminine-products aisle. On the bus, I wrapped the package in as many bags as I could so that no one could see my dirty little secret. And when I lost my virginity a year after that, I would tell no one but my journal, and even there I could not bear to tell the truth. I rewrote and reimagined the whole thing—it was romantic, and the man thoughtful and kind. In reality he was much too old and drunk and he never called again and I was not ready as much as I felt like I just better get the whole thing over with. I had never been valued up to that time in my life by those closest to me, so how could I begin to value myself? It would take me years of learning to love and create safety for myself before that would ever be possible. I wish I could tell every young girl how special and valuable they are. I wish someone had told me.

All that was years away. That day I sat in the car, twisting my torso this way and that, experimenting with the strange new feeling around my chest, wondering if anyone at school would notice the next day, not sure which I dreaded more—boys noticing or not noticing.

I was a regular visitor at Diane's house. Her mom liked me, and Diane and I often played after school, dressing up and listening to the radio, dancing for hours to songs like "Girls Just Wanna Have Fun." One day she and her mom had to leave for some errand, and for whatever reason they left me alone in the house. They told me to make myself at home. And boy, did I ever. It began with me trying on Diane's necklace that was sitting on the bedside table. Black plastic beads made to look sort of like pearls. It was like a fever came over me. I wanted it. I put it in my pocket, thinking she would never miss it. Then I saw a pair of leggings I'd coveted peeking out of her closet. I took them as well, rolling them tightly and fitting them into my jacket pocket. I saw that pink geometric-patterned sweater and I had to have it in my life too. I gathered so much stuff that I went down to the kitchen and found a garbage bag to fill. And I filled it. I had no plan. It was as if there was a black hole hidden in me that I had unwittingly ripped wide open, this terrible need in me like an abyss, sucking everything I saw into it, trying to fill the void.

I think I carted the heavy bag several miles home and hid it away. I couldn't wear any of it without being caught, but I didn't give it that much thought. Within the hour Diane and her mom came home and there was nothing subtle about what I had done. Diane's mom called it a cry for help and asked my dad to go easy on me. And he did. He did not yell or hit me. He seemed to see I was in trouble, and lots of big, sad concerned eyes were cast upon me, which strangely didn't make me feel any better. I still had this emptiness inside me. No one seemed to be talking about how to fix it. Needless to say it put a strain on my relationship with Diane. School did not get easier either. I was diagnosed with dyslexia that year, which explained a lot.

That summer, after school ended, we moved back to Homer, thank God. Back to the barn. And I prepared for seventh grade. I was so nervous about junior high, and did my best to fit in by asking the most popular girl for a picture of herself so I could get my hair permed the same way. Again I recognized that embarrassed look of pity as she stood there on the stairs, late for third-period English. Little did she know I would befriend her and then rob her. Kidding! My stealing stopped for a while after the Diane incident.

I managed to make a few friends with the outcasts, and thought I was doing pretty well in general. Despite my difficult home life with my dad, I acted bright and cheery in class and in the hallways, but I must not have been fooling the school faculty, because I was enrolled in a special workshop in relaxation techniques and meditation. I noticed all the kids in it were "troubled." A group of five or six of us met with a woman who would turn the lights down low in the small classroom. We'd lie on the floor as she guided us through several exercises in a low, soothing voice. First relaxing every muscle in our bodies, then imagining different colors sweeping through our bodies, melting away any tension the colors came upon. She would tell us to imagine a place we felt safe, what it smelled like, what it looked like. She asked us to taste fresh cool water that might be running through our favorite spot. My place was at the head of the bay, where I often rode on my horse. The smell of cottonwood trees and timothy bluegrass, and the cold, crisp taste of the water I would drink from a spring. She asked us to listen to the sounds of our special place. That was easy for me—the hermit thrush had a three-tone call that I had spent entire afternoons listening to, along with eagles' cries high up in their nests, and the sound of the wind strumming the leaves like a harp. I often fell asleep in meditation, which the teacher said was a sign that I was learning how to fully relax.

I put the techniques I learned to good use. My aunt Stellavera (my dad's sister) also taught me Transcendental Meditation. I was so often stressed just being alone. There was no stability, no certainty, and no predictability in my life. The visualizations brought such a peace and allowed me to live in my own body and enjoy the space and calm in there for a little while. Meditation helped me to access the same thing my writing did: my intelligence and my instincts beyond the turmoil that inhabited the forefront of my mind. It was addictive, and a well I could draw from any time I wanted. I lay down on the floor and did my visualizations before I went to bed each night. I was able to engage my creativity and come up with other techniques that worked for me as well. I began a gratitude practice after looking back at my journals and discovering that I was surprisingly negative in my writing. I never complained in my day-to-day life, or to anyone, but when I held my writing up as a mirror to myself, I saw someone who worried and who always expected the worst. Seeing myself on the page, in black and white, was startling. I wanted to focus on what was good in my life, and so before bed each night, as a sort of prayer, I said all the things I was grateful for that day. I always managed to find a lot. It often had to do with nature and feeling taken care of by the land. Animals taught me not to feel sorry for myself, because animals accept things and stay in the moment. If an animal lost a leg, for instance, like one of our dogs did, it did not question God or sit around and mope. Animals did not wonder what on earth they did to deserve this and make it about their own morality—they learned to accept it and move on. And sometimes to stay out of the road next time. I learned to practice walking meditations, to still my mind as I explored the meadows or the beach. In these sessions I learned we need one another and are connected, whether we see it or not. I learned that connection is invisible. It dawned on me in science class when we put drops of food coloring in the water of some store-bought carnations, the flower would soon turn purple. In my mind I colored the wind purple, I imagined my lungs taking it in, and my skin turning the moody tint. I followed my exhale as the trees absorbed it, the leaves changing color. A chain reaction followed until the ocean, the birds, and each living thing were all variations of the same shade. This gave me such a profound sense of peace, and sense of how we all live interconnected existences.

I really tried to be mindful of when people were kind to me. I experimented with this mindfulness in other aspects of my life. I noticed my anxiety lessened the more present my mind was in my daily activities, and I began to find a meditative state while weeding the garden or our five-acre potato patch. I wasn't great at it, and rarely could sustain it for very long, but it was the foundation for something that would help me greatly in my life. I was trying to make good on my promise to do no harm to myself. To find positive ways to fill the emptiness that had measurable impact, rather than negative ways that, while distracting or numbing, ultimately would only set me back further.

eight

an invisible thread

During the summer after seventh grade my aunt Catkin came to visit, the youngest of my dad's siblings. She had risen to captain in the Marine Corps and we hit it off. She invited me to live with her and her two-year-old daughter and husband in Hawaii. I didn't hear much she said after that. Hawaii conjured up images of blue seas, balmy breezes, and easy living. The opportunity to escape that dark barn and all the ugliness inside seemed like a dream come true. No weeding gardens, no milking cows in subzero temperatures, no looking for lost calves in the frozen still of night, and no coal stove to bank. No dad yelling at me. Sign me up! The hitch was I had to earn the money to get there. I worked hard at my usual jobs: babysitting, driving hay equipment, singing with Dad. My aunt took care of enrolling me in school, and I bought my one-way plane ticket just in time to get there and get settled before school started. In hindsight, if I could go back and advise myself before leaving, I would tell my younger self to always buy a round-trip ticket. I would also caution myself against expecting Utopia to exist anywhere. Hawaii wasn't so much going from the frying pan into the fire, but it was at least like switching frying pans.

When I stepped off the plane, the air embraced me with tropical-scented arms. My eyes tried to take in the different scenery—the deep blues of sea and sky, the busy roads, the lush green mountains. However, by the time we walked out to the car that had been sitting in the sun, I almost had heatstroke. It was hot. Really hot. Like over seventy degrees hot. I didn't think I would ever get used to that heat and humidity. But I was sure willing to try. Catkin was cheerful and showed me a few sights as we drove to the far side of Oahu to the town of Kaneohe, which would be my new home. She also filled me in about the local public school as we drove, and said most white kids went to private schools because the locals were known for being very tough, but that I would be fine. At their house I met her now ex-husband, Larry, a lieutenant in the corps. Larry was the picture of a fit, clean-shaven Marine. He was Filipino and had a lot of family on the island. And then there was their daughter. Half Swiss and half Filipino, she had caramel skin and golden green eyes and curly locks of hair. She was sweet and funny, and I knew we would have a great time together.

We lived in a subdivision, with identical homes lined up neatly and indiscernibly on streets that looped with mazelike precision. All seemed well. Until school started. I learned quickly that my school was properly called something like the King Kamehameha Junior High, but was mostly referred to as the King Zoo. The kids in the seventh and eighth grade school seemed to outnumber the population of my entire hometown. But private school was beyond my reach, and so I tried to steel myself and hoped for the best.

The campus was beautiful—all outdoors, no windows, just slats separating indoors from out, and so the breeze swept through each classroom. Hallways were open, no walls, just canopy coverings for protection from daily rainfall. I was optimistic, but all illusions were shattered within five minutes of my first class, when a young boy said something clearly rude to the elderly math teacher in what I assumed was another language, but later learned was a broken English dialect the locals call pidgin. The student then took the teacher's toupee off his head and flung it out the window. I was gobsmacked. The teacher just hobbled outside to get his toupee and the kids laughed. My heart shrank.

In the days and weeks that followed, I was called tuna (slang for "slut"), haole (pronounced "howly," derogatory slang for "white"), and many other new and colorful terms I wished I'd had a dictionary for. *The White Girl's Guide to Being an Underdog*, it might be called. It's an odd thing to know you are being insulted and have to ask someone to define the insult for you. I nearly got jumped every day, and learned to keep my head down and be as invisible as possible. I found a few other white girls to form loose alliances with, and stayed out of trouble mostly. Every day at school felt like living in a powder keg—one wrong look at a local girl and she would say, "What you lookin' at, haole tuna? You like beef?" "Beef" meant a fight. I had to ask about that one too. At first the term made me hungry, and I almost said, "I would love beef!" but once I caught on, I would say, "No, no, I would not like to beef," so properly that it would elicit giggles. I kept my tail between my legs and was able to walk away most times, but one day a local girl accused me of liking her boyfriend. I said I didn't even know who he was. When she enlightened me, I said, "Him? I don't even think he's cute." I thought for sure this was a great way out of the mess. It was true. He was not cute. I had no interest in him. Of course she was insulted and said, "Oh, so you think I'm dating some dog?" Oops. I saw the error of my ways but was unable to take it back, and soon a group of girls surrounded us and were yelling, "Beef, beef, beef!" Soon the circle closed in and I could hear chants of "Knock dat grin off dat haole's face!" I did not want to fight. I had never hit anyone, but I had been hit enough to know I hated it. And this girl was big, half Samoan, and outweighed me by a lot. That, I was wise enough to not point out. But still, here I was, facing certain death and feeling more like throwing up than like fighting. My antagonist leaned in to push me, and as she did, she whispered in my ear, "Next time I push you, just run." I looked in her eyes and could see she had no fight in her. We were both victims of the group around us. But the others had formed such a tight circle I didn't think I could break through it without one of them hitting me for running. Luckily, there was a guy who stopped in a beat-up old Toyota truck when he saw the commotion on the street. He opened his door and he hollered, "Hey, you need a ride?" I had no idea who this man was, but just the presence of an adult made the blood lust dissipate in the group, and I walked to the truck and got in. He didn't say a word that I can recall. I told him where I lived, tears quietly streaming down my face. He was kind enough not to ask me about it.

My home life began to turn sour as well. Larry, it turned out, was controlling, rageful, and mean. It started with small outbursts, where his anger didn't match the trigger—after doing chores one day I covered an unused portion of dog food with Saran Wrap and put it in the fridge so it would not go bad on the counter. He found me in my room and screamed that he would now have to throw everything away because I was so disgusting as to put animal food in the fridge with our own.

Another time, a neighborhood friend and I were playing in the storm drains with some other kids, throwing rocks and yelling in the long tunnels to hear our echoes. I lost track of time and Larry came looking for me and heard us playing in the storm drain. He ordered me out like a drill sergeant, grabbed my wrist, and dragged me home. He was a quiet volcano during the walk to the house, but at dinner he exploded and let me have it. I was eating peas and they kept falling off my fork, which seemed to be driving him nuts. My aunt was chatting nervously, trying to keep the peace as she felt the tension escalate, and to keep Larry calm. The veins began to bulge in his face like a rabid pit bull. "You make me sick! You are a fucking slut and you make me sick! You fucking whore! I bet you have been fucking all the boys you were playing with today!" My aunt just kept saying, "Now, Larry, let's stay calm, Larry." I remember looking at her and thinking, *It's your job to be protecting me. What are you doing?* It was then I thought she must have been in denial, or that she had her hands full protecting herself and she couldn't protect anyone else. All I knew is that I had to keep the tension from spilling too badly onto my little cousin. I already knew how to toe the line and be as small a target as possible, to just do my time.

I had no money to get home, and I couldn't sing or raise money easily in the suburb we lived in. I was stuck until my Alaskan dividend came through. Every Alaskan resident is paid a royalty from the oil the state sells, as long as you have been a resident for a year. I would have to stay in Hawaii half the school year while I waited for the check, and I often listened to music as an escape. I remember Kate Bush helping me to pass much of my time. I wrote to my mom about how miserable I was. She reminded me to hold the pink stone she had given me a few years earlier. It was a piece of smooth round rose quartz. She said she had one too, and to imagine an invisible silver thread that tied the two together. That tied us together. I would fall asleep at night with it clenched tightly in my hand.

School life at least eased up a bit once all the local kids learned I could yodel. I dare say yodeling saved my life. Well, it saved me from a lot of fights, anyway. There was a very proud cultural heritage among the locals, and many of the kids performed traditional Hawaiian dance and music. I noticed how the voices of the singers often cracked, similar to the crack employed when you yodel. The Hawaiian version was much more melodic, more similar to what I would call a Swiss style of yodeling, whereas German is more rapid. On the bus ride home one day some kids were practicing, and I began to visit with them about their singing. I showed them how I could yodel. Before I knew it, one of the local girls told the whole bus to "Shut up and listen ta da haole girl yodel!" And yodel I did. The whole busload of brutes turned to me and I yodeled for all I was worth. From that day on, anywhere I went on campus, I heard, "Hey, dere's dat haole girl who can do dat ting wit her voice, check it!" And like some organ-grinder monkey, I yodeled on the spot. In hallways, classrooms, on bus rides. I didn't complain; it was way better than nearly being beaten up every day.

nine

my own ladder

After that first semester, my money came in and I got a ticket to Alaska. The plan was for me to go live with my mom and brothers in Anchorage. When I left for Hawaii, my dad had moved off the homestead again, staying with a string of girlfriends, and I never had a place to stay. I learned early on to farm myself out, sleeping on a girlfriend's couch, sometimes with my aunt Mossy, helping her run a bed-and-breakfast on her ranch. I ran hay equipment in the summer and sang for money. But my dad was always in control and we fought horribly. I was so excited to finally live with my mother. I got on the plane in sunny Hawaii and got off in gloomy, dark Anchorage, where it was ten below zero. Snow was piled high and the sun set around 4 p.m. My mother lived in a seedy part of town, called Bar Alley, in a small pink house sandwiched on a block between the infamous Chilkoot Charlie's bar and project housing.

My mom and her boyfriend-slash-business partner had converted the front room into a showroom for glasswork. The back had a small kitchen, bathroom, and bedroom, where my brothers and I slept. My mom slept downstairs in her studio, a basement with a workbench full of sheets of stained glass, soldering tools, a sandblasting booth for etching, and a small bed in the corner. We would go to an alternative school around the corner, called Steller, that had a reputation for being the place where social rejects who couldn't make it in regular public school were sent. All the kids there had a story. Some were openly gay, some were pregnant teens, some were failing out of other schools. It was full of individual oddballs, and I felt much more at home, even after transferring in half-way through the year. I fell in with a group of kids from the projects. Dionne was half Aleut and half African-American. She looked Polynesian somehow, with exotic almond eyes that were the deepest brown they shone like a watery midnight peering back at you. Bethany was full-blooded Athabascan. She was tall and slender, with the grace of her culture. Her mother came to school occasionally, and had the traditional facial tattoos of her tribe. Dutima and Kalindy were twins, half East Indian and half French Canadian, and they modeled in their free time away from school for catalogs and the like. They were tall, with eyes the color of the brightest yellow gold that were set off by skin that was creamy olive. They introduced me to Garrett, whose dad was black and mom was white, yet he hated all other white people. He was very reluctant about becoming friends. On the fringes of our circle were Sam and Tyrone, who were Cripps (yes, the Cripps and Bloods made it to Anchorage). I heard that both have since been killed in gang-related violence.

Dionne and I became the closest, and by the end of the year I was staying at her house more often than my own. Her mother, Eleanor, became a sort of surrogate mother and the three of us did a lot together. Eleanor was a full-blooded Aleut (Alaska native), and as a child had lost her right hand just above the wrist but could use the bit of wrist she had quite handily to carry things like grocery bags. She was a single mom and worked hard, and she was very close to her daughter; they were like a team that stuck together. I craved that closeness. They lived in the projects, and Eleanor was putting herself through school, taking odd jobs where she could without losing her welfare status. They lived on food stamps but she fed me as if I were one of her own.

I learned to adapt to the city as a teenager, and my pidgin slang came in handy as it made me sound a little more urban. Or at least I thought it did. I began to dress like my new friends, very mid-'80s. I relinquished the grubby secondhand homestead gear and work boots and saved up some money for flats, pegged skinny jeans, black stockings with short black stretchy miniskirts. White button-down shirts with bolos, tank tops with blazers (sleeves rolled up of course), and then there was the ever-present smell of enough hairspray to be a fire hazard when we were all gathered for lunch. The school operated more like a college, where we could attend and create class schedules with some flexibility. Garrett and Sam would often hot-wire a car and take me out for lunch, then we would return it an hour later, no one ever the wiser that I knew of. Garrett and I became close friends, and he often confided in me about his home life. Sometimes his dad beat him so severely that he had to miss school so that no teacher would call social services, staying home for a week to let the bruises heal. I had never been beaten like that. I hoped never to know that feeling. Dionne and I would ride the city bus to his house and visit with him during these times. He was stoic and hard on the outside, but as I got to know him I could see his heart was tender and breaking behind the wall he was building to survive. He was, after all, still just a child. I knew that feeling.

Life with my mom was not mean at all. She was seemingly the opposite of my dad. She did not yell or hit. She was soft-spoken and calm and full of artistic imagination, always making me feel anything was possible. But all her time was spent reading or doing artwork, and very little was spent with us. I remember her crying a lot. We could hear her through the floorboards.

My favorite times with her were in her studio, where she taught me how to do glasswork. I watched as she drew a design on paper in Sharpie. She could draw freehand very well. I would then help her cut each shape and number them. We laid the paper cutouts on sheets of colored glass she had selected and then drew an outline around one using the glass cutting knife to carefully free the unique form from its generic former self. We'd wrap copper foil around the edges of the glass, and slowly a mosaic would come together as her drawing was reassembled, fitting together like a jigsaw puzzle. Then the fun work of soldering each piece, the lead melting like mercury when I touched it to the hot tool, and hardening again almost as quickly. I would accompany her on installations, going to rich people's homes, listening in like a fly on the wall as the owners marveled at their new purchase and my mother waxed on about the philosophical and spiritual undertones of her work. On a few occasions my mom and I got singing jobs this way. She and I worked up an a cappella set, and she would offer to sing at any functions for the same clients. A few took her up on it, and we would dress nicely and walk around parties in backyards, singing songs for partygoers much like magicians walk around performing tricks in similar settings. Soon my mother would be talking with all the guests as if she were one of them. I took everything in, always from the outside.

My mom began to turn me on to music she liked—Odetta, Josephine Baker, Tracy Chapman. I listened, transfixed, as lyrics stirred my soul, and raw voices transmuted hurt and fear into hope. I had gotten hold of her copy of Leonard Cohen and Jennifer Warnes singing "Famous Blue Raincoat." I listened to the story a dozen times in a row, seeing Leonard's lyrics come to life like a movie in my mind. I wanted to inspire that kind of tragic passing of two ships. I wanted to be able to write in a way that imparted the angst, the longing and moody undertones, an entire psyche as much as a scene or feeling. It would be the inspiration for "Foolish Games" five years later: *I watched from my window, always felt I was outside, looking in on you. You stood in my doorway, with nothing to say, besides some comment on the weather.*

My brothers and I continued to drift apart, as we had slowly begun to do after the divorce. I think we all became so preoccupied with surviving that it drew us each inward in solitary fashion, slowly causing us to separate rather than grow closer together. When I moved to Hawaii, Shane moved to Wyoming to work for an outdoor guide. By the time we were back together in Anchorage, the drift had become more pronounced. We went to the same school but hung out with separate crowds, and Atz Lee tried his best to fit in, though he always struggled the worst. He switched schools often to escape bullying, and looking back I wish I had taken more time with him and helped him. I was so busy trying to save myself and find friends to fit in with that it took all my focus, it seems. I was still operating under the belief that my little brother was the enemy because he was my dad's clear favorite. I spent much of my childhood trying to feel better about myself by knocking down Dad's favorite. Such a sad and misguided energy, one I aimed toward my brother but should have rightfully been focused on my dad.

At the end of the school year I went back to Homer, drifting with my backpack between couches again. Around this time Dad and I began to tour farther across the state, picking up a band here and there if a bar wanted a more up-tempo set. This was my first introduction to playing with bands, though I was just a backup singer. We still did covers mostly, old Hank Williams Sr. stuff, Jim Croce, Clapton, anything that the folks could dance to. I began to sing lead on a few songs, like Kris Kristofferson's "Help Me Make It Through the Night" and "The End Is Not in

Sight" by Amazing Rhythm Aces. I sang "The House of the Rising Sun"
and learned to get the crowd going by belting it out. People requested to
hear me sing for the first time, which was fun. Adjusting to a band was
easier musically than it was socially, mainly because a thirty-five-year-old
musician kept making moves on me. To save money on hotel rooms, we
would pitch a tent on the beach in the wee hours after the gig and lay our
sleeping bags out. It became an unspoken game of chess as the musician
waited to put his bag down after he saw where mine was. I learned quickly
to put myself against the farthest tent wall, and my dad's bag next to
mine.

The bars in the interior of Alaska were different and fun to play. I
can't recall the names of some, but remember that it seemed like they
were in the middle of nowhere, strategically located so that folks from the
many outlying towns could drive about the same distance to drink and
socialize. The chasms between my school life and social life and my night
life widened. I blended in with the adults quite easily, and the social aspect of kids my age became increasingly difficult to navigate.

For the next school year I wanted to continue going to Steller Second-
ary School, but my mom had moved into a new house, where we joined
her. Our new home was a black house with white trim that sat all alone
across from a cemetery in downtown Anchorage. It was not a good area.
The project housing nearby had been demolished and heaps of crumbled
lives were left for years in the lot down the road. Ours was the only house
left on the block. I thought it was fitting the house was dressed in mourning colors for those who slept eternally across the street from us.

I remember the first bum I saw freeze to death on our sidewalk. The
alcohol made him sleepy and the cold soon made him numb and he
slipped from this world. *His spirit making the short journey from our side
of the street to the next*, I thought to myself. In the dusky twilight an ambulance came and lifted his stiff body into the back. From that time on

we kept a number taped to our fridge that we would call when we saw a drunk asleep on our sidewalk. Good Samaritans would come and load them up, some groggy and spitting, others grateful and compliant, as they were driven to a safe, warm place to sleep for the night.

We may have developed a reputation for being helpful to the homeless, as several started camping on our street and coming by. My brothers and I were home alone in our basement when a belligerent drunk knocked on our front door. Shane went upstairs and peeked around the corner to see the man's red face, swollen with anger and drink. "I need some aspirin!" he was saying. He looked scary and we decided not to answer. We returned to our video games downstairs, and the drunk followed from outside and rapped on the tiny basement windows. He was on his knees, hunched over, face pressed against the window, hands cupped up to his eyes to reduce the glare. "I can see you in there! Goddamnit! I can see you in there! I need some fucking aspirin!" He began to shatter the window. We picked up the phone and shouted that we were calling the cops and he left. We of course did not call the cops. They would not have come in time anyway.

The window remained unfixed the rest of the winter, the cold air seeping in and making our rooms down there bitterly cold. We kept our doors shut and turned the heat up in our rooms, and avoided the basement as much as possible, although it was where the TV was, which is powerful motivation for three teenagers. So we would grab all the blankets off our beds and wrap ourselves in them and enjoy some mindless distraction in arctic temperatures.

My mother took the master bedroom on the main floor for herself but she never slept in it. There was a separate apartment upstairs with a private entry that would have been perfect for renting out, but instead that was where she stayed. When I heard her get home, I would go up the stairs in the back. I loved to visit with her. She seemed magical and calm and serene. She talked about art and her dreams. She said some people in life were dreamers, and others were warriors. She said she was a dreamer and told me of her elaborate visions. She was like a medicine woman, full of portent and premonitions. She said I was a warrior, a doer, and capable of handling anything. This made me proud. It reminded me of a time years before, when we were visiting her after the divorce. I was about nine. I finally confided in her that Dad had started hitting Atz Lee and me. I'm not sure how I expected her to react, but it was somewhere in the realm of protecting us. Maybe taking us away from that place. Taking us back. I hoped. Instead she looked at me and said, "Jewel. You have a steel rod in you. You cannot be broken. Atz Lee is more fragile. You need to look out for him."

Children are incapable of comprehending the whole picture. Incapable of being angry at a parent and saying, *Hey, that isn't what I need to hear right now. I need you to protect me and want me and love me. I am fragile too. I'm afraid I'm breaking.* Instead I saw my mom as most kids do, especially because I had so much need. She was a deity and I assumed she must be telling me the truth. In a way it was the truth, and I knew that down deep too. *I can take anything. I will not break.* It was like being given marching orders to get back in the trenches and *take it, take it, take it.* And at age fourteen I could add *I am a warrior and a doer* to the list. I had no idea the dreamer was grooming me to be her servant; at the time she was pure oxygen for me.

My mom worked with glass mostly, but that winter had begun working with ice. She liked the impermanence of ice, she said, that her art would be experienced for only a moment before it disappeared. She said it made the experience more special. I felt the fleeting moments of our interactions were the same. Special, ephemeral, and intense before she disappeared again.

In our backyard she covered female mannequins with satin sheets and lay them on the ground. Each day we used a water bottle to spray the sheets down so that a new layer of ice built up each night. After a week she lifted the sheets off the mannequin and the ghostly, silken frozen forms of women were propped up all over our backyard. It was eerie and beautiful.

Large chunks of glacial ice would come off barges and she did installations like launching ice lanterns filled with candles into lakes against the backdrop of the black Alaskan night. Now that I write this, I can't remember whether she actually did this one or only talked about it. It's hard to say whether my imagination took over or whether it happened in real life. Much of my experience with my mom was this way. My mind filled in holes and vacancies with vivid and beautiful experiences to keep my heart from breaking with the ugliness of the bitter truth.

One art installation I do remember. She took over a three-room gallery and filled it with ice carvings of women with berries placed inside their bodies. I imagined they looked like frozen molecules of blood in a crystalline flesh. My mother placed rock salt in their hands, which caused them to melt—symbolic of the way women embrace what destroys us so often, I overheard her say. Leftover salt covered the floor except for paths that led from one room to the next, lit with tea candles. A song she recorded a cappella played on a loop, an old folk song with a haunting melody. The ice fragments shimmering like wet crystals in the candlelit darkness. It was stunning and she was brilliant. I could hear those who walked through comment on the symbolism of it all. They were moved.

One day at the graveyard house she came downstairs from her apartment, sat us down, and announced that she had cancer. It didn't dawn on me to ask what kind. I was so scared for her. She said she needed to go to Hawaii to heal. I think she got money out of my dad to go for treatment. Not much changed with her gone. We got ourselves out the door as usual. When she came back several weeks later, she told amazing tales of vision-questing and sleeping in caves, where she had dreams of lizards that taught her things about life and the universe. She brought me back feathers and rocks and taught me how to make medicine wheels. She also brought me totem animal cards, and we would stay up for hours as I asked the cards questions about my worries and fears. She would help interpret the cards I turned over, teaching me about myself and what I could do to improve my life. I was always looking for deeper meaning. She was always happy to help. We sat on her bed and I asked the cards about boys and school. She never mentioned the cancer, and when I asked her about it, and where it was, she said dismissively, "Oh, it was something small on my leg. It's gone now," and it was dropped.

Money was scarce. Things were disjointed and fractured. Other than these encounters in the evening with my mom, we rarely saw her for breakfast or dinner on a daily basis. My brothers and I fended for ourselves. I often stayed with Dionne and her mom, over in the projects on the other side of town. I took the city bus several connections to school, her house, and back to mine at times. I met lots of interesting characters on the bus lines, and saw a lot of life. Girls giving boys blow jobs in the women's bathroom at the bus station. Drug baggies quietly exchanged. I remember one pimp who got on the bus, then stopped in alarm and said loudly, "Am I in Hollywood?" He began to walk down the aisle toward me in the back, the petite white girl wearing a miniskirt and leather jacket complete with an '80s tidal wave of bangs. I knew enough by then not to take the bait and kept looking out the window, sensing a punch line coming. He made it over to me and said, "'Cause, honey, I am seeing *stars!*"

It was the first time I'd heard this line, and it did make me laugh. I would have the opportunity to hear him say the line to others many more times that year, as we always seemed to be on the same bus line.

I took care of myself, and took jobs where they came up. I gigged quite a lot during this time, which is how I bought many of my nicer school clothes. I was frugal, though, and saved everything I could, keeping my cash in a box in the cupboard. Sometimes my dad and I traveled on weekends to remote towns for shows. Sometimes I would sit in with other bands or players I had met through the years.

One such musician was Paul. He was the father of three young girls and had a nice wife. My dad and I had been to his house several times to rehearse. On this occasion my dad was back in Homer, and Paul asked me to do the gig solo with him. I was probably fourteen. The gig was at the Gaslight Lounge, a small, dingy place, but it paid two hundred bucks, so I learned the songs—a blues set—and he played rhythm and lead. When the gig was done, we went into the small back room to get our jackets. Paul turned to hand me my coat, leaned in quickly, and tried to shove his tongue down my throat. I was afraid and frozen and quiet. I pushed him away without saying a word and walked out without my coat. He let me go. I walked down the street at 1 a.m., in broad daylight. I had never been so thankful for the midnight sun, lighting my way to our little black home with the white trim. It was freezing out, but I did not shiver. A numbness settled over me, and a fear that touched something much deeper in me. This feeling would take years to understand as well.

Around this time my mom picked up and moved to Seward. There was a fire sale of her art and antiques, everything was sold. Shane was in Switzerland on an exchange program he managed to get into, Atz Lee went back to Homer, and I stayed alone in the house across from the cemetery so I could finish out the school year at Steller. I made my own meals and got myself to school just like I had always done, but I didn't have my favorite roommate upstairs to visit with anymore. To remedy that I would hitch rides to Seward on weekends to see her.

My school's administration was flexible, and when I realized I was able to fulfill my credits and class duties in four days each week, I was free to commute to Seward the other three days to be with my mom. I had a room there that I plopped my duffel down in. My mom lived upstairs in the attic, which had been converted into a living space, and she had a roommate as well. I cried a lot in this house. I was too busy surviving to cry in Anchorage, but in Seward a sadness and a fear came over me. My mom seemed sad too. She said she had developed a heart condition and had to rest a lot, and I did not see her much. I spent my time riding my bike around the idyllic town and pushing my body on runs over Resurrection Pass, a famous trail where a race was held each summer. Running had become a freedom for me. I would run as hard as I could to get beyond anxiety and to a feeling of calm. Flying across the mountaintops, down steep valleys, hearing nothing but my breath and my heartbeat. And my thoughts.

In Seward I had a lot of time on my hands, and heard through the grapevine that there was an American Indian powwow up north—a large gathering of many tribes open to anyone who wished to learn more about their culture. I had long been drawn to Native American culture, and my mom had taught me to do medicine wheels. My mom's roommate and I hopped a train up to Denali, where the gathering was held. I had never been to Denali National Park and the sight from the train was breathtaking. I was warmly welcomed by the gathering and its organizers, who invited me to join in the opening ceremony, a talking circle. It wasn't until this moment that it dawned on me that I was far from home, and I knew no one else there. I got incredibly shy in an instant, especially as it dawned on me that I would have to talk. A talking stick is passed around the circle, and while it is in your hand, you may say anything that is in your heart. When it was handed to me, I clammed up. I held the stick and I looked down at my lap. This was so much more personal than singing onstage. I passed the stick to the next person without saying a word.

When the circle broke, I considered grabbing my backpack and hopping right back on a train, when I was swallowed in a sudden shadow. I looked up to see two large Ottawa Indians standing over me, blocking the sun. One of them said I needed to walk with them. So I did, a raven-haired brave on each side of a small blonde girl. They both began to chuckle. I asked what was funny and they pointed to a tattoo on one of their forearms—two dark mountain peaks with a sun rising between them. It looks like us, one said. I laughed as well. They took me to a quiet place and sat down with me and became very serious. They said Great Spirit had told them that I would need to learn to speak from my heart. I explained that I wrote a lot from my heart. They said no, that was not what they saw. There was more. They said they'd had a vision that I would speak to many people one day and that I would need to learn to *speak* truth and with honesty from my heart. I was speechless. I was completely unable to do that. I went to a mountain by myself later that day and tried to say something to the clouds but nothing came. I began to cry. I had no idea how to say anything real. My feelings were so deeply hidden inside myself that the only way I knew to express them was through the tip of a pen. I stayed at the gathering that day and practiced in the talking circles. I grew very close to my Indian uncles, as they called themselves. I was close with them and the culture for decades to come. They started me on my path and were angels in my life.

I was committed to staying in Anchorage because, for the first time in my life, school was a bright spot for me. It was the first school I had attended for more than one year. I had a teacher named Ken (all teachers went by first names there) who taught a philosophy class. Reading philosophy felt like the first breath of oxygen I'd had in a long time. I was drowning in my life, and here were these amazing minds reaching through time, speaking to me. I was severely dyslexic, and reading was very difficult for me, but I was so passionate about the ideas in these books that I finally developed a system that worked for me. First I learned to focus my eyes in a different way, so that the black type showed up, instead of all the white negative space. I could focus like this for only a line or two, and so I would paraphrase what it said in my own words in the margins before continuing. This helped my mind internalize the ideas and I would stay up late into the night, adrenaline running through my body as I contemplated the words and teachings of everyone from Pascal to the Buddha, Thucydides and Socrates, to Dostoevsky's Grand Inquisitor.

Reading the great classics transformed my life. I went from being a scared teenager who was stealing cars with friends on lunch breaks— complete with big hair and miniskirts, flirting with the local dime-bag dealer in the hood—to feeling like a semi-self-confident and self-possessed woman who had learned she could think. My teacher saw my love of the work, and in ninth grade he offered to let me have my own group of eighth grade students. I would get the reading assignment from Ken, and then it was up to me to get ten kids through the material and ready for a large symposium where other groups would join in. It turns out my dyslexia was a blessing in disguise. The system I used to help myself read also worked well for the other students. I watched these books transform other kids as well and build their confidence, showing them they could care, and they could think. I saw their clothing and their hairstyles change, and their posture change, just like mine had. My group shone with comprehension and ownership of ideas. They were able to internalize the concepts and speak from their own lives, debating difficult material. It was good to feel proud of myself instead of scared and sad.

Ken invited me to speak with teachers at neighboring schools and to lead symposiums. It was funny to watch teachers react to a small blonde student showing up, and many were dismissive and condescending, though it was also fun to surprise them by being prepared and to shake them out of their hubris with wit and a sharply placed point.

I felt so empowered by all the ideas in the books I was reading that I got a bit drunk on reason. It felt safe. If I applied logic and the dialectic process to my life, perhaps I could turn it around. Perhaps I could beat the fates and the stars I was born under. Even my journal writing at the time became less reflective and emotional, in favor of treatises and essays. I learned to hide in logic, and shutting my heart down felt safe.

One day my teacher wisely said to me, "Jewel, you are also deeply feeling. You might like some of the poets." Another great change in my life. I began to read the works of Pablo Neruda, Octavio Paz, Gioconda Belli, and eventually Charles Bukowski and Anaïs Nin, and I felt the other half of my spirit find expression. My intuitive emotional self found a voice along with my analytical self. I began to understand that my mind and my emotions could be the ladder out of my life. Reading these works and feeling the ripple effect they had on my soul and creativity made me hopeful. They made me dream. Something I had lost.

While talking with my mom in Seward, I shared that I dreaded going back to Homer to live with my dad again, as was the custom in the summer. He was building himself a house on the homestead, and he and Atz Lee were living in a makeshift cabin there. My dad had a bed in the kitchen and Atz Lee had a tiny loft, narrow as a pocket, that he could barely crawl into, no room for sitting up. There wasn't really room for me and I didn't want to be back in a volatile cycle with my dad. My mom, always full of surprising ideas, said, "Why don't you move out?"

Looking back now, I realize this is absurd. Most moms would say, Honey, you can always stay with me. You should never be afraid to live with a parent. You are safe here. Instead, she suggested I move out on my own. At fifteen. And anyway, why not? It's what I had already been doing in many ways, though I'd never paid rent or bought groceries. That part would be new. But honestly the choice was not that hard: I could live in a cabin with an asshole, or I could just live in a cabin.

I did some asking around and found out my uncle's cabin down the road from my dad's place was vacant. I made a deal with him for four hundred dollars a month, and when I went to find my box of cash for rent, it was gone. I searched the house frantically. I asked my mom if she had seen it. "Maybe some movers took it when I was selling all the antiques," she offered. It didn't seem a likely scenario. In the meantime, I went about gigging, babysitting, driving tractors, and cutting hay to earn the first month's rent. I was relying heavily on the fact that a steady, if small, stream of cash would come in from doing shows with my dad.

ten

a sea change

I didn't have much to move in with, other than a few cups and dishes my dad gave me from his storage shed, as I had been living out of a duffel bag for years. I was so proud when I moved into my little cabin. It was a tiny one-room box with an outhouse in the backyard. A kitchen counter with no sink. No plumbing. No refrigerator other than an icebox outside, a wooden box lined with foam insulation. You could put a chunk of ice in there and keep milk cold for a few days. There was a single bare bulb that hung from a wire in the middle of the room. A bed on posts, so you could store things underneath, a plank of plywood on two sawhorses for a table, and a window looking out at the trees. There was enough grazing around the cabin to stake a horse out on, which was a lucky thing, because I would need to ride my horse to work, as I was too young to have a driver's license.

Work was in town, about fifteen miles away, so I rode my horse two hours by beach if the tide was low. I would stake him out in a field at my aunt Sunny's, who lived near town, hitchhike the last three miles, then ride home, thankful again for the long hours of daylight. Horses lack headlights. Sometimes I could be seen on the weekend at the McDonalds's drive-thru, my horse in line with all the other cars. He would stick his head in the window as if ordering his own fries.

Other times I'd hitchhike, though it could be hard to get a ride home late, as few people go that far out of town after 7 p.m. or so. Sometimes I'd be stuck, unable to catch a ride, and stayed in town with a friend for a few days. I always carried a backpack with some extra clothes.

I returned home once, after being gone like this for several days, to find the plastic tub of dishes I'd forgotten about had grown a mountain of mold on them. I was thoroughly disgusted. I had run out of the house late one morning, intending to do the dishes when I got back that night. No such luck. Days had passed before I got home and I was now staring down a nasty chore. Not only did I have to contend with the mess, but I had to run to the creek and get water, fill up the five-gallon jug, wrestle it back to the cabin, and heat it up on a camping propane burner. Dishes were a real sore spot for me. I can't tell you how many fights took place over washing dishes. My dad yelling that I wasn't doing it good enough, me rewashing them, failing inspection again. Redoing them again. This went on so long once that I was grounded until I'd cleaned the house with a toothbrush. I hated dirty dishes. I hated the sight of them. Then it dawned on me. There was no more Dad. No one could make me do them. I was an independent woman, and my own boss. I grabbed a shovel from a neighbor, went outside, dug a hole, and buried those dishes. A perfect fifteen-year-old's solution to a problem.

The next day I bought paper plates. They were also a good fire starter for the wood-burning stove. Another solid solution, I thought to myself. Plus, fewer dishes meant more time for writing and reading after work. It was time to take everything I had been theorizing and philosophizing about and see if I could apply it to my life. It was time to work on an internal ladder that might get me out of where I was. Could I use my reason and my mind to change my internal landscape enough to climb out of what seemed like a predetermined cycle and beat the odds? Nature versus nurture. I had to try. I knew I didn't want to be a human full of holes. I wanted to be a whole human.

The first summer on my own was a great summer. I turned sixteen and eventually got my license, though I still had no car to drive, which meant I hitchhiked a lot. I was headed into town for work, and an older guy, maybe in his twenties, picked me up around Fritz Creek. He introduced himself as Lee. I said, "I'm Jewel Kilcher." I didn't know it at the time, but he was a friend of my cousin Dylan, who had told him that I was a singer. About a week earlier, Lee had been working on a fishing boat and overheard some of the crew talking about this blonde Kilcher kid, Dylan's cousin. So when he realized who he had picked up, Lee wanted to warn me to be careful hitchhiking. He started out by saying, "You know, you're a very pretty girl, you should not be hitchhiking." I said, "Thanks, I'm pretty careful." This didn't seem to satisfy him, so he said it again, "You are pretty. You shouldn't just hitchhike around." "Got it, thanks," I said curtly. "I mean, you could get raped out here." He said it again, and I got the creeps. I pulled a four-inch skinning knife from my boot and swiftly stuck the tip neatly under his chin while he drove, and said, "Are you gonna fuck with me?" I don't know what I was expecting, but his response caught me off guard. He laughed. Hard. I could tell in an instant that I had misread him. He was a nice guy who was genuinely concerned for my safety. As I slipped the knife back in my boot, he added, "That was so *hot!*" Ah. And he was gay. We were destined to be best friends.

Lee was a real source of support. He knew I never had firewood at my place and would drop some off for me. I never had money for food, so he would feed me out back of the restaurant where he worked as a chef. I also went down to the docks, and took all the halibut heads the tourists had thrown away, and cut the cheeks out. They were a delicious cut of fish, and best of all they were free.

Lee often drove me out to my cabin if I was stuck in town, or let me crash with him in the converted old school bus he lived in. He introduced me to his friends, although I never told people how old I was. I was embarrassed by it. I just let people assume I was older. Lee heard the first drafts of my early songs and later toured with me through the heights of my career. Today he lives with me, and in addition to being my best friend, he's manny to my son, Kase.

It was harder than I thought to make ends meet, because shortly after I moved, my dad announced he could not sing with me anymore. He said he had talked it over with his therapist and it was just not healthy. Well, most likely it hadn't been healthy long before this, but to stop now when I really needed the cash was a huge blow. I didn't know how to play guitar, I was just backup and sang harmonies mostly, so getting a gig on my own was not a real option.

I got busy finding other jobs. I worked for a cowboy on the Spit, giving horse rides to tourists. He would run a string of horses and take folks for rides on one side of the beach, and I had my own string that I was in charge of farther down the beach. It meant long days in the saddle, and you always had to be on your toes, but I enjoyed the work. It just didn't pay a ton.

One day I saw a flyer posted on the docks for a dance clinic that would be in town for two weeks. I had never danced but thought it might be fun to try. As it turned out, I was not a promising dancer, but the teacher, Joe, found out I could sing. I usually stayed after classes asking questions, and as we became friendly, I invited him to a show my whole family was putting on as a lark—a Kilcher talent night. My aunts, uncles, and cousins are all very talented and had decided to get together and have an evening of entertaining each other. After Joe heard me sing, he told me he thought he might be able to help me get a scholarship to the school he taught at in Michigan, called Interlochen Arts Academy. I was flattered he thought I had the talent to go, and the idea of going to a private school like this excited me.

Joe got me the forms I needed. I wrote the essays required and we got my school records together from the six different schools I had attended. The hitch was that I had to submit an aria for a vocal scholarship. What the heck was an aria? I was a bar singer who belted out blues songs and did covers of Jim Croce and the Eagles. I had no idea where to start. I told my mom my problem, and she helped me audit a music class in Anchorage. I picked a French aria and learned it by ear. As I could not read music, I asked the teacher to help me learn melody. A friend of hers loaned us a studio and somehow a nylon-string guitarist came on board. I had never sung in my falsetto before, and I enjoyed the soft, clear sound. I did not have much volume in that range at that time, or fullness, so I relied on purity and clarity of tone. No vibrato. I had no idea whether my pronunciation was correct. It had an innocence to it that I hoped would be appealing, because I didn't have much else to offer as far as technique or education. I recorded it and shipped it off, never thinking I would be accepted. I was wrong. I got a letter a few weeks later saying I had been awarded a partial scholarship, and I could attend if I paid the balance of tuition. A mere ten thousand dollars. And if I wanted to enroll for my upcoming junior year, I had to come up with it in three months. Shit.

My mom proved helpful. She taught me a system I still use when looking for a solution to a problem.

Her: Write your goal down on a piece of paper, Jewel.

Me: To go to Interlochen in the fall.

Now write down what you need to accomplish that.

Earn $10,000.

Now write down ways you can earn that.

I thought and thought and finally came up with the idea of a fundraising concert. I wrote that down.

Now write down a date to play the concert.

I chose one month before school started.

Now write down what you need to do in order to pull off a concert.

Get help organizing it.

Who can do that?

Maybe friends will help.

What else do you need to do?

Find a venue.

And there it was in front of me. How to transform an idea into reality. All I had to do was execute what I had written down. And that's what I did.

My uncle Otto's wife, Charlotte, was a graphic designer and helped me design a flyer. Otto's ex-wife, Sharon, was an accountant (I often babysat her kids, Eivin and Levi) and offered to help with the books. Nikos's mom suggested I get local businesses to donate items we could auction off during intermission at the show. I got the local high school to donate the theater for the evening of the show and set a date. I taped flyers everywhere and advertised the fact that I was going to be doing a concert to raise money for school on the local radio station. We were all set except for one problem. I couldn't play a solo show. I didn't play an instrument. I would need to hire a piano player or a guitar player. An old family friend, Jimmy Anderson, played piano, and so I asked him to help out. I went about learning enough material for a solo show, mostly Cole Porter songs. The entire town turned out to hear me. The auction went off well. I had no stage banter, and had never carried a show before, so it was a bit jilted and awkward, but I got through it somehow. And the hometown crowd was more than kind.

Sharon tallied up the total, and I was still five thousand dollars short. That's when local celebrity Tom Bodett (it's his voice in the Motel 6 commercials saying, "We'll leave the light on for you") wrote a check for that exact amount. My aunts showed me how to write thank-you notes, and I wrote hundreds of them. Practically my entire hometown of 3,500 people helped me get to that boarding school.

I still had to earn money for a plane ticket, and managed to scrape it together just in time. My dad was kind enough to buy my horse from me, which gave me a little extra money and also meant I wouldn't have to buy hay for him while I was gone.

When fall rolled around, I packed my trusty duffel bag with my few things, and made sure I had some blue flannel shirts in there. I bought some khaki pants from the thrift store in town so that I would comply with the school's dress code of navy and khaki, and I boarded the plane for Traverse City, Michigan. As I sat on the plane, I was filled with excitement. I had no idea what lay ahead of me. All I knew was that it was going to be a change. And that couldn't be too bad a thing.

eleven

turn toward the pain

After many connections, delayed flights, and canceled flights because of weather, complete with nights spent unexpectedly in hotel rooms the airlines had to pay for, I finally showed up on campus a little worse for the wear. I had long messy hair and a vintage leather biker jacket, and was dragging my duffel bag down the main road of campus, garnering a few stares. I was promptly escorted to the dean's office and nearly kicked out of school my first day on campus. Apparently showing up with a large skinning knife fastened to your side was frowned upon in classier establishments. The dean asked me where I was from, and when I said Alaska, he seemed to relax a little. He explained that I was welcome at school, but that my knife was not. I promised I would keep it locked away.

I was shown around campus, but someone may as well have been giving me a tour of Mars. There were kids wearing crisp navy blazers and sharp pleated khakis and pearl necklaces. They all seemed to feel perfectly at home on the sprawling campus. And there were parents. Everywhere.

Parents unpacking their kids in dorm rooms. Parents sharing meals with kids in the cafeteria. Parents handing kids their schoolbooks for the semester. Wait. Schoolbooks? Schoolbooks! It had never dawned on me that I had to buy books for this place. My dorm counselor sent me to the bookstore, where I found out how much it was going to cost me to have books for school. And for food. I was such an idiot. I'm sure the paperwork said something to that effect somewhere. I must have missed it. I had no money for books. Or food.

Back to the dean's office I went. I remember him asking whether I had parents or if anyone was helping me. I explained that I had, indeed, been conceived through the traditional methods. He only smirked slightly. Apparently smartass humor was frowned upon as well. I explained how I'd gotten there, how my town sent me off, and how I didn't have all the funds needed. He said he could help me find a job on campus and that in the meantime he would help me procure some used books.

It was arranged for me to be a model for a sculpture class during my free period. I was not thrilled about this job, as I had to dress in a leotard and tights and stand on a pedestal at the front of the room. Mortifying for any teenage girl. But I sucked it up (and in). I felt fat, but did it anyway.

The harder part of school for me was the social aspect. I had gotten quite used to living alone and making my own rules, as well as hanging around Lee and other adults in their twenties. The strict regulations of a boarding school for young teenagers made me feel claustrophobic. I didn't like being told what to do and when to do it one bit. We were not allowed to swim in the lakes. We were not allowed out of our room after curfew. Lights out at a certain time. Walks through the woods at only a certain time. It would take some getting used to.

Apart from the few friends I'd made and left in Anchorage, I had never spent much time around many kids my own age. I went to school, but kept to myself, engaged with teachers, and sang in bars. I had been around so many adults, and dealt with so many adult emotions (even though I had a limited understanding of them), that I rarely had much in common with other kids. They looked at me like an alien, and I them. Many of the kids at school were a new breed as well. They were not hard-scrabble do-it-yourself-ers like most Alaskan kids; they were privileged and entitled and their minds seemed to know a lot about specific things but lacked common sense. But then, I was the one wearing ridiculous pink tights and a leotard, standing on a podium for them . . . I really had no room to judge.

To make matters worse, I began to suffer from panic attacks. I shared a room with a roommate, and a bathroom with suitemates. When I was younger and the stress and anxiety of my life became too overwhelming, or when fights with my dad got too bad, I would go running outside into nature. The mountains were my church. I would go off by myself like an animal to heal. At boarding school I could not leave campus and there was nowhere to be alone. I think that the tension, combined with enough distance from home to feel somewhat safe, is what brought the attacks on. It would be years before I learned such terms as "PTSD," "trauma survivor," and "trigger." When I felt panic coming on, I would sneak out of class, go back to my room when it was empty, curl up in a fetal position, and cry from way down deep in my bones. I learned to pet my hair as I rocked back and forth, to soothe myself. I learned to tell myself things as if I were a parent caring for a frightened child. Sometimes I could find words for my sorrow. *I'm scared. I'm lonely. I don't know what I'm doing.* I was on my own. No family, no safety net, and I was hurting. I turned to my pen for comfort, trying my best to feel my feelings rather than numb them.

Once I came back to my room between classes to find my suitemate crying on her bed. I figured she must be having a panic attack. I went to her and petted her hair and after a time I asked what was wrong. She looked up at me through tear-stained cheeks and stammered, "My dad won't give me a Porsche when I come home if I don't get all A's." I was a bit stunned. It was my first encounter with real wealth. I remember looking at her and thinking, *Holy shit. Being spoiled is worse abuse than being hit.* At least I knew that being hit is wrong. But being spoiled ruins you. This girl was a great person, but her life had robbed her of the opportunity to find strength in herself and a sense of self-worth. This was the same journey I was on as well, but I felt fortunate in that moment because I knew it was up to me to make the changes in myself. I developed tools for dealing with my panic attacks. Under extreme duress, especially as a child, I would disassociate, just shut down and become robotic when the stress or emotions were too overwhelming. I could basically pop out of my body. Shut down my thoughts and leave. The effects of dealing with long-term stress were more subtle; I was not even aware I was doing it. I just got tough, and a bit desensitized to the anxiety. It was a dangerous habit, because our feelings are our best defense system; if prolonged trauma becomes the norm, you become desensitized to pain, and cut off your ability to perceive danger as well. We learn to tolerate the intolerable—a problem that would vex me for decades.

At school I learned better coping mechanisms, ones that allowed me to keep my feelings intact. Instead of escaping or shutting down, I learned to get in touch with my body and mind more. This seemed the opposite of a good idea at first, because my body was often the source of so much pain. But the only way to actually be safe was to turn toward the pain, not away from it. I practiced a meditation when I felt panicked or anxious. I would visualize myself as an ocean. On the surface were frightening storms and turbulence—raging winds, lightning strikes, and huge waves. Then I would imagine myself swimming deeper down into the ocean of myself. The farther down I swam, the calmer it became. I reached all the way to a smooth and sandy ocean floor. Rays of light filtered in, like enormous beautiful curtains dancing in the body of the water. I would notice the colors change from stormy grays on the surface to rich and tranquil sea greens near the bottom. I would change my breathing to be deep and rhythmic. Several counts to inhale and longer, slower counts for the exhale. This regulated my heartbeat and brought calmness into my body along with the visualization. I would imagine the sounds around me muted, as if I were underwater. With the lightning far above me. I would look up at the surface and from this safe distance I could watch the storm far away, not so frightening. Sometimes I would stay like this for a long time. Other times I learned to take quick trips here, when I needed a calming or relaxing moment between classes. In time I learned to take the exercise further, and I began to see what was triggering me, or what was frightening me, and I would ask the storms for answers to my questions. What do you fear? Not knowing. Why do you assume you don't know? Because I'm just a kid, and I keep getting into jams. If you knew the answer, what would it be? And often the solution was right there in front of me. Start at the beginning. Get a job. Take a step. Take action.

Otherwise, I found myself stimulated by academics and all the classes I took. No longer a big fish in a small pond, I thrived in swimming with these kids who were so skilled and educated. They had all been practicing their craft as long as I had, or longer, and they were powerfully talented. There were music majors, all specializing in classical music or musical theater. There were writing majors, vocal majors, visual arts and theater majors. I was in heaven.

My voice lessons were a foreign concept for me. I had never been trained before, and I was behind all the other kids who had already been studying for years. Two of my suitemates were die-hard vocal majors, complete with the water bottle attached to their hip and a near-religious devotion to vocal warm-ups and drills throughout the day. I was the only student who did not read music. My teacher liked me, though, and helped me. I learned a lot about my range and how to unlock different registers. I learned to sight-read music and also how to sight-read terminology in German, Italian, and Latin. I had no idea what the words meant, but I knew that in Italian two *c*'s made a "ch" sound and that one *c* made a "k" sound. My teacher Nicole was very nice, though, and she seemed to genuinely enjoy my voice and was even a bit protective of me and my talent. While she taught me a lot about how to use my higher registers, she seemed to enjoy that I didn't fit a traditional mold and she didn't try to change that. I remember feeling very insecure about how I'd been trained mostly by bar singing, while all the other kids knew everything there was to know about composers and theory and technique. I was shocked when she said that when she heard my audition tape, she felt that my voice was very special and that she couldn't believe I was going to be her student. I didn't know how to absorb that, but it felt good and gave me the courage to keep going. I will always appreciate that she listened to who I was and supported that, rather than teaching me to be generic vocally. A lot of parents want their talented kids to take voice lessons as early as possible, but I often caution them against it. Unless a child is bent on going into opera or classical, too much training at a formative age can make you a correct singer, but not a very interesting one. It can also make you mental—formal training gets you into your head, and you become worried about technique and little more. Audiences don't care if you sing correctly. They care if they feel something. If they don't, they forget you. Emotional honesty creates loyalty and a lifelong connection above all else. And for that, there is no substitute for old-fashioned practice and self-discovery. The thousands of hours I spent listening to Ella, Sarah Vaughan, and Maria Callas while riding my horse, doing chores, and walking to school taught me to swoop, swell, brighten, narrow, and warm my tone. And now Nicole was teaching me to sing in my higher registers, but was thoughtful enough to go about it in a way that supported who I was, rather than making me overthink the rules.

Many parents want to support their kids' talents and dreams, but it is up to the kids to have the drive and curiosity to discover their own way. They have to have the impetus and courage within themselves to develop their own creative voice. The best advice I can give any young artist is to never assume someone knows more than you do about your talent, desire, and creativity. Go inward, into your heart, and engage in the darkness and the unknown. Grope and feel around for what you respond to. An artist's most valuable asset is individuality. You can't learn it from a teacher. It has to be sussed out and nurtured. Wrestled out of the silence within you. It has to be fed—our best teachers do not always live in schools but inside ourselves, in the books the masters wrote and the music they recorded. You must cultivate a large appetite for the things that move you. Let them wash over you as you begin to build yourself as an artist and as a person. Seek out good teachers and go to school, but protect your own process of discovery and know it is sacred. We must wrestle with ourselves to get to the good stuff. I am so thankful that some of the teachers in my life were wiser than I was in this regard, that they recognized an artist in me and had the respect to guide me and also leave me be. I did not understand this at the time, but, as artists themselves, they recognized it, whereas I was years away from thinking of myself as the same.

I enjoyed classical music, but all the other vocal majors had dreams of musical theater and Broadway or opera. I did not have those ambitions. I didn't have any real dreams or goals. Those were for other people. I loved learning to sing in this style but found the rigidness of classical music stifling. Visual art, on the other hand, was a wide-open frontier for expression, and I became absolutely enamored. Modeling for the sculpture class turned out to be tremendously stimulating both intellectually and artistically. The teacher, Gene, would instruct her class using my body as an example. "See, the plane changes here," she would say, putting her hand on the curve of my arm, where it receded into the distance. She spoke of perspective, form, function. I was smitten. I asked lots of questions and tried to ingest everything she was saying. She was often kind enough to stay with me after class and elaborate about a point that she had made that day. Finally I asked her whether I could stop modeling and join the sculpture class.

So after settling into school for a while—I forget how long—I decided to take on two majors, in voice and visual art, and two minors, in dance and theater. Back to the dean's office I was sent. He explained that it was just not done. They encouraged kids to focus and hone a particular craft. I knew it was a big workload, but explained that my academics were solid, and that if I skipped lunch hour and ate in the art room, I could pull it off. I wanted to maximize my time there and take advantage of everything I could, partly because I had no idea if I would get to come back the next year. The dean squinted at me when I said that, and after a heavy sigh, said he would let me see how it went, but reminded me that I had to keep my academics up.

I had a tightly packed day, and went about it with a starving man's mentality, devouring everything in sight. Figuratively and literally. I had put on at least ten pounds since I had been there. I blamed it on the fact that I had so much food available to me, and that none of it was fresh or homegrown, and I wasn't out hiking, running, and riding horses. Fitting into my leotard for my general dance class was embarrassing, but I did it anyway, and just tried not to look in the mirror. Still not a great dancer. Joe's wife taught the general dance class. She was patient and kind with all of us non-dance majors. The bright spot of the class for me was the live piano player, Ray. He was a disheveled, odd guy, who only half successfully covered the smell of the previous night's booze. He played waltzes or little simple rhythms the teacher required for whatever steps we were learning, but I often heard him warming up before class, and I could tell jazz and blues were in his wheelhouse. I struck up a conversation with him and eventually we got together and jammed.

Ray was soft-spoken and reminded me of characters from old movies, a half-drunk who lost himself in learning piano but never got his act together other than to scrape by. He was a pool shark, narrow of frame, with greasy hair under a fedora, rumpled jacket, and pocked skin, but was every inch kind. And talented, with a real old-school sense of honor when it came to the classics. His playing was tasteful and understated, and he knew his music history. Since I'd quit modeling to be in the sculpture class myself, I needed cash, so Ray and I decided to audition for a regular gig at a piano bar in Traverse City. I had never auditioned for a gig before, so it was kind of new to me, but I followed Ray's lead and sang the material he had given me to learn. We got the gig, and started that Saturday night. At first Ray tried to teach me to play bass so we would have a fuller sound, but I had no real talent for it. He would shake his head and show me a bass line again, but soon he gave up and in his soft-spoken tone said we'd be better off if I just sang and he played. I wore a black dress, and Ray a sharp fedora and a crumpled sports coat. Some people sitting at the bar paid attention. Some didn't.

Ray turned me on to a lot of old blues songs I had never heard. "St. Louis Blues" (which one day I got to sing with B. B. King himself on the Jools Holland show in England), "Gimme a Pig Foot and a Bottle of Beer," "Peepin' and Hidin'." All the good ol' stuff that any writer or singer should have as a foundation. I had listened to a lot of standards, but these were more obscure, raw, sexual in a bawdy underground way, not the clever highbrow sounds of Cole Porter or the coy lyrics of many classics—these were full of speakeasy grit, sass, and swagger. Ray would cringe when I would introduce a song as being by Harry Connick Jr., rather than invoking the original artist or composer. I had to learn that these songs were heirlooms passed on from generation to generation, and they deserved to be treated like treasures, and most important was where they'd started rather than who had drawn attention to them in the moment.

It never dawned on me that singing in a bar with a faculty member would be frowned upon, but soon I was summoned to the dean's office. Again. He scratched his head as I sat across from him yet again. "Jewel, I've heard you're singing in town. At a bar. With a faculty member." "Yes," I said. "With Ray." "Jewel, we can't have a student in a bar with a faculty member." This got me in a panic. I told him I'd grown up bar singing, and that I needed the money. He was worried it would look inappropriate, a sixteen-year-old and a faculty member in a bar. I assured him Ray was nothing but professional, and invited him to come see us. I don't recall whether he ever came, but we got to keep the gig. I invited my vocal teacher Nicole one night and got her up onstage. She sang "Smoke Gets in Your Eyes" in full operatic tone. She had been singing opera so long that she had no street voice left. When I turned to look at Ray, he was shaking his head and rolling his eyes while he played backup, pained to hear such a beloved song sung so stiffly and operatically. I appreciated that he was so protective of songs, but still I loved Nicole's version. It's not always about the song. It's about the singer's heart and the courage to step beyond their comfort zone. Nicole saw me step outside my comfort zone every day, and she was always proud and supportive, and I damn sure wasn't going to miss the opportunity to get her up to sing. I was flattered she came out to support me and had fun.

twelve

who will save your soul

At Christmas break all the faculty left campus, the school shut down, and so it made sense that students could not stay. This didn't seem to be a problem for any of them but me. In the weeks leading up to the break, everyone talked excitedly about the friends they were going to see back home. They spoke of favorite meals and family, who a mere few months earlier they'd been eager to escape from. I didn't have the money to get back to Alaska, and did not advertise the fact that I had no place to stay. This would be a problem at every break and holiday, and each time I would have to come up with a solution. As Christmas neared, I felt like my best bet was the modern dance teacher I'd made friends with early on in the school year. He was a tall and imposing figure, hard to miss on the campus street. American Indian, with long black hair, a classic profile, high cheekbones, and wearing a bright red leather jacket with fringe. He reminded me of my Indian uncles, the two men who had adopted me a year earlier, and we became good friends and often took trips to the sand dunes and talked about the importance of ceremony in life and how to imbue deeper meaning into art. I knew he was leaving to visit his partner in Seattle and asked him if I could stay in his house while he was gone.

I really had nowhere else to go. He thought about it a few days and decided to let me stay, but he made it clear it was against the rules and I had to keep it quiet and lay low. Luckily, it was a small two-bedroom house situated by itself on a lake. When all the other kids went off, I packed my bags and was intentionally vague with counselors and dorm leaders when they asked in passing where I was headed.

I arrived and found the key where he'd left it for me. His place was modest but nice. I set my bags down in the guest room and stood in the living room, looking out at the frozen lake covered in a thick blanket of snow. There is something so peaceful and quiet about land covered in snow. It muffles all sound in a quietness so unlike the hum of summer. No birds in the trees, no rippling of live water. The isolation reminded me of Alaska, and I decided to take advantage of the opportunity to go into silence myself. Winter is a time for going inward. For tending to the unseen. I had brought my drawing pad and my pastels and my notebook for writing. I had taken the school's shuttle bus into Traverse City the weekend before for groceries. I think I ate butternut squash with honey and salt, canned black beans, and rice cakes with almond butter the entire time. It was a prolific couple of weeks, as there was little else to do. I had begun drawing that year with pastels and made several self-portraits, and tried to capture the folds of fabric for the first time. I sat in the living room, where there was good light, with a small mirror I found. I talked to no one and read a lot. It was complete isolation.

As Christmas drew near, I became a bit blue. It was sad to be alone and have no presents. I was sad that I had no one to take care of me. Before I could become sorrier for myself, I made my way to town to see if I could bring some cheer to the little house and for myself after all. I stuck my thumb out and caught a ride easily. Hitchhiking on holidays always brings generosity to people's hearts. It felt good to hear the bright noise of cheerful conversations and holiday music in the stores. I had a little money for fresh rosemary twigs. Rosemary is a quick way to make any meal taste like Christmas. If you can't afford the turkey, the herbs are a good substitution. I also bought two pretty metallic silver and gold drawing pastels that were so creamy and luxurious they looked like candy. I saw a pretty fuchsia empire-waist dress with a scoop neck and fell in love with it. I knew instantly that it would be my present to myself and didn't bat an eye before stealing it. I looked at it as spoiling myself a little.

Back home, I got to work decorating the house. I took out my drawing pad and, using my new pastels, drew solid sheets of gold and silver, then cut the paper into long, thin strips and hung them on the meager houseplant like tinsel. I drew red circles and cut them out, hung them like ornaments from the leaves that looked sturdy enough to hold them. I spent hours drawing a rather Klimt-inspired geometric pattern of black, gold, and silver, and when I finished, I carefully folded it around my colorful dress. I made a goldfish-orange-colored ribbon to tie around the package and set it under my little makeshift tree. My heart leaped with happiness each time I saw my little tree with my pretty present beneath it. On Christmas Day I made spaghetti squash with browned butter and rosemary, lit a candle, said a prayer of gratitude—thanking the universe for my health, for poetry, for school, and for my friend who let me stay in such a pretty cabin—and ate while looking out on the lake. I opened my present and danced around the living room in my new dress singing classical arias I had just learned in school and finished the evening with my favorite Christmas carol: "Have Yourself a Merry Little Christmas."

IT WOULD'VE CHANGED my life if I'd gotten caught stealing that dress. It would've been horrible. I'm sure I would've been kicked out of school.

I didn't assess the risks. My behavior was very compulsive. I remember once stealing some bathing suits in Michigan. Though I only really needed one bathing suit, I couldn't decide which one I wanted, so I stole maybe four of them.

I made a few other unexpected friends who helped me, like Elena, who worked in the kitchen at Interlochen. She was a kind, elderly Hispanic woman who let me stay at her house on school breaks when I was not allowed on campus. She gave me extra food, and needed to nurture someone as much as I needed nurturing. We saw each other only in the cafeteria during school and said a quick hello, and when I stayed with her, I'd see her only in the evenings because she worked as a maid in her free time to keep the lights on. Her husband, who had Alzheimer's, was nearly incapacitated. The first time I came to her house, it had the cluttered, musty, and slightly abandoned feel of the elderly. And a shocking surprise. Elena kept her husband locked inside a large closet during the day with food, water, and a toilet, so he couldn't wander out of the house. Which he had done once, nearly getting hit by a car. As I got to know her better, I learned that she deeply resented having to care for him. She had been abused by him her whole marriage, and now she was a slave to changing his bedpans and working three jobs to support them both. I felt that there was a small part of her that liked to lock him up like a dog. When I stayed at her place, I watered her plants and slept in her bed, as it was the only option, and came down with a terrible case of scabies. A horrible affliction. It made me feel terrible for Elena. There are so many people living lives that nearly crush them, with no support for the physical, much less emotional, freight we all carry.

When spring break rolled around, again I didn't have the money to go back to Alaska. This is when I concocted the brilliant idea that I would hobo by train across the country and then hitchhike through Mexico, like all parents hope their children do one day . . .

I took a Greyhound bus from school to Detroit and stayed the night in the bus station. Note I did not say "sleep" in the bus station. A chilling experience. I decided to learn guitar so I could street sing along the way and earn train fare as I went. I never played guitar as a child—my dad was the musician in our act—so before I left campus I learned four chords: A, C, G, and D. In that order. I could not play them out of order because I did not know how. I could not learn cover songs because I didn't know any other chords and couldn't read tab, and so I decided to just improvise songs about what I was seeing around me. I figured as long as I sang well, no one would care what I was singing about. Before I left, I saved enough money from tips at the piano bar to buy an Amtrak ticket from Detroit to Chicago, got off, and made my way to Michigan Avenue. It was my first time seeing a big city like this, or America, for that matter. Alaskan culture, especially where and how I was raised, was about as opposite from pop culture as one could get without being part of a Pygmy tribe in the rainforest. I began to make up lyrics about what I observed. Televisions could be seen in every restaurant and bar. Celebrity worship. Words began to flow off my tongue. All the poetry and prose I had written for all those years, all the books I'd read, from Plato to Bukowski to Neruda, all the bars I had sung in, the thousands of cover songs I had sung since I was five—it was like I'd been in life's music school for a decade and for the first time I was able to combine music and words. And it felt like magic happened as I wrote my first song: I found my voice. Not my singing voice, but my voice as an artist. *People living their lives for you on TV, they say they are better for you, and you agree. She says hold my calls from behind those cold brick walls, says come here boy, there ain't nothin' for free.*

I took the money I made busking to the ticket counter at the train station. I counted out crumpled dollar bills and random change and asked how far it would get me. Sometimes it was enough to get a ways down the road. Sometimes it was just enough for a sandwich. I eventually made my way to San Diego, my first time there, and crossed the border into Tijuana. A girl, a backpack, and a guitar. And her skinning knife. I hitchhiked to Cabo, using the "large trucks only" policy I devised after hearing horror stories on the train about small cars being run off the dirt roads by larger trucks in Mexico. I made it to Cabo, where I sang on the dock to earn a ferry ride to the mainland side of Mexico. To supplement my income, I made a little sign that said, "Reflexology," and gave foot rubs to blue hairs. Once I had ferry money and made it to the mainland, I hopped trains (the Chihuahua al Pacífico railroad) and went all throughout the Barrancas del Cobre, a beautiful and rugged time capsule where traditional Mexican natives lived in the mountains still, wearing handwoven clothes and eating corn and simple foods, tucked into the cliffs and canyons.

I met up with my mom and her roommate and we rode trains, sitting with chickens and goats in boxcars. We stayed in hostels and I sang in restaurants in exchange for food. I talked a boy into letting me ride a horse he was feeding dry corncobs to and, without a saddle, rode the animal, which was more goat than equine, through the dry, rocky mountaintops. The roommate and I took a ferry back to Cabo, stayed in La Paz, and hung out with some locals I met at the beach who were windsurfing. And finally, we made a sign that said "Norte Por Favor" (the extent of my Spanish) and stuck our thumbs out. In the name of safety we passed on anyone we didn't feel good about (a practice I had honed in Alaska) and only accepted a ride that was going all the way to the border, so we would not be stranded in some small town in the middle of the desert. After several hours we got lucky and two nice young men said in broken English that they were going to Tijuana, and so we hopped in the cab. Between our lack of Spanish and their lack of English, we all smiled a lot and communicated the way souls do who find their lives suddenly thrust together. They were warmhearted and generous of spirit, sharing their food and water. The drive was too long for one day, and so they pulled to the side of a dirt road at dark to sleep. They offered to let us sleep in the cab, but we opted for the empty tractor-trailer. They had hauled pinto beans, and a thin layer covered the floor. I got out my sleeping bag and was quite comfortable—like sleeping on a beanbag, with all those pintos beneath me. I left the doors to the trailer open, wrote more verses to my one song until it was too dark to see, and stared at the *estrellas* until I fell asleep. *So we pray to as many different gods as there are flowers, but we call religion our friend, we're so worried about saving our souls, afraid that God will take his toll, that we forget to begin, but who will save your soul if you won't save your own . . .*

The next day our new friends dropped us off at the border. I crossed back into the States, all without being murdered or raped. So that was good. I busked back to Michigan, editing and refining the song I had been writing. I kept playing those same chords over and over, simply changing the melody to denote the chorus. As the pink desert of Arizona, the mountain majesty of Colorado, and the fertile goodness of the midlands dreamily floated by my train window, I sifted through thirty or so verses until I had what I felt were the best ones.

We try to hussle 'em try to hussle 'em try to cuss 'em the cops want someone to bust down on Orleans Avenue . . . some are walking some are talkin' some are stalkin' their kill got social security but that don't pay your bills . . . there are addictions to feed and there are mouths to pay so we bargain with the devil say we are ok for today say but who will save your soul if you won't save your own . . .

A less welcome gift of my trip was a bladder infection I contracted while busking my way back across the States. Too ashamed to open up to a stranger about what the heck was happening to me, I sucked it up and toughed it out for three painful days instead of asking for help. I had a fever and curled up in my train seat, shivering and sweating it out. By the time I hit Illinois, it had passed, and I returned to the Greyhound station in Detroit feeling so grown-up and independent in one way, yet so devastatingly alone and helpless in another. I dragged myself, my sixty-pound backpack, and my guitar off the bus and hitchhiked with no success the few miles to my school, just in time to be hospitalized for the first of what would be chronic kidney infections. But I had my song. I titled it "Who Will Save Your Soul."

I returned to school with a world of experience and a song of my own. I was hooked. Songs began to pour out of me. Emotions and anxieties finally had an even more focused outlet.

I began writing myself lullabies at night, when terrors came over me as I lay down to sleep. I wrote "Raven" when I was about sixteen, to soothe myself. Writing music carried the freight for me. It relieved the pressure and let me see my own inner workings plainly. Writing songs offered different tools like melody and tone to convey and release emotion, unlike journal writing. It takes seeing a thing first to be able to change it. Our unexamined feelings swim like restless schools of fish inside us; they stir up and muddy the waters. Self-examination organizes our moodiness, and helps us identify the stimulus that caused those feelings, and calms the water. Had I never become a professional writer, I would still write every day for the same reasons I began to: as Socrates suggested, "The unexamined life is not worth living." I knew that because I had come from living it.

There were, however, unhealthy ways I coped as well. My compulsive eating was becoming more difficult to ignore. Control is a central theme for anyone who steals or has an eating disorder. I felt helpless and out of control, and I cracked under the pressure in heartbreakingly human ways. I tried to comfort myself with food and tried to take control by stealing. They both gave me a sense of power, the illusion of providing for myself. I tried not to turn a blind eye on my actions. I kept writing. On paper, I saw myself commit crimes, binge eat, and run to my dorm room midday to break down and cry. I also saw myself write songs, go to work, sing and make money, I saw myself thrive in art. I tried to be honest about it all, if only on paper. Good and bad. I knew it was imperative to be honest with myself, even about my tremendous flaws, so I wouldn't lose track of myself entirely. I couldn't be perfect, and the only shot I had at ever getting better was being realistic about where I really was. In many ways I was in trouble, and in many ways I was doing well. Both were true and I had to accept that until I could grow differently. I continued to work hard at school, and prepared to graduate a year early because I didn't think I could get the funds together for another year at Interlochen and going back to regular school didn't sound fun. With all my academics out of the way, I was going to wrap up and head back to Homer with no real plan for the future, when I was informed that the school was prepared to offer me a full scholarship to return. I couldn't believe it. I explained that I was done with my academics, though, and that if I came back, I wanted to study only art—and they said that would be fine. I was instantly energized with a sense of excitement that propelled me into a happy and productive summer back in Homer.

thirteen

internal permission

I returned to my hometown and drifted between my aunt Mossy's place and my dad's cabin-in-process. All I remember is writing a lot. And gardening and hauling water up and down the hill on the homestead. I slept in the unfinished basement while Dad and Atz Lee stayed in the small outdoor shed. I helped my aunt with horse pack trips in the mountains and I stayed by myself a lot at her remote cabin at the head of the bay and wrote and read. I hung with Lee and his friends, who read and traveled and were trying to figure things out, like I was. I was glad to be away from the drama of high school girls and boys. I could relax a little around my Alaskan friends, who were self-sufficient and engaged in the adventure of life. I wrote "Little Sister," "Can't Take My Soul," "Billy," "Money," and many songs that summer and played them for the group that hung at Aunt Mossy's farm.

Mairiis (Mossy) was my dad's eldest sister. She was part surrogate mother, part boss, part pixie. I'd worked at her bed-and-breakfast and taken tourists on pack trips from about fifth grade onward. Being her helper was pretty fun. She was chipper and upbeat, always a song on her lips, a spry woman of infinite energy that was at odds with her years. She is to this day the embodiment of the Alaskan can-do pioneer woman. Every bit my grandmother's daughter. She built her own houses and shod her own horses. There were always campers in tents in the fields (at five bucks a night), tourists in the B&B, and long-term renters in tiny cabins along the long dirt road. I changed sheets, saddled horses, and packed saddlebags. Her farm was called Seaside Farm and it was closer to town than the homestead, though still pristine and lovely. The barnyard was a happy place teeming with baby colts and fillies, calves, goslings, and one bunny named Caramel. There were no other bunnies, so Caramel was raised with the chickens. The chickens loved that bunny, and Caramel grew up as one of them. She would sit on their nests and hatch eggs for them. She would line nests with her soft fur, and hop around herding up baby chicks as they wandered this way and that. She even ate like a chicken, stabbing her head forward and sort of pecking at feed and grass. This delighted me to no end as a child—an orphan bunny who found love with a different tribe. It also made me think—what if I were a bunny being raised by chickens? How would I ever know my true nature?

I began to look at everyone around me, at other girls at school, at other parents and families, and what I noticed was there were other ways of doing things. Other systems, other ways of interacting. I knew I was an unhappy child. I knew I was scared and hurt and at risk of never finding peace or happiness. I realized that happiness was not some bird that landed on your shoulder by accident, but was a skill that was taught, or not taught, in certain houses and families.

After summer drew to an end, back at Interlochen, I took art classes all day long. I majored in visual arts and voice, with minors in dance and theater. I began carving marble and doing head busts about a year after I began writing songs, and credit sculpture for teaching me more about melody than any other thing. I had grown up listening to great melodies by Gershwin and Porter and other Tin Pan Alley writers but had never sat down to study what makes a memorable melody. I had been turned on to Joni Mitchell and Neil Young. I loved listening to them, but never studied their songs' structure or form. I was more of a storyteller and I knew what a chorus was and a verse was, but knew little else about writing a song. To get around my ignorance with the guitar, I began to experiment with tunings. I would work the pegs and drop strings to lower tones, or sometimes higher ones, until I found a harmonic combination that was pleasing to me. When I discovered my own open tunings, it freed my head musically and lyrically. Open tunings allowed me to find melodies and voice more complicated chords with much less work, and it was more aligned to my way of thinking, because down the fret board were lower chords, and up the fret board were higher chords, much the way a piano is laid out, I imagined. I told stories and wrote songs and fell in love with music without ever really thinking about the strength of melody, or breaking down intellectually what a great melody needs. We don't always know why abstract shapes and patterns and colors affect us, but we know when they do. Melody has its own shape. The shape has to have focus, have movement, and evoke a feeling. Form is everything. It has to be clean, clear, recognizable. It has to have purpose. It has to have variance and contrasts to be interesting. I immediately recognized the similarity in melody and abstract sculpture. Simple geometric patterns always emerged from beneath the complexity and interpretation that was unique to the artist. It is melody slowed down to the point it is frozen in time. It communicates without language and affects the viewer with the emotion the artist experienced while creating it. Modigliani's long necks. The exaggerated bend of Klimt's necks. Brancusi, Noguchi, Lipchitz, even the painters who used geometric design within their paintings to create their compositions. As I studied the songs that became beloved and popular for generations, I could see a spiraling melody. A melody that climbed to an apex, then back down to create a pyramid shape. Square shapes that went up, over, down, and back to the root like a square. The Beatles' songs are great examples of this type of melody—deceivingly complicated ideas and forms wrapped in simple singsong-patterned melodies. And Joni Mitchell, while more complicated tonally and structurally, still adhered to the basic principles of a pattern—hers more like the mathematics of a bumblebee or hummingbird. Delicate, intricate, gravity-defying. I was fascinated by how much could be communicated with pure sound—by creating a strong shape with it that in and of itself communicated emotion before words were ever added. Then the layering of elements over one another. Juxtaposing a provocative lyric with a sweet melody, changing timbre from pure and crystalline to a growl and a snarl to portray irony, or anger laced with humor or a wry wink. Lay this on a bed of minor chords that might ascend to a major and yet more is communicated about longing and a hope of where you wish to end up. Nuance could be achieved in song the way visual artists use light, focal point, value, and color.

I made some very good friends my second and last year at school, and had a new roommate named Madella, who was from Mexico and a wonderful music enthusiast. I wrote "Don't" this year, and I remember she loved it and encouraged me to keep writing songs. She was a very funny, larger-than-life character who I have such fond memories of. I began singing my songs and yodeling at open-mic night on campus. There were lots of guitar players, drummers, and pianists at Interlochen, but it was hard at first to find fellow musicians to jam with, because so many of them were trained in reading music but not in improv.

I had the same bifurcated sense that I was doing really well while also not doing well at all. I gained fifteen to twenty pounds from stress eating and was horribly upset that I could not control my diet. I had heard about twelve-step programs from my mom. She told me she had gotten into a twelve-step program and was learning to make amends. I asked her if she was an alcoholic and she said no. I'm not sure why she was in the program. I forgave her, of course, just as I had forgiven my dad when he came to school with the bagged lunches. It seemed so vulnerable and honest to come to your child like this. I went to the library at Interlochen and found a book there on twelve-step programs, and saw that there was a group specifically for eating disorders called Overeaters Anonymous. I read the book at night when I was done with my schoolwork. It was like reading my diaries, the uncontrollable binge eating, the comfort eating, the euphoria followed by the intense shame and self-loathing. And I knew I didn't have the worst case—not yet—but that something was wrong with me. I didn't want to wait until I was a hundred pounds overweight, rather than twenty, to do something about it. When I couldn't find an OA chapter to join, I decided to start one at school, with the help of a school counselor. There was a running joke on campus that after lunch you could hear every toilet in the dancers' dorm flush from so many girls purging. Our first meeting was quite small, and it never really grew much. I remember one very nice young girl in the group—there were only three or four of us. She was anorexic and said she wore black to the meeting so she would look thin. There was a sixteen-year-old boy, a dancer, who was bulimic, and he felt so much shame that he had a "girls'" disorder. Brené Brown, the author of *Daring Greatly*, describes the issue beautifully as the web women are trapped in: "Be pretty, but not threateningly pretty. Be a go-getter but don't threaten anyone or be a bitch. Caught in this web of contradictions, we have to be everything for everyone and we lose the ability to explore who we really are." She goes on to describe the trap society sets for men as a box, where they must be strong and brave but unemotional and shutdown. For the first time in this support group, I saw that these dynamics play out over and over in everyone, as girls and boys, men and women, try to break free from unnatural confines and live as whole humans—to give ourselves the *internal permission* to be as emotionally conflicted and confused, and as strong and confident, as we are at any given time. We had all been judged by the outside world, and all of us had learned to internalize that critic and use it against ourselves. We all indulged in acts of self-hatred to gain feelings of control in our efforts to build self-worth.

This was about the time I really began to think about the fact that I had to be a good parent to myself. I had loathed how my dad criticized and emotionally abused me, and here I had begun doing it to myself. I'd relabeled it "perfectionism," instead of abuse, which seemed kind of sexy—I got results, I told myself. I pushed myself hard and expected a lot, and it worked for a while, until the internal critic eclipsed everything else and I floundered rather than flourished. I've often thought of this dynamic, especially as a professional years later. High standards are great in many ways. Challenging yourself and expecting a lot is great. But perfectionism gets you results only to a certain altitude. It propels you up a mountain, but if you want to move around in the rarified air of the summit, it takes creativity and freethinking—and you can only be genuinely brave in your ideas and vision if there is enough safety to take risks in your thinking and push your art. Negative self-criticism is an iron chain that will never let you ascend to real greatness. I had been hard on myself since I moved out. It had gotten me pretty darn far. But now it was crushing me. Nothing was enough. I lacked the ability to be proud of anything I'd accomplished. I knew I had to start practicing something I had never been given or shown in my family. Kindness. Patience. Tolerance. Being allowed to mess up without feeling that my self-worth would go down the tubes with one poor performance. Or that love would be taken away if I did not behave just so, or to the standards of my caregiver.

I didn't know it at the time, but between my panic attacks, the need for control over my life, and my self-defeating behavior, I was experiencing what it is like to be a trauma survivor. Something would trigger a memory of a past trauma, my fight-or-flight response would kick in, and I would freeze, gripped in terror much the way a soldier experiences PTSD. The reaction never matches the stimulus. Sometimes I felt my body being transported back to a time, adrenaline flooding my system with terror. Sometimes it was a wave of fear as I froze, feeling helpless. I had to learn to trust it like the tide—the episodes would come but they would pass. Sometimes the tide was just out, but nature dictated that it would always come back in.

In many ways I was a grown-up, navigating grown-up things, but in other ways I was so young and I desperately wanted to belong. I had parents who I called home to, but they were not like normal parents. I wanted them to love me, I had some connection to them, but they didn't function like normal parents. Not like other kids' parents. I just started to handle things on my own. When I got letters from my mom, I read and reread them so many times the writing began to fade. I remember one in particular where she said she admired me, and that we were twin flames. She said we were not just alike, but the same soul in two different bodies. For a lonely girl, it was music to my ears, and made me feel that I belonged, and that she wanted me. I was able to explain away all the reasons she was not in my life with those few words. We were the same soul in two bodies. How I wanted to believe it. Her words set a trap, though— when your soul is tied to another's, you feel responsible for them. You feel their will by an extension must also be your will. Her values and desires in many ways became mine.

fourteen

the wisdom of silence

When I graduated from Interlochen, my parents came to the ceremony, as well as Atz Lee. My dad made a memorable entrance, dressed as a sourdough, wearing steel-jaw bear traps slung over his shoulder, a hat with a bullet hole through it, a flannel shirt, and Carhartt pants with the legs rolled up to reveal rubber boots—the Alaskan cowboy boot. He came rolling into the lobby with a hunched-over posture and began to sniff the fine ladies in their pastels and pearls, saying, "Where's that girl?" He made a rapid pass through the lobby, sniffing the air and different folks, repeating, "Where's that girl?" When he saw me, he said loudly, "I wanna see what an educated girl smells like!" Everyone already thought I was some wild animal, and now they could see I came by it honestly. It probably would have embarrassed most teenagers, but I thought it was hysterical. The horrified looks on the faces of the well-to-do families was fairly priceless, and I appreciated my dad's flair for drama. I have fond memories as a child of my dad involving me in elaborate skits he planned for girlfriends. He would dress as the Birdman from *The*

Magic Flute, his wings made of odds and ends we'd bought at the second-hand store and sewed to his shirt, a beak made of construction paper, and he would serenade his beloved with an aria. Another time he dressed as Caesar and stood in the airport with a wreath of leaves we had sewn for a crown, while reciting some improvised oratory. My dad was creative and spontaneous, and I learned a lot about taking risks from him. He never wrote a set list, opting instead to read the crowd—still a habit of mine today.

I worked feverishly to finish my final marble carving right up to the graduation ceremony. I could hear that the ceremony had started and I waited until they got to calling for the kids whose last name started with *H* before I threw my gown on over my clothes, which were covered in marble dust and sawdust, and pulled my cap on over my messy hair and ran for Kresge Hall. I remember being a bit embarrassed by the attention of walking onstage and accepting my diploma. It was very hard for me to feel proud of myself, and I think I threw the diploma away as soon as I got offstage. It was just a piece of paper, and the school was much more than that for me. Plus it didn't fit in my backpack, and I had a strict policy: if it didn't all fit in there, I didn't keep it. I was brutal about that, and didn't save any of my student art. Instead I took pictures of it and threw the actual art away. I had no home lined up and didn't want to ask my dad to keep it in a shed somewhere. I decided philosophically that it was better to just keep things light and avoid clutter. Part of me still believes this, and I subscribe to the less-is-more theory to this day. On a subconscious level, though, it was a way to protect myself because I knew I was not in a position to be able to have much, and this made that harder reality seem like it was my choice. I didn't have money to buy a yearbook, and while I secretly longed to have one, I reasoned away the mixed emotions about graduating and the uncertainty of my future with a laissez-faire attitude.

All the other kids had plans to go to amazing fine arts colleges like Juilliard, and I was planning on nothing, really. For some reason it just didn't dawn on me that college was in the realm of possibility. No one had ever mentioned it to me. Counselors at school didn't bring it up. I didn't think about music being an option beyond how I always had—bar gigs and getting by. I would have loved to pursue something in the visual arts, but I never really felt I was talented enough to go further, much less obtain another scholarship to a college. Not to mention I felt the reason I got a scholarship to Interlochen was because of Joe's suggestion and help. I didn't have an "in" anywhere else. Applications and the like were still a mysterious world that I knew very little about. I'm sure if I had asked, someone would have helped. Perhaps my parents thought the school handled that stuff, and the school thought my parents handled that stuff. I did have one promising proposition. My vocal teacher mentioned she would like to mentor me if I wanted to pursue classical singing, and while I was flattered and really enjoyed singing classical music, I loved the freedom of writing my own songs and singing my own melodies without the structure and rules. Knowing there was nothing left there for me, I was ready to leave the rigidity of school and the difficult social navigation and just get back on my own and be free again. Into the great wide open. My dad could not bear to see me throw away my marble carving and bought it from me for two hundred dollars to give me some cash.

My first postgraduation adventure was a road trip the day afterward, with two girls, a sculptor and a painter, both friends from art classes. Atz Lee piled in as well, and we headed off in the Bronco that belonged to one of them. We were headed west, where they would drop me off in San Diego to see my mom, who was working at an alternative health center called Optimum Health Institute and attending its program for her seemingly persistent health problems. We all made it as far as Seattle, where we had a falling out because I could not afford my share of the gas money. My little brother made his own way down to San Diego (he was only sixteen, but somehow in our world this seemed normal, and I didn't worry or look out for him), and I stayed in Seattle, busking and writing. I found busy street corners and yodeled and sang "Who Will Save Your Soul" and newer songs like "Money" until I earned bus fare to go on.

Eventually I made it back to Alaska for the rest of the summer, and I got a small cabin at my aunt Mossy's. I wrote feverishly, spending two weeks in silence. I cannot overstate the importance of silence to young artists, or to anyone seeking a creative voice. It takes great influences to find your way to unique self-expression. You must stand on the shoulders of artists who have gone before you. Read great works. See great arts. Listen to great voices. This sets a bar for your spirit and psyche to work toward. Then you must dive inward into silence. Stand on the rippling edges of the expansive universe within your own being and create from there. Don't compare yourself with what's popular. Doing so is like one child comparing himself with another. Greatness is never achieved by trying to imitate the greatness of another. Greatness is chipping away at all that does not belong to you and then expressing yourself so truly that others can't help but recognize it. It is in silence that we discover ourselves. The silence and the unknown can be frightening, but with time it stops feeling like there is nothing there. The darkness and silence will begin to feel like a void in a positive sense—the womb of creation. It is the magical nothing that something is birthed from. Feed yourself a diet of great work, and then go away by yourself and listen alone to your soul speak to you. Silence will be your greatest teacher.

That summer I fell in love with a young man named Phillip, and by fall we had decided to take a road trip across the States, eventually winding up in Boulder, Colorado, where I planned to move in with a girlfriend from Interlochen. Like the kids we were, we slept in the back of his pickup truck and showered at rest stops. I thrilled at seeing the country change as we headed east. Phillip, or Musse as I called him, was fairly fluent in Swedish, as his family hailed from that part of the world. I tried to learn how to speak some as we drove, writing down notes and pronunciations of each word.

"How do you say 'dolphin'?" I'd ask, looking out at the sea.

"*Delfin*. But you say it like del-feen."

"How about 'wolf'? Would it be 'voolf'?" I asked, sort of kidding.

"No, that's *varg*, pronounced va-ree." Oh, not too similar this time. The music of each language is so particular; which words rise and which ones fall determines and describes as much as the words themselves. It was like learning a difficult song, as exciting an adventure as the drive itself.

"*Hoor mor doo? Tack, yag moor brah.*" Does that sound right?" I would ask.

"Yes, that's right, but do you even know what you are saying?" Musse asked patiently.

"How are you? I am fine, thanks," I answered, all teeth, beaming with pride. "Where are we? Arizona? How do you say 'Arizona' in Swedish?"

"Arizona," he answered in a flat tone, staring at me with a smile to make his point.

"Riiiiiiiiight . . ." I said sheepishly, and looked out the window. I tried to see the subtle beauty of the desert that had inspired O'Keeffe and so many others. I didn't get it. I missed the explosive drama of the land that raised me. "Shit!" Musse said. I stayed quiet as he pulled off the road. Our engine seized, made one loud clank, and then quit right then and there. He got out and opened the hood.

"I ran it out of goddamned oil. Son of a . . ."

I got out to investigate. Musse kicked the dirt and flagged down a passing car. He explained what had happened and asked if they would be so kind as to stop in the town up the road at the service station and have them send us a tow truck. They said they would, so we watched them drive off. We began to wait. There was plenty of daylight and it wasn't too hot. "How do you say 'broken engine' in Swedish?" I asked, trying to lighten the mood, but Musse wasn't interested. He just stared out the window.

It took a few hours, but a tow truck came and we drove into a small dusty town, where the mechanic surveyed the damage. He turned to us slowly, wiping his hands on the oil-stained legs of his coveralls. "Well, you are gonna need some parts that we ain't got." He watched the thoughts cross our faces: *Where will we stay and how long will that take?*

"But, I can get the parts," he continued, clearly enjoying himself. We stared at him.

"It'll take a week." He raised his hand as if to stop us from flooding him with questions, then answered them before we could ask. "There's a cheap motel called the Cactus Inn up the road. You can stay without settin' ya back too much. If you didn't know, this is kind of a resort town. You can go sightseein' down there at Havasupai, maybe take you a mineral bath," His mouth shut again, this time for good. The tow-truck driver turned to us and offered us a ride to the motel.

We grabbed some clothes out of the back of the camper shell and shoved them into a bag. The motel was cheap, but not cheerful. I have always hated depressing places. I guess I've always been depressed enough on my own that any extra provided by a dismal environment was just more than I cared to bear.

I asked the lady at the front desk if there was anywhere else we might stay, perhaps the mineral spa I had heard about. She was tired and couldn't have cared less if we rented a room from her or not. She told us if we were the adventurous but broke types, we could hike into the Grand Canyon, and after several miles along the bottom, we'd find an Indian village. No hotel, but there were places to camp and hot mineral springs. A local man named Gary would drive us out to the trailhead. A week camping somewhere would beat a week of sitting around bored. We walked into the lot and saw a worn and dusty burgundy Cadillac, with a man just getting into it.

As Gary drove us out, I tried to pay attention as he told us what to expect. We had a six-hour hike ahead of us.

Musse and I had spent the night before in the back of the truck, backed up to a lovely vista overlooking one of the branches of the Grand Canyon. We had risen early to the sound of wild horses as they snorted sharply, approaching our vehicle with equal measures of curiosity and caution. I lay there and watched them scrounge for food among dry grass and sagebrush. I had no idea when I'd awoken that morning that later in the afternoon we would be afoot, hiking into that massive canyon I'd stared into as I stretched, rubbing the sleep from my eyes.

After about thirty minutes of driving, Gary pulled over at a rest area, pointed us to the unmarked trailhead, and wished us luck. It was only noon and we had plenty of time to make our way down to the bottom. I marveled at the red dirt trail that cut like a ribbon through the hard rock canyon walls. Deep purple clay wove in and out of the steep cliffs, and the downward pull was hypnotic, impossible to disobey. It had warmed up considerably with the sun high overhead. I tied a bandanna around my head and took in the vast landscape. It really was beautiful in its own way; nothing like Alaska, which was full of bold colors, water, mountains, and varied landscapes. This terrain was muted, just variations of one color. The canyon was massive—my eyes boggled to comprehend the twists and turns of sandstone cut by the invisible sword of millions of years of wind and weather. As we descended deeper, the walls grew taller, like massive wings that unfurled around and above us as we walked. Sounds changed as we descended. At the top our voices were tiny and lost in such a big sky, but at the bottom the slightest whisper carried and echoed as it rattled around the canyon walls.

We walked for some ways like this, seemingly at the bottom of the world, along a narrow path of pebbles with womblike canals unfolding before us. Even though the sun was at full strength, the carved canyon walls remained cool. I listened as our footsteps clattered brightly and echoed against stone. Soon I heard something familiar: the crisp and precise sound of hoof on stone, many hooves. We rounded a corner and there was a short straightaway, where we could see a mule train coming toward us. An Indian man rode a sinewy horse, and in his hand was a lead rope with a train of maybe six mules tied nose to tail. They were packed with garbage, mailbags, and random items that were being brought out. I introduced myself and said we were looking for a place to stay at the falls. I asked him about his mules and told him I had run a few pack trains on hunting trips in Alaska. His eyes brightened.

"I have two cots in my yard in the village underneath a cottonwood tree. You can sleep on them if you want for free. You can stay as many days as you need if you run the mule train up to the top of the canyon once a day for me."

I turned to Musse, and then back to the Indian. "Sure! It's a deal!" We shook hands and I asked his name.

"Indian Joe," he said with a broad smile. "Follow the trail to the village, and the first house you see on the right just before the village is mine. My wife's name is Sue, and tell her I said you may stay on the cots in the yard."

We followed the trail to Joe's. Without opening the screen door between us, Sue pointed to the west, and in the distance we saw a tall cottonwood tree, such an usual sight for the desert.

I pulled my sleeping bag off my pack and laid it out on the single bed closest to the tree. The sunlight was dancing through the canopy overhead, creating a kaleidoscope of color and sound as dry leaves chimed in brittle tones. I lay down and stared up at the shock of green leaves, so rich and vibrant against the monotonous landscape. The canyon walls rose around me at every angle. It almost caused a feeling of vertigo. I felt like a tiny shell laying there, an archaeological artifact, a brief blink and breath of fragile skin.

We set up camp by our tree and shared our food and talked until we both grew quiet under the spell of the evening's music. Hawks cried in a far-off corner of the canyon. Dogs barked, trying always to get the last word. Chickens clucked from the safety of their evening roosts. Then all was silent but for the great collective hum of the desert. Bugs and frogs, insects that rubbed their wings against trees like locusts, all blurred into a white noise.

I went to that place I rarely find: a deep and restful sleep with no ghosts nagging. I felt safe and happy in my soul, surrounded by beauty and God's music . . . then, a woman screaming.

I startled awake, my eyes shot open with alarm. Adrenaline rushed through my body as I tried to comprehend the sound. I sat disoriented, trying to find the source.

"What . . . ?" Musse stammered.

My God, I thought, *a woman is being murdered!* I knelt on my bed, turning around as I tried to make sense of the painful screeches bouncing off the canyon walls. I looked in the direction of the house and saw no lights. I could hear no one stirring. The scream would stop as abruptly as it started, then a deafening silence. In the utter confusion, we waited for another outburst.

"From over there?" I pointed to the northeast, just behind the house. The cobwebs of slumber had cleared now and on the second scream I was able to pinpoint the source a bit more clearly.

"My God, it sounds like someone is hurt!" Musse said.

But I began to recognize the sound, and it slowly became clear. It was the incredibly sad and mournful crying of a . . . mule. I half laughed.

"No way!" Musse proclaimed in disbelief. Sure enough, shadowy four-legged figures could be seen, restless in the shadows in the small pens on the other side of the house.

I sat for a minute and contemplated the comedy of the situation. It had to be a nightly occurrence, as not a single person besides us seemed bothered by it. The mule in question kept it up for only another hour, but it had set pins and needles loose inside my skin. I kept thinking I felt critters crawling around, though I knew that up high on that bed it was unlikely. I was sure glad I wasn't sleeping on the ground.

Dawn came and the air was cool and damp with the difference. Indian Joe must have had an eye on us that morning, for as soon as we rustled around, I heard his voice bark from a distance.

"Morning! Come on over when you get up."

I had wondered about our deal, and if he was serious about letting a complete stranger run his mule train. Apparently he was very serious. I rounded the house and headed to the wooden pens.

"Sleep good?" he said with a grin. "My mules scream. Very scary if you don't expect it. Look, after breakfast, we'll pack the mules. You'll ride Rocky, my horse. Just follow the trail. Real easy, the mules could do it themselves but they are lazy and wouldn't go if you didn't make them."

Sue made eggs and fresh salt bacon. It was the first real food it seemed like we'd eaten in a long time. Afterward Joe placed his dishes in the sink and told Sue he had the day off since he was putting Jewel to work. Sue was quiet and winked at me as I picked up my plates, said thank you, and headed for the door.

Musse helped us pack, as Joe explained that the mule train was critical to life in the village, the source of groceries and mail, among other things. We gathered the tail of each animal and tied it up so the hair created a loop. We tied the lead rope of one animal through the looped tail of the one in front of it and so on up the line. We used a knot that would release if it was pulled on really hard. A quick-release bolen. On the steep trails, if one of the animals were to lose its footing and fall down the steep patch, the rope would come undone to prevent dragging the whole pack train down with it.

I measured my stirrup length and he gave me my instructions. Just follow the trail up to the top. Be careful on the steep parts. Someone would be waiting up there to meet me. Unpack and repack the mules with fresh supplies. I encouraged my pony to head out, which he did ever so reluctantly, and I felt my lead rope tighten as the mule behind me protested. Then he slowly started and I felt another pull as the mule behind that one pulled slightly, uneager to start, and so on down the line until we were all moving forward toward the trail.

I waved my hand and cheerfully chimed, "*Hej!*" The Swedish greeting that meant both hello and goodbye.

"*Vi ses snart,*" Musse answered—he'd see me soon.

Though I was a bit nervous at first, I began to relax as I saw that my horse, Rocky, knew his way at each small fork in the trail. I was just there to provide motivation. I sat back and enjoyed the scenery. An hour passed and I began to see the ground rise at a slow and almost imperceptible grade. I pushed the train on at a slow and steady pace and the canyon widened with each foot we climbed. In a few hours we were on the steepest part of the trail—we switched back and forth, zigzagging up the steep cliffs. I stopped every now and then to let the sweating animals catch their breath. As we walked, I watched small rocks knocked loose by my horse's sure feet tumble down behind us. I listened to the tiny clanging sound until I could hear it no more, drowned by the steady rhythm of hoofbeats. The sun was high and directly overhead as I neared the top. My tummy was growling and the mules began to nicker as they knew the top meant lunch was near.

As I cleared the last turn, I could see a powder blue form start to appear at the apex of the trailhead. The crown of a pickup became slowly discernible, then a straw hat, and then the face beneath it, folded arms, legs crossed, until finally I was at the top of the hill and could see the whole man. I must have been revealed in the same fashion: first my horse's ears, then blonde hair, and so on.

"You're not Joe," the Mexican stated in an even tone.

"No, I'm Jewel." I had not spoken for the last several hours and had inhaled so much dust that my voice sounded shockingly loud. That was that. He seemed to require no more explanation.

It took us at least an hour of quietly working side by side for us to re-pack the mules, being careful to distribute the weight evenly on both sides of the animals. Packing mules is quite an art, and the Mexican, who never gave me his name, was quite a hand at it. I helped as best I could, and tried not to get in his way.

The ride back was peaceful. A *hoo-hoo* of an owl out in the day, the scratches of a rabbit as it scurried, always fearful of discovery. It felt so pleasingly familiar to be on horseback, by myself, wandering as I had done on the bluffs of Alaska. Here I was, many miles away, in an ex-tremely different climate, running a mule train in the bottom of the Grand Canyon for a guy named Indian Joe, who lived in a forgotten vil-lage belonging to a tribe I never knew existed. Unbelievable.

As I neared the house, I called out. There were kids in the narrow paths that they used as streets, though really they were nothing more than dusty trails worn smooth by so much foot traffic. I headed to the general store and began unloading the supplies. Musse and Joe showed up, and Joe said, "What a nice day off I had! Sue did not let me out of the house—I lived the good life today!" His smile was broad. It was three in the afternoon when we got the last bit of tack off and put away, and cur-rycombed each mule. I was beat, but eager to look around. And a hot mineral bath sounded good.

Down the trail we went, and it felt so good to be out of my hiking boots and restrictive jeans. The heat and exertion made my limbs swell, and walking in sandals was a delight. We followed a chalky path as it wound deeper into what seemed to be an oasis. Soon I could hear a distant roar. We rounded the corner, and I quickened my pace and then stopped suddenly in disbelief. I could not believe my eyes. And even writing about it, you will think I'm lying unless you've seen it too. Blue does not begin to describe the supernatural color of this water. It glowed like neon, even beneath the full light of day. It was so blue it almost quivered against the red cliff. And it was no minor waterfall—it was a sixty-foot monster pouring from high above, straight out of the stone. A large pool gathered beneath it and white spray frothed and foamed and settled ultimately into rippling robes that furled and unfurled in widening concentric circles, gently lapping at the dusty edge. I stepped out of my sandals and headed straight in. It was cold and exhilarating. Apparently these were not the hot pools. It is still one of the most exotic and beautiful places that I have ever been, or even heard about.

"God bless you for not checking the oil!" I said as I waded deeper, goose bumps running up my legs and fanning down my arms as the chill soothed my sore feet and caught my breath.

After a short time we went farther down the trail to the hot springs. I laid myself flat, resting my head on a rock for a pillow, just my face above water, and felt the heat penetrate deeply into my muscle and bone. Magical. I breathed in deeply, the sculpture of the canyon and mineral smell of the water mixed with the fine dust and the dampness of the evening as it cooled. I was weightless, completely cradled by the womb of the water as it gently rocked me. I stared up at the sky as it darkened slowly, a deep indigo bruise that was spreading from the east. I couldn't help seeing myself as if from above. My wet hair fanning out like tentacles. Limbs weightless in the water. I burnt that image into my mind's eye, saving it until I could draw it one day. Green eyes and pale skin floating in a tiny pool, nestled into red earth. I was watching my own becoming. I was witnessing it all unfold. A knot was loosening, and I was more than just a child running scared. I would stay there, I would work and run the mule train for the week, I would go on to Colorado, and God knows where after that, but I wasn't as worried. I could slow down inside myself a little. Enough to enjoy this moment.

I tried to imagine more of the unpainted portraits of the woman I would become, but I could not see them. They were still waiting to be drawn. I was not certain about the exact shape I would take, but I knew in that moment that if the past was an indication, if the amazing amount of life I had managed to live in eighteen years was a clue, it was going to be an adventure. I was already a ragtag study in contrasts. I was a kid on a dog sled in the Arctic Circle on my way to sing for Inuit villagers in the land of the midnight sun, a traveler in the desert running mules for the Havasupai Indian, a kid in the slums of Anchorage, a bar singer, a graduate of a prestigious fine arts school, a scared girl, a brave girl, a student of nature—all these impossible things were all strung on the same thread that was me. An accidental poet, trying to suck beauty from the driest places. I would try to be as bold as that blue waterfall that had the audacity to liberate itself from stone. *'Cause I am a painter and I am painting myself a lovely world . . .*

FARMERS OF LIGHT

shimmering
faintly
something I see
from the
corner of my eye
but disappears
when I stare straight at it

hope
perhaps
not close
but existing
for me
in the future, even
is enough
to buoy my heart
a little
and keep me going

so dark these days have been
that I do not see darkness
but only stars
. . .

I stare at stars
at the beauty of night
for if I let myself
study the darkness
I would get lost in
just how absolute it feels

yes darkness
you are there
I have brought you into my life
in my ignorance
in my half wake state
and you descended creating
a long dark night of the soul
but I will not lose myself
in you
I will not let myself founder
or falter
or cease to believe
in the existence of a better day
. . .

instead I will trust the rhythm
of nature
with each death a rebirth
with each night a dawn
with each empty tide
a full one follows

today is just a hard day
it has just been a hard year
because I fought you, Darkness
for years
instead of letting myself
accept you as my teacher
to see what it was I had to learn
from you

now I busy myself
mending my net
examining my holes
doing the work the dark is good for
looking inward
repairing the habits
fixing the holes in my
self-love
that got me here
in the first place

I stare at the stars
my heart is quiet
in the winter of itself

but I will not be made idle
with despair
I will be a busy little animal
trusting nature
trusting rhythm
readying myself
for when that glimmer
on the horizon
shifts
for when the shimmering
grows more sure of itself
when the light in me
calls forth the light
in the world
sure of my own
worthiness
and ready to step into a new day

I bless this darkness
for without it
I would never do this work
I would be distracted continually
but in the dark
robbed of my sight
I must look inward
and while it is painful
I bless the wisdom
in me
that brought me here

. . .

I will try to be the best
student I can
of the night
for I sense
the quality of
myself here
is the quality that will come
    with me
as I walk through the rest of
    my days
and my willingness to really
roll up my sleeves
to do the hard work
will determine my experience here
in the long night of my soul
and will determine the length
of my stay
and will determine
I think
even the length and quality
of my return to day

so quiet, body
I know you are afraid

you crawl out of your skin
with the fear that
this darkness is here
forever
and quiet, mind
focus
on your mirror image
see the starlight within
and grow those points of light out
until the light swells across our
    internal
horizon
spilling outward

we are not in the business of
fighting darkness;
we are farmers of light

so stay quiet, body
stay focused, mind
stare at the stars
quiet yourself
and know

I am alive in here
waking inside myself

fifteen

the servants of
our thoughts

After dropping me off in Boulder at Andrea's house, Musse and I parted ways, unsure of when we would see each other next. He was off to the East Coast to visit family. I would see what life in Boulder had in store for me. I got a job working the register at a funky secondhand store and made enough to cover groceries, but not much toward rent. Thankfully Andrea was kind enough to share the apartment with me anyway. We had a lot of fun together. We cooked and read books aloud to each other. We talked about art. Andrea was a dancer but played piano and sang as well—it was she who had taught me my first chords on guitar in high school. I admired Andrea and had written her a song called "A Dance Between Two Women" about a year earlier, about the specialness of female friends. Someone who wanted nothing from you other than support and solidarity. It was a very safe and reassuring thing, to have someone else who was struggling with art and trying to make a life that included it.

I went back to street singing for extra cash. Pearl Street promenade was a busy spot and I could always make a little money this way. I met a lot of locals and made friends as people would stop and strike up a conversation. I discovered that street singers had a way of looking out for each other. One day I was walking down the promenade, stressed because I had no money for food. I walked by a busker who asked for five dollars, and in exasperation I declared, "Man, I don't have five dollars!" He looked at me, stopped playing his guitar, reached into his jeans pocket and said, "Here, have what I made today." It was such a touching gesture.

For Thanksgiving we went to Andrea's parents' house. It was fairly impressive, and I did my best to feel the warmth of the holiday even though I was in a new and strange place. There was something a bit cold and stilted about the atmosphere that was hard to put my finger on. Andrea was clearly enjoying being in her childhood home and around her brother and family though. After the meal I was surprised when her dad invited me for a walk, just the two of us. He was a sober and thoughtful man, it seemed. He'd watched everything carefully that day, I could tell. As we walked, he asked me a lot of questions but the conversation didn't seem friendly somehow. After listening to me talk about my plans, or lack of plans, for the future, he began to speak. He chose his words precisely and it took me a while to realize that in the politest of ways I was being invited to leave Boulder and stay away from his daughter. He clearly thought I was riffraff and would go nowhere, and he feared his daughter was drifting with no focus and that I was the cause. In the spaces between his words, in the subtext, he made it clear that he was paying his daughter's rent, not giving me a free ride. Finally he suggested that I earn enough money to move on.

I never told Andrea about it, but began to look for better-paying work immediately. Sadly, I wasn't qualified for much. I applied for a nanny job with a nice family. They had three lovely kids. I didn't have a car, so the husband gave me a ride home after my interview. They wanted a long-term commitment, and I just wasn't sure I would be in Boulder that long, but I really needed a better job to earn a plane ticket out of there. The husband told me to think about it and that he would touch base with me soon.

He called and asked what my thoughts were a few nights later. When I told him that I liked the idea but that the logistics might be a bit complicated, he invited me to dinner to discuss it. I was excited by the prospect of a hot meal, and hoped maybe there was a way to work something out short-term. At dinner I explained that I needed to leave town in a few months, and that while I'd love to take the job, I wasn't sure I could commit much further than that. He asked how much money I needed. I said about a thousand dollars. "I have that much in my pocket right now," he replied. I didn't see what he meant until it suddenly dawned on me that his posture had changed. He was leaning forward. He had assumed a powerful energy and an opportunistic one. He was a shark sitting across from me and he smelled blood in the water, and I was no longer a kid. The difference a birthday makes on the eighteenth year was suddenly tangible. It dawned on me that we were eating at a restaurant in a hotel. A nice hotel. I had learned that the best way to diffuse a volatile situation was to expose it, and so I said, "Are you propositioning me?" He stiffened. "Don't you think you're putting the cart in front of the horse?" he said, feeling clever about turning it back on me, trying to make me doubt my perceptions. "Well, am I?" I responded. He said, "Look. You seem nice. And I'd love to help you get to wherever you're going next." I sat back and took it in. I'd like to tell you I told that man to take a hike. I'd like to tell you I immediately told him off. But the gravity of the situation was hitting hard. A thousand dollars would take me months to earn, and I was not welcome to stay where I was. It was shocking to think I could get the money in a matter of minutes. I see why girls take guys up on things like this. He was handsome. He was going to cheat on his wife with someone. I needed the money. I'm not above saying I was also flattered by his attention. I felt so down-and-out and lonely, how could I not be flattered by the attention? But my heart spoke loudly and there was just no part of me that could get on board with this. I found my way back to the apartment and told Andrea all about it.

Giving myself up like this would divert my energy from my writing and derail me from becoming my own best work of art. I had a lot to figure out, and this was not a solution. It was a terrible temptation that would be a devastating distraction I could not afford. I believed in myself, despite the odds. I believed I could dig in and figure things out on my own. I felt frightened and overwhelmed but my Alaskan pride was intact. I remembered my gratitude ritual to help me focus my thoughts on everything that was working for me. I had a roof over my head. I had food. I had a job. I was young. I had health and energy. I was better off than so many.

I read books about physics, which inspired me to think anything was possible. If light particles could be in two places at once, or be a wave at times and particles at other times, then what else was possible? How did our thoughts affect our reality and interact with the world on a quantum level? How do you describe having an idea and then, the artist's job as alchemist, transmute that invisible thought and give it actual form in the real world? I saw so many correlations between science and art and they inspired and intrigued me greatly. Ever since I was young, I have seen shapes and patterns when I sing. They are three-dimensional and they expand and contract, collapse and climb. They have different colors and move when pitch changes. The colors change when the tone and vibrato change. They shimmer, snap, bend, all in reaction to what I'm singing. I began to read books about interference patterns, and when I saw drawings of fractal patterns, I was blown away—these were two-dimensional images of what I saw in my mind when I sang. When I tune my guitar, or find pitch, I see the shapes in my mind and they vibrate at different rates. When the notes are the same pitch, they unify and vibrate at the same rate or frequency. Onstage, I hear or see wave patterns that move through the air more than I hear the note in my ear. Sound pushes through the air in a different way if I am hearing a tone in headphones. It's harder for me to match pitch when I wear headphones because I feel cut off from my feedback system of hearing the sound wave move through the air, where I can then match my tone and vibrato to it. This has always made singing in the studio hard for me even though I am hearing my own voice clearly. Though I can hear an instrument to match pitch to, my own pitch will be way off. When I take the headphones off and listen to my voice through speakers, hearing the sound travel through the air, the patterns will come back and I can find my pitch instantly. I have learned that if I tighten my throat and brighten my tone, the shapes respond and tighten, making them appear rounder. When I darken my tone and slow vibrato down, the edges of the shapes are more visible and move slower. If I add emotion in, the frequency and color intensify.

I knew my reality was my perception of reality. Perception was everything. A glass half empty and a glass half full were both true. Schrödinger's cat was both alive and dead. I learned years later that my gratitude practice actually helped me form new neural pathways. The hippie rituals of positive affirmations are not just baloney. Gratitude doesn't exist only in your mind—you have to *feel* it in your whole being. Feelings are the shadows of thoughts. When we have negative thoughts, our emotions mirror them with anxiety. You can often see what you are thinking by reverse engineering and studying your feelings. I worked hard to identify my feelings, and when I grew anxious, I came to see that my thoughts were often skewing negatively. This is where I had a chance to stop the cycle. I didn't have to be a victim of my own mind. I thought change was going to come in big dramatic moments and grand gestures. Instead I realized change came in small and seemingly insignificant ways. It came by breaking a thought or a feeling down to its fundamental building blocks.

I buckled down and after a few months scraped together money for a ticket and headed back to San Diego, where my mom was. She still had health issues, and I was going to live with her and help out and enjoy the beautiful climate. The palm trees and blue ocean were calling me. Plus it would be nice to be around family and I would have someone on my side looking out for me.

Since I was a kid, my mother would have these mysterious bouts that would disrupt everything suddenly. I remember one Christmas, when I was about fourteen, she became faint and said her heart was hurting and lay down on the floor, asking us to call the paramedics. We were at my aunt's house. I worried and held her hand as she lay there, my dear mom whom I loved so much. The medics found nothing, but I still worried. She had a tranquil face that belied her failing body. I was totally hooked.

At Optimum Health Institute, she learned about nutrition and proper health and I loved learning about them too. I sang at the open mics at the institute and did cleanses in the program. We met people who were as passionate as we were becoming about health and spirituality. They introduced us to a group that gathered once a month to listen to an amazing teacher, they said. We went out of curiosity, and it was *so* California. There was a woman named Jacque (pronounced "Jackie") who channeled a male entity named Zarathustra. I had never heard of channeling before, but I had read Nietzsche's *Thus Spoke Zarathustra*. I was beyond skeptical, but once I saw it for myself, it was hard to refute. Her face would transform as the new spirit came in her body, and her posture and very essence were unrecognizable as her own. Zarathustra's spiritual and philosophical teachings were simple, but all of us there felt we were getting intriguing guidance somehow. It seemed as though pure love poured from him and he taught us to be always more loving, more unconditionally gracious, more thoughtful. The world seemed wide-open and science seemed to be blurring with spirituality. Who was I to say channeling wasn't possible. And really, I didn't care if channeling was real or not—I just enjoyed what was being said. It was basically what I heard in church as a child. The point was that our future was up to us. It was inspiring. It was metaphysical. It made me feel anything was possible. I was in control of my life, and my future.

Eventually my mom quit working at OHI, and we moved to Poway, into a beautiful house that was, as usual for my mom, nicer than we could afford. I got busy working two jobs to pay rent. A friend in L.A. gave me a beater car he was going to leave with the junkyard. It barely ran, but I got a mechanic friend to tape it together so that if I never took the key out of the ignition, and if I turned my head just right and stuck out my tongue, it would get me to work. I worked as a hostess in an Italian restaurant. I also got a job as a barista at a local coffee joint called Java Joe's.

Java Joe's had great live music every night. I enjoyed listening to the local singer-songwriters, and one night a guy named Steve Poltz came offstage, walked up to the counter, and asked for an herbal tea. Poltz was tall and lean with messy brown hair and impossibly innocent, round brown eyes, like a kitten's. His devilish smile, boyish charm, and offbeat humor endeared him to every man, woman, and child in the audience. He was a quirky and highly creative songwriter. We struck up a conversation and I told him that I sang. He got me up onstage during my next break and I told him to play a blues in E. Wearing my barista's apron, I improvised lyrics about the patrons in the coffee shop. A harmonica player got up and belted out a solo. I got offstage and went back to my duties of caffeine pimp, but felt excited to have found a community of musicians who cared about the same things I did, who were looking to find their own unique art inside themselves. Folkies, blues cats, traditional ragtime, jazz writers, and anyone else gathered at Java Joe's to hear each other play. On nights off I came in to sing and hang with everyone. This was the first place I debuted songs I was actually writing.

The owner of Java Joe's was an okay guy who got some stuff right. He recognized that his business depended on live music and he had a genuine fondness for local artists. He treated the musicians well and everyone thrived. But he was also human and fallible, and it showed up when he started talking about doing a calendar that he hoped us girls would pose for. I quipped that he could keep dreaming. He never asked me about it again. I stepped in and said the same thing to him another night as he was pestering someone else about it—and got fired on the spot. I took my apron off and walked outside and sat down at one of the only empty tables. I must have looked stunned, because a man sitting at the next table asked if I was all right. I told him I had just gotten fired. He said, Do you want a job? I looked up and he did not appear to be joking. What is it, I inquired. Answering phones at a warehouse. What a lucky break. I said yes, and reported to work the next day. I wound up playing a show at Joe's after I was signed, ironically, to commemorate the first place I'd performed my original music.

My new boss seemed nice. He hired a small team to fill orders at a warehouse. I had no marketable skills but was able to handle this job of answering phones and taking orders. It wasn't a fun job by any means, and I can't say I was a very passionate or valuable employee. It was just a job to pay rent. After a few months my boss took me aside to have a talk with me, I assumed to reprimand me for not putting more heart into sales. Instead he propositioned me. By this time I thought I'd perfected the art of the turndown, one that uses humor to disarm and wit to protect myself while protecting a man's ego so we could both move on with pride intact. He didn't come on too strongly, and I joked it off, saying I was dating someone and it probably wasn't a good idea. The conversation didn't seem overtly tense or strange, and ended with some talk about work. All was well, I thought.

The next day my rent was due. We had a very nice landlord, but had been late so often with my rent that he said he would have to ask us to move out if we didn't start to pay on time. I always struggled to make rent. All my money went to paying it. I would steal toilet paper from public bathrooms and bum food off friends who worked in restaurants. Often the last few dollars of rent money was paid in change, as I was scrounging to get by. I walked in my boss's office that day and cheerfully said, "Good morning. Just came in for my paycheck. My rent is due today and my landlord is busting my chops." My boss didn't look up from the papers he was working on. I waited a second to let him finish, but he never looked up. "Um, hello? I just came by for my check." He acted like I was a ghost he could not see or hear. I stood there awhile as he kept on quietly working. I broke out in a sweat. I was powerless and humiliated. I had no idea what to do. What recourse does a person with no education and no resources have? I walked out of his office and out the front door and sat in my car for a long time. I felt hopeless and doomed. I would never make it in the world. My only value seemed to be in men's perverted interest in sex. I felt hollow, worthless, and incapable. I drove home slowly, still in shock, knowing full well that we would be kicked out of where we were living. I would be letting my mom down. She was depending on me to pay rent. Where would we go?

I pulled up to the house and found my mom in her room and I started crying. I told her I'd been fired for not sleeping with my boss, and that our landlord was going to evict us. I expected panic and tears on her end, but her reaction was just the opposite. She got very calm, and said, "Well, let's move into our cars. That should take the stress level down a bit. Yeah, why not?" At first I thought she had temporarily lost her mind, but the more I thought about it, the more I realized it did solve a lot of problems. I had no money for a deposit on a new apartment, even a modest one. I could live in my car for a few months, get a new job, and with no overhead I could save up the money for a deposit and get back on my feet. San Diego was perfect for living in a car—heck, having a car to myself in a lovely climate was nowhere near as rough as living in Alaska, in an unheated saddle barn, sharing a room with two brothers. It might even be fun!

I went about another round of getting rid of everything that didn't fit into a backpack. I had continued with my drawing and had begun my angel series in the Poway house. Angels in blue jeans who were topless, wearing pearls and with dark blank faces. My drawing has always been a deep reflection of things I'm struggling with internally. I think of Interlochen as my skeleton-alien phase—so much self-loathing and pain in my body. Boulder was about studying those near to me, like Andrea. In Poway I tried to find innocence and intrinsic worth within myself. I tried to learn how to have something other than poverty in my life, without trading nudity for worldly possessions. I also wrote lots of songs. "Innocence Maintained" was one that I started there. Another was "1000 Miles Away," where my little green car has a starring role.

Being properly out of financial recourse, I had taken a Zen approach to mechanics, hoping that if I somehow fixed myself, the universe would reward me with a car that actually turned over when I started it. I saw parallels between my car and me: *a little run down, a little beat up, maybe just a little green. Maybe it's my battery, maybe it's my starter, maybe my heart's too weak.* When I got sick or when something was not going well in my life, it was always my fault. In a way, that was a beautiful point of view, because the only person each of us can control is ourself, so I took every responsibility on myself, in hopes I could change everything if I just tried hard enough. What no one told me is that everything is not my fault. It does not signify anything about our morality that bad things happen to us. When bad things happen, all we can control is how we respond to them. That's a much healthier and more productive mind-set to have, because a sense of shame is not initiated each time something bad happens. I was a long way from understanding this though; it was just not how I was raised. My mom taught me that every single thing that happened to me was a reflection of my own thoughts—I was responsible for everything, all the time, and it was exhausting. Most parents take their children to the doctor when they are sick. My mom told me to sit and meditate it away. She did the same thing. She never went to a real doctor that I'm aware of for her heart problems. She would shut herself away and meditate more. She seemed to be doing fine, so I tasked myself to try harder, always harder. I would be sick and shivering and feverish, with no idea that letting unbearable pain go untreated meant I could become septic from blood poisoning when my kidneys shut down.

It was around this time that I almost died in the parking lot of a hospital. A kidney infection had not been mitigated with cranberry juice and wishful thinking. My mom drove me to the emergency room but no one would see me without an insurance card. I sat in my car, throwing up all over myself, when thankfully a doctor who had seen me get turned away tapped on my window and gave me some free antibiotics and his card. He said he would treat me for free, and did so for many years. After my career took off it felt good to be able to pay him. He was another angel in my life.

I was so earnest and eager to please, and my mom seemed to know this about me. What often seemed like deeply spiritual and even supportive advice always seemed to serve her best. Instead of going back to live with a parent after high school while I figured things out, I was paying rent on a house I could not afford, and after a few months of living in our cars, she went back to Alaska and left me in San Diego, where I fended for myself.

But none of this seemed weird. It was just my life. My mom seemed so caring to me, or at least I needed to believe so. I had no contact with my dad at this point. I was by myself, living in a car that broke down all the time. I was hitchhiking to get spare tires when one busted. I was often sick and couldn't afford antibiotics. While I was able to find a few jobs, I lost them quickly by taking too many sick days, which I spent alone in my car waiting out yet another infection. I became agoraphobic and was gripped by terror if I tried to leave my car. I was absolutely convinced that if I stepped foot outside my car I would be seized by illness. It was irrational and totally paralyzing. I had never been afraid of being out in the world, and yet here I was with agoraphobia. It was debilitating. I rarely left my car, and when I did, it was to pee in someone's yard or behind a bush, or to shoplift food.

The stealing began again with carrots, which apparently are the gateway vegetable, because soon it led to all manner of produce theft. I had quit stealing for a while, but now the need seemed to be back in full force. I was able to limit it to food until one day I saw a sundress that I really coveted. It was frilly and girly and I wanted it so badly. I went in the dressing room of the store to try it on, thinking about the best way to go about stealing it, but instead a strange thing happened.

I tried the dress on. It was ivory with forest green flowers and vines all over it, and smelled new and clean, like someone else's life. Someone's life that I wanted. I wanted to feel clean and new. If I could get it for myself, it would help me deny that I was destitute, in such dire straits that I could hardly eat, much less wash my clothes. I looked in the mirror, happily turning this way and that—the key to these things is not to think too much. Just do it. For some reason I looked at the price tag. Why on earth did I do that? If you're stealing something, it doesn't exactly matter what it costs. But I looked down at my grubby little hand wrapped around the pristine price tag and saw that the dress cost $39.99. I don't know what it was about that moment, but a bolt of lightning hit me. When had I lost faith in myself? I looked in the mirror, the ridiculous frilly shoulder straps puffing up around my face, my stringy hair falling loosely over them. My proud Alaskan body and tan skin and biker boots underneath this white summer dress. I looked like a dog wearing pajamas. The dress wasn't even me. I looked straight into my own eyes and stared. I had once been so confident. I had believed I could do anything I put my mind to. Hell, I had two jobs and paid rent at age fifteen. I put myself through private school and traveled around the country. When had I stopped thinking I could earn forty dollars for myself? I had never thought of stealing as being hurtful to anyone. It felt like getting even with life. It felt like I was in control, doing for myself what fate seemed always to leave out for me. It made me feel taken care of, to provide myself food or something nice to wear. But suddenly I saw that the only person I was cheating was me. I was showing a complete, utter, and total lack of faith in myself. I stared in that mirror, embarrassed, my pants half pulled up around the dress I was attempting to cover up with my clothes. I had been lying to myself. Stealing was not about evening the score—it was about the fear that I would never be enough or have enough. And it was a total stress response. I can look back at every time in my life that I stole (because the times came and went) and it was always directly related to a feeling of extreme duress.

My little green car had been recently stolen, my guitar and all my belongings along with it, which sucked. But at least I hadn't been in it. I was faced with sleeping on the beach or crashing at people's houses as I met them. One guy at a coffee shop said I was welcome to shower at his place while he was at work. He gave me a key and seemed nice enough. I made sure he told me where he worked and what his hours were. I stopped by his job, which was walking distance, just to make sure he was there when he said he was. After a few weeks of showering at beach rest stops, a proper hot shower called to me. I took the key and went to the address he had given me. I let myself inside and saw that I was not alone after all. There were several women in the living room of his tiny apartment. After a slightly awkward hello, one of them asked if I was waiting for a job. No, I said, just here to shower, and walked briskly to the bathroom. I looked around the place for any cameras. None that I could see. As I undressed and bathed I kept wondering what she had meant. I washed out my underwear in the shower homestead-style, dried it with a hair dryer, put on my dirty clothes again, and went out and struck up a conversation with the girls. They were older than me, in their early twenties. One was lying on the couch hardly moving, complaining that she felt like a tractor was parked on her chest. I learned she had just gotten a boob job and came back here to recover from surgery. Another girl was waiting for a call. Apparently this kind stranger ran an escort service on the side. Ah. It was all coming together now. One of the girls asked if I danced. I said I had studied in high school, though I knew that wasn't what she meant. They danced at a local gentlemen's club as well and said that it was great money and I should try it. The girl with the imaginary tractor on her chest said she wasn't going to do it forever, just until she got through school. I asked how much they made. A thousand a week. Gosh. A thousand a week sounded good. And easy. I just could not imagine dancing onstage in my skivvies.

I loved talking with the girls about what their lives were like when I came by to shower—they were generous in sharing the details of their work with me, and I listened to them like a writer does, paying attention to the details, without judgment, but I did not listen like an apprentice. I had seen girls my whole life who gave up just a little of themselves only to see it was a slippery slope—the line they said they would never cross kept moving farther and farther away until they hardly recognized themselves. I sensed this would happen to me if I gave up that little piece of myself. It felt dangerous, not that I didn't consider it. It was an option. But for whatever reason there was something in me that just would not bend on this subject.

In the dressing room, I had to face myself. No more kidding myself. This was not an amazing adventure. I was not doing well. The terror and hopelessness were going to drown me. Jail, disease, or death were certainly in my future if I did not get a grip, get serious, and turn things around for myself. I looked back down at my hands, that forty-dollar price tag still clutched between my fingers. I looked back at the mirror.

"What are you afraid of?" I asked myself.

I answered. "That I'm always going to be alone."

I choked back silent sobs. What else? That I don't know how to take care of myself. What do you know how to do? Write. And learn. Do that then, until you know what else to do. Remember, do no harm. Hard wood grows slowly. No shortcuts. Fear exists in your mind. Master your mind. It's all you can do. It's literally all you have. I took the dress off, hung it back on its hanger. I was shaking with fear. It was as if only at that moment the reality of all I was facing actually hit me.

Unsure what else to do with myself, I walked to the public library and thumbed through Plato's allegory of the cave, one of my favorite works. It invited me to engage my imagination, intellect, and creativity in understanding my world and my perceptions. It felt comforting. I remembered what Buddha said: Happiness does not rely on what you have or who you are. It relies on what you think. If this was true, then what did I think? On the outside, I was a fairly optimistic kid. If you met me on the street, you would never know I was homeless, really. If you met me on the street, you'd think I was upbeat, outgoing, and friendly, with a smile on my face. But the anxiety and fear that seemed to be controlling my inner life and thus my actions became untenable.

Again I looked back through all my journals to get a better picture of what my real feelings and thoughts were. My journals were my prize possessions, and the only things I had managed to hang on to over the years. I carried them in my tattered backpack everywhere I went. I wrote my poetry, thoughts, feelings, and lyrics in them. I opened the cover of one I'd finished recently to see my familiar dyslexic scribble, as thoughts tended to pour out faster than I could write. I was shocked by the pattern I could see laid out there clearly in black and white. I was not an upbeat, optimistic kid. I was deeply negative. I was living in the past and projecting it all on my future and I was being completely robbed of the opportunity that lies in the now. Even in my honest writing, I wasn't being honest with myself. I had hidden my terror. Every action I took—writing and stealing alike—was for the sake of avoiding reality. Where my feelings were, I was not.

Looking back now, I recognize that the disconnect between the negativity and fear in my writing and my happier day-to-day appearance to other people was sheer compartmentalization. I didn't learn that word until recently, but it was a survival skill that worked for me, almost too well. Compartmentalization is what kept me from experiencing real fear when I did dangerous things like hitchhiking, whether to see my mom or busk through Mexico. I had become so used to stressful, high-risk situations that they felt normal to me.

If you are not present, you are unable to have an effect on that unique, fleeting moment called now that truly determines what happens next. Now is the only creative moment we have. Fear was causing me to project my past into my future, never allowing me to engage in the now. Worry and fear are thieves that rob us of our ability to change. I was simply surviving each day, running scared, sure that yesterday's hurt would be tomorrow's pain. Change was not possible like this. I vowed to try to stop the cycle I had fallen into.

I invented a new exercise to tackle my agoraphobia. I focused on what my biggest obstacle seemed to be: fear. I shut my eyes and tried to sit in my body and just feel the terror. To really feel it. Study it. When it overtook me, I shook and cried, gripped by paralysis. It crashed over me like a wave and I was at its mercy, swallowed in its infinite yawn, until I found myself on the other side, exhausted and spent. I had to find a way to interrupt this cycle. Next time I tried to move toward the oncoming wave with awareness. By choice. I shut my eyes and took a deep breath, using some of the meditation techniques I'd learned as a child. I tried to visualize what terror looked like. It looked like a knot, real and concrete and impossibly tight. I felt the knot in my body. In my stomach. I felt nervous. Edgy. Jittery. Hmm, jittery. When I got nervous just before going onstage as a kid, I would get butterflies in my stomach—it was a jittery feeling, but exciting. Maybe I could work with this. Maybe I could pretend my fear was actually nerves, the kind you get right before doing something hard but exciting. I decided every time I had an overwhelming feeling of terror, I would consciously force myself to flip a switch and pretend it was excitement. I liked the idea of a switch to flip. I painted one in my mind's eye—a giant white light switch. I practiced looking at the knot of terror and then seeing a light switch, and when I flipped it, I imagined the knot turning into a thousand butterflies that fluttered away. I felt my body relax. It felt odd and strange to play this game, like pretending—and it was. But the terror was imagined as well. This was a conscious choice to choose a different experience. To be in the moment and to use that moment to influence the next one.

At first I had to flip my imaginary light switch about a thousand times a day. Before I knew it the knot would be back. Flip. Butterflies. Knot. Flip. Butterflies. Knot. But after some weeks of practice and mindfulness I was able to see the butterflies more and more, even follow them and watch where they went. What was I excited about, anyway? If I wasn't using my energy to imagine and plan for bad things happening, what could I redirect my energy toward? What good things might be possible? As creative as I was at that age, I was so hampered by fear that I could not imagine one good thing happening. Not one! After all, what good could happen to a homeless kid? People walked away from me on the street. People looked at me like I was subhuman. I looked dirty and lost, and frankly I was. Flip the light switch. Follow the butterflies. Imagine them outside going into blue sky. Where did they go? What did they want to do? Maybe I could follow them outside. Maybe I could street sing for some food money. Maybe I'd make someone smile. Maybe they would smile at me. Slowly I expanded my comfort zone, and after that made my way to a street corner, where I sang a song that I'd written. Some skater kids came by, three young guys about seventeen or so. They stopped and listened and I looked them in the eyes as I sang. They gave me five bucks and one kid said, "You sing good. Thanks for making my day a little better." I was floored. I had manifested something good in my life! It was almost magical. How quickly I had forgotten that I was capable. Here I had focused on something in my mind and I had made it happen! And it was something positive and not destructive. I continued to work hard at flipping my light switch, at forcing myself to see things as opportunities and putting my nerves to work for me.

At first it seemed impossible to notice my thoughts—they came and went too quickly and I was not attentive enough to slow them down and assess them while they were happening. Instead I watched my hands. My hands were the servants of my thoughts. They carried out the physical impulses going on unseen in my mind. I spent several days trying to be present and just witness what my hands had been doing. They had been stealing. They had been writing about all the bad things that had happened to me and that would surely happen again. They were hypervigilant in predicting the next bad thing that might happen, so that I might somehow avoid it. They obsessed over when I would become sick again.

They dwelled on all the belongings I did not have. They were not engaging in the opportunity that lies in the present moment. If I couldn't change my thoughts, perhaps I could reverse engineer the process. If I changed what my hands did, perhaps that would force me to change my thoughts. I began to notice and write down how many doors I had opened for others in a day. Then I tried to open more doors than I had the previous day. I found myself holding a door open for strangers even when I wasn't going into the building. I began to notice and look for others who needed help. Helping others helps you get over yourself and your own problems. Instead of staring down at my feet I would look someone in the eye. This would force myself to remember we were all connected and help me let go of the illusion that I was alone. These were all practices in being present.

Whether it's a trick or not, I managed to gain some power over my sense of perception—I could experience myself feeling in control of my life, feeling capable, not being a victim. And the more empowered I felt, the more empowered I allowed myself to be. And the more my confidence bubble grew—from a street corner, to maybe a couple blocks away, to maybe surfing during the day, to allowing myself to look at the blue water and say, I'm okay, right now this very second, I don't know what will happen an hour from now, but in this moment I'm okay and have all I need. I learned that if I could get through second by second, if I could allow myself to experience that right here, right now, and then just to sink into that moment and expand it, and let myself *feel* that, let the energy of that move through my body, let my tension and my tightness melt away, I actually felt some joy. Real joy.

I began to document what I was learning in a song. Worry was wasteful. My hands being my own, no matter what life was throwing at me. Neither God nor anyone else owes us. I owed myself. And in the end, only kindness matters. I called it "Hands," and it would become a hit for me on my second album. This song was a gift for me, not only in the moment I wrote it but years later. In 2001, my husband, Ty, and I were camping for a week in the mountains of Northern California. We came back to civilization on September 14 to see the flag at half-mast on the ranch where we were staying. The flag at the next ranch was at half-mast. We saw handwritten notes along the side of the remote dirt road that said, "God Save Us," "God Bless Our Country." When we finally had radio reception and learned that a few days earlier the country had been attacked by terrorists and that the towers had fallen, we sat in complete disbelief. Then the DJ dedicated this song I had written at such a dark and pivotal time in my own life to everyone in America experiencing the same. It was a genuinely surreal and humbling moment.

sixteen

safety in vulnerability

I couldn't hold down a normal job because I kept getting sick and then getting fired for taking too many sick days. Medicaid was difficult— the appointments I had to keep were too far for me to walk to, and I had learned that hitchhiking in Southern California was just not an option. Having no address and no money and fielding all the suspicious questions was so demoralizing that it was more trouble than it was worth. I decided to try to get a gig in town—maybe I could do cover songs in a coffee shop or a local bar. I walked into several coffee shops in Pacific Beach where I had seen musicians play. After speaking with one manager, I found out that musicians generally played for free or for tips. That seemed absurd to me; I had been raised with the notion that bringing in patrons or entertaining them deserved pay.

One day a friend named Gregory Page invited me to play a solo acoustic gig with him. I was excited because he was the bass player in the Rugburns with Steve Poltz, and I knew that the band got paid. I got to the coffee shop—I forget the name now—and it was packed. A man stood at the door taking a cover fee just to get in and listen. We both sat onstage and swapped turns singing original tunes. I was an unknown with no following, but Gregory had quite a few fans from his Rugburn shows, and the night went well. I saw that the tip jar at the foot of the stage was fairly full of ones and fives by the time we got off. I was excited to finally get paid and get some warm food, and headed toward the owner to see how the split with the door money went. I was stunned when she informed me that she kept it all. "But they came in to see the music. How about we split the door money in thirds?" She said no, flat out. "Okay," I said. "You keep the door money. Gregory and I will split all the food and coffee sales." She looked at me with an incredulous smile on her face. Gregory seemed like he wasn't too worried about the money. I turned back to the proprietor, and she said, "You and Gregory split the tip jar. I keep the coffee sales, and the food sales, and the door money." I was dumbfounded. "The reason all those people came tonight was to see music. And I need the money. I don't have another job." She looked at me, unmoved. An anger rose in me and suddenly I found myself at no loss for words. I put my small finger in her face and said, "You are stealing from the people who are helping your business thrive. You're not a nice person. Your business will fail. Mark my words. I'm going to tell every musician I know to boycott this place because you are willing to cheat the very folks who are putting food on your table. Your greed will end up starving you, not me." Then I added, "I'm going to find a place to sing that lets me keep all the door money. You can keep the tips from tonight. You're going to need them." She didn't seem too worried as she said, "Good luck. This is how every coffee shop operates."

While I enjoyed the drama of giving her the tip money, it didn't take me long to regret it. She was right: every coffee shop charged door money and expected to have musicians play for free. For the privilege of the "exposure." Where was everyone's pride? I couldn't understand being onstage for hours and not being paid something. I wasn't looking to get discovered, I didn't think an A&R agent was going to give me a break onstage at a tiny coffee shop in a beach town. I just wanted to earn enough money to get an apartment and get off the street.

One day I was walking to Turquoise Beach, a local surf spot with nice waves for longboarding. I would often hang at the beach and befriend a surfer and borrow a board for a few waves. I also showered in the public rest area there. This particular day I took a less frequented street and noticed a coffee shop quietly tucked away. It piqued my interest so I walked inside. No customers. Funky mural art on the walls. There was an older woman behind the counter who told me after we'd talked awhile that the business was struggling because there was no foot traffic in the area and that she would have to close the doors soon. I asked if anyone ever sang there. Not really, she said. Confidently, I told her I was a singer (even though I had never played a solo gig of my own material before) and said maybe we could help each other. If I brought folks in to see me sing, I could keep the door money and she could keep all the coffee and food sales. We shook hands on it and I left with my own gig. Now all I had to do was get people to actually show up. Considering I had no following, that was a tall order.

I asked Steve Poltz, who had a large local following, how he did it. Singing in town for years, developing a reputation, he told me. I didn't have that kind of time. Steve suggested that, for starters, I sing the same night every week, so folks would know where to find me consistently. It was hard to compete with Friday and Saturday nights in town, as everyone went to bars to drink and see bigger bands, so I made flyers inviting people to come see me sing at the Inner Change Coffeehouse every Thursday night. I wore a cute velvet jumpsuit I had gotten at a thrift store when I had a job and walked the boardwalk handing out my flyers, mostly to surfers who said they would come see me play. Sure enough, that first week three of them showed up. It was a start.

I assumed I had to play five-hour sets, like we had when I was a kid. I had set about writing five hours of material in a panic. I still had no ear for teaching myself cover songs on guitar, plus writing my own was so much more fulfilling that I never really tried to learn. I wrote about everything I was learning about myself. About my fear. My longing. My need to be strong in a true way, and not in a pumped-up false one that was simply hiding a fragile ego. I wrote poems and put them to music. I wrote short stories and put them to music. No more secrets. I gave voice to my deepest fears, insecurities, and dreams. I stepped onstage that first night and with all the courage I could muster, opened my heart, and let it bleed out for all the world to see. Or three people. But still, it was scary. I wasn't sure whether people would walk out or tell me I was weird. But the opposite happened. I felt seen for the first time, because I had let myself be seen. And unexpectedly, the folks in the audience felt seen and understood too. My own fears were not so unique. Talking about my shame and fear actually caused others to accept me. True safety was not in having armor. It was in vulnerability. I was also a ham and chatted up the folks who watched, creating a very personal connection.

The surfer guys were blown away. They told their friends and more came the next Thursday. Before too long I had a regular and loyal crowd coming to see me. Nancy, the owner, kept her word and let me have all the door money. The word spread that Nancy gave a fair shake to musicians and so other songwriters came to play. Her place began to develop a reputation for having an audience that would listen more than it talked. Now that I was no longer doing cover songs, I hated audiences who talked while I sang. It was hard to bare your soul while someone was talking to their friend about a new sweater they bought. From my first show I asked people to use the potty before I started and to please wait until the end of a song to get up and order coffee or food. I asked Nancy to run the espresso machine only between songs. I would tell stories and the like between songs so she could catch up on orders. The fans I found in those early days were caring, thoughtful, respectful, loving, loyal, and supportive. I don't think I ever told anyone I was homeless, but they all seemed to want to take care of me and help me out. They reinforced my courage to be honest and transparent, poetic, thoughtful, silly, and brave in my writing. I got to be me. All of me. It was liberating.

After several months there was standing-room only around the edges of the small shop. People showed up early to get a seat and to avoid my calling them out for showing up in the middle of a song. Nancy installed small speakers on the back patio so people could hear me sing while they watched through a large window that looked in. When the back patio filled up, Nancy put speakers out in front and folks would stand out there on the dirt and watch me sing. The feeling, the excitement and admiration, was so tangible that I would get goose bumps as I told my stories and sang. I remember one night I was lost in a song and opened my eyes to see it was dark and pouring rain outside. There were people with their noses pressed against the glass, soaking wet, who had been standing there listening to me sing for hours. It was staggering.

I was making enough money to buy food and gas and even to occasionally splurge on books and clean clothes for the stage. I bought vintage clothes from the thrift shop like marching band uniforms and 1950s bathing suits with cute sewn-in skirts that I wore with go-go boots. I wore antique prom dresses and old ballroom numbers with lots of chiffon. It was fun and absurd and it made me happy. It felt like dressing up, even if on a dime-store budget. I was saving up for the deposit on a new place as well. Meanwhile, I'd borrowed a thousand dollars from Musse to buy a VW bus to live in. I had never borrowed money in my life, but I knew I would never make it on the street with the other homeless kids I'd met. Most of them hung out in Ocean Beach. They formed their own kind of family unit, and they welcomed me in. It was an honor to get to know some of them and their stories. Like me, many of them came from hard-knock backgrounds. No kid leaves home at a young age because they think it's going to be fun—they leave home because living on the street feels safer to them than their home life. Most people assume drugs lead kids to running away or becoming homeless, and this is not so, based on what I saw. Many of those I met had been in dysfunctional government programs like foster care with abusive caretakers, their biological parents long since missing from the picture. Others had home lives that were intolerable, so they struck out on their own, and, like me, they'd started off well until there was one glitch and the poverty cycle became too hard to crawl out of.

Homeless kids have a natural mistrust of adults, as adults have typically taken advantage of them. They have a natural mistrust of the law, as laws and officials have rarely cared or advocated for them in meaningful ways. They are prime targets for streetwise criminals as well. Being homeless and underage is a particularly hard prospect because you are not old enough to get a legal job. You either have to forge documents to get a job or you just take to panhandling or selling dime bags for local dealers. Having no address and no skills equals no legitimacy.

There was a family-group dynamic that was an appealing aspect of hanging out with these kids—they looked out for each other and had each other's back—but my instinct told me it would not be a good scene for me to fall into. Avoiding drugs was the best thing I could do for myself, along with finding healthy ways to mitigate my fear. There was also this quality about the group that I sensed. I felt they were giving up their hope and succumbing to disappointment. On some level I knew that this was the most dangerous thing of all—to lose hope. To accept my circumstances. I was so lucky to have something these kids did not have—I could sing. I had a skill that also happened to double as a healthy coping mechanism. If I kept trying, I could make an honest living and hopefully save up for a deposit on a new place, if I could keep from getting sick and keep my expenses low.

I bought the blue and white VW from a mechanic, a nice family man who also surfed. He caught on quickly that I was on my own and would be living in the car. I told him I was a singer and offered to give him free tickets to my shows in exchange for helping me repair the van if it broke down. He kindly agreed, and he and his wife came to see me regularly and became supporters of mine, bringing me food and books to read. Two more angels in my life.

Each time I got a little money saved, I experienced a setback. My VW was broken into and my guitar was stolen. Another time Steve Poltz's car was repossessed. It was towed and he had too many unpaid parking tickets. He couldn't afford to pay them, and couldn't get to his shows. I pulled out all the cash I'd saved and handed it to him.

I worked hard to pay Musse back. I knew which bars had a happy hour and ate potato chips and peanuts for months until I had saved the money. In the meantime I was very happy in my little van. It was an amazing upgrade from living in my tiny green car and sleeping all scrunched up on the backseat, jammed between my guitar and my few possessions. I found a tacky brown Formica dresser, and my mechanic friend bolted it to the floor so it would not fall over when I drove. We removed the fold-down seat in the back, and he built a simple wooden frame. With a little scavenger hunting I found an old futon that did not look too diseased. His wife gave me a couple of blue Mexican horse blankets as curtains for a bit of privacy. For an Alaskan girl who had lived in a saddle barn and shared a room with her brothers, it was not shabby at all. Once I had a couple hundred dollars saved up, I bought a new guitar at Taylor and that's still the guitar I play. I love it. I call it Bird. It's a beautiful guitar and sounds amazing. It had a flaw on it, some indiscernible little crack that nobody could see, and they sold it to me at a discount.

Soon the word about my shows began to spread and other musicians came to see me play regularly. A local program director named Mike Halloran from 91X, one of the biggest stations in the country, came in one night. Mike was and still is a genuine lover of music and musicians. He has always had his ear to the street in his community. I remember everyone whispering that night that he was a big radio guy. Mike was a big guy physically, too, and right in step with the grunge movement, complete with blue flannel shirt and goatee. Halfway through the show he began crying while I sang "1000 Miles Away." I knew right then and there I liked him. There I was in some Ginger Rogers frock, goldfish orange with a sequined bodice, and after my usual five-hour show he invited me to the station to record a song, saying he would play it sometime. I recorded several songs, I think—new ones like "Angel Needs a Ride," "Mamma's Little Hero." I thought Mike was nice, and was excited about what he said, but I wasn't exactly going to hold my breath. As a kid bar singing, self-proclaimed entrepreneurs and wealthy men sometimes told my dad that I had a great voice and that they would help us make a record. Or local studios would have me record a song and swear they had connections, but things never seemed to pan out. Lots of good intentions, no ill will, but things just dissolving after the initial excitement faded. And that was okay. I was realistic. I heard what was played on the radio and I knew I sounded nothing like that. The records I liked had been out-of-date for decades. I wasn't a size 2, I wasn't cool, and I wasn't that good. I was earnest and sincere, and those things made me feel honest. I was beginning to feel happy with where I was. Maybe I wouldn't need another day job, maybe I could get out of my car by singing like my dad had done to support us. A blue-collar musician making a living. I was excited by the prospect. I loved writing songs about real things. It was making me happier.

When I was younger, I'd thought of happiness as a capricious bird that, if you were lucky, landed on your shoulder and sang its bright tune with a will all its own. Happiness seemed arbitrary, and I hoped for it to find me as if I had no say in the matter. Well, perhaps in the way they say you make your own luck, you could make your own happiness. If it was a bird, perhaps I hadn't built an attractive home for it. If my mind was chaotic, unorganized, negative, closed off, or resentful, there was no place for happiness to alight. I thought about what kind of house I had built, and what it was attracting. Were my windows open wide or firmly shuttered? Was I taking the time to build a foundation and invest in a structure that would hold strong? Or was it only halfway conceived, reactive?

I began to watch people who appeared to be happy. They got outside. They exercised. They did things they found fulfilling in some way. They took care of themselves. I imitated them. Being homeless and relatively jobless afforded me a tremendous luxury if I did not waste the day on fear. I had time to experiment and try new things. I made myself exercise every day. I attempted to keep my van tidy. I imagined that my thoughts were food, and asked myself often whether I was feeding myself junk or higher-quality, nourishing thoughts and feelings.

I also paid more attention to literal food and nutrition in an effort to heal my kidney problems and improve my health. At this point in my life, the subject of nutrition and health is one I could write an entire book about. I was blessed to have been raised on a ranch where the whole foods we raised and grew were so good for us.

Buying healthy food on a budget was more than just a little challenging. It was impossible. I read about the foods that were good for kidneys and that plenty of clean water was key for flushing infections and proper function. On the homestead, we had a hose that went from a creek right up through a hole in our sink for our "running" water. It was ice cold and tasted sweet and delicious. Granted, the system was a bit flawed—in the winter we had to keep the water source from freezing over, and during the spring thaw worms and critters flooded the hose. I remember coming downstairs to find my prized possession, a pink frilly scarf, had been put to work as a filter, folded over the faucet and wrapped with rubber bands, keeping a large bulge of worms on the safe side of the equation. There was no room to be precious on the homestead, a lesson that served me well while homeless. I was shocked to discover that people in the Lower 48 hardly ever drank tap water and by how much stores charged for bottled water. I could hardly afford the two gallons I needed a day. I knew firsthand what it took to haul water by hand to clean vegetables or dishes, how we saved every precious drop we could, and I was appalled by how many people let their faucets run while they brushed their teeth and watered lawns in the desert. Seeing the water crisis we were facing in America, I wondered what it was like in foreign countries for communities that had no opportunity to buy water, and vowed that if I were ever in a position to help, I would. Fortunately, in 1997 I was able to form my charity, Project Clean Water, which has put clean water wells in more than fifteen countries so far. In addition to founding PCW and healing myself with herbs and food, one of my proudest moments as a parent has been feeding and teaching my son about nutrition and the amazing machine his body is, and how to properly give it what it needs to be whole and healthy. We lack education about food in America.

My mom had influenced my interest in nutrition quite a lot. She had moved to California originally to live at the Optimum Health Institute for what I thought were her heart and cancer issues. It was a place folks went to cleanse and included a raw vegetarian diet, wheatgrass, and enemas. She taught a small class at one point in exchange for receiving treatment, and I went with her to cleanse as well. A good food for the kidneys was watermelon, so while homeless, I hatched a scheme to find free watermelon. Every Wednesday OHI served watermelon to its members while they gave their cleansing testimonials. I would pose as a participant and eat all the watermelon I could, for the minimal price of having to come up with a cleansing testimonial. I was convincing enough—my stories about a particular cleansing crisis or a breakthrough I'd experienced while imbibing too much wheatgrass and not enough food drew emphatic "amens" and "atta girls" from the group.

One day at OHI, freshly stuffed with watermelon, a song idea came to me, and since there wasn't anywhere to sit alone inside, I sat in the parking lot with my guitar working on it. A guy wearing funny sunglasses came by and stood listening. I didn't really look up until I had worked out a phrase, and I instantly recognized him. Flea from the Red Hot Chili Peppers. His band was absolutely the biggest at the time. It was unmistakably him. In a parking lot. At a cleansing institute. He sat down next to me and told me to play some more, so I did. He said I was good and asked if I had a deal. No, I replied, not even remotely. Flea asked if I knew any good waves, and I said I did. So we went surfing. He meditated and was sweet and kind. We didn't talk about music anymore, only about life, and he told me to give him a call if I was ever in L.A. We would end up becoming lifelong friends. I never asked him for help in the music biz, and he never offered. I was on my own path and I figured whatever was to happen would be up to me. It was never my style to ask people for help, but when I got signed, he was one of the first people I called. Flea played bass on "You Were Meant for Me" and played with me on TV as part of my band in the early days, when I didn't have one. Even though he was a rocker, he helped me believe in my folk music and to be true to myself.

There seemed to be a buzz building about my music. Mike Halloran had kept his word and played one of my acoustic songs on his station.

Between that and word of mouth about my live shows, I noticed tonier folks showing up to my little shows. I remember Daniel Lanois drove down. Someone in the crowd recognized him and told me he was the producer for U2. I introduced myself and asked him if he could help me make my system sound better. He looked at me a bit puzzled, but we fiddled with the knobs awhile, before he was kind enough to find a gentle way to say the system didn't suffer from the wrong EQ settings but from a lack of quality. It was just a sucky system. He stayed for the whole show and we grabbed tacos afterward. I picked his brain about his creative process and the bands. I was surprised that he treated me with so much respect, asking me about how I wrote and whether I kept journals.

Ike Turner came in one night. The movie *What's Love Got to Do with It* had been out not long before, and the coffee shop was abuzz. In the room, dead quiet apart from my own voice, he commented loudly on my singing to his friends. At one point, I stopped in the middle of a song and asked him to kindly be quiet. The regulars were expecting me to, but still, when I did, a bit of a ripple went through the crowd. Ike nodded as if he was impressed, and didn't seem to mind the extra attention in being shushed, but instead of settling in quietly, he stood up and handed me a signed eight-by-ten photo of himself. After the show I looked at it. He handled being illiterate with flair, "signing" his glossy with a stamp that said, *What's love got to do with it? Not a damn thing! Ike Turner.*

seventeen

imperfect, full of mistakes—but honest

The song I had played for Mike at 91X was requested so often by folks calling in that it made it to the top 10 countdown. Record labels spend a lot of money to get their artists in the top 10 and they all began wondering who this girl was with nothing but a guitar getting played between Nirvana and Soundgarden on one of the biggest stations in the country. Suddenly I felt like Cinderella. Limos began showing up outside the Inner Change. Men in suits sat conspicuously out of place next to the surfer, beach-town crowd, and if they dared to get up halfway through the four- or five-hour show, I would call them out. It was a lot of fun. Afterward they would take me out to a dinner that cost more than I had made in the last two years combined and then ask, "Where can we drop you off?" "Oh, here . . . is good," I would say. They had no idea I was homeless at the time. Nancy would get calls at the coffee shop from executives asking her to save them a seat for that night's show. When she'd find out what label they were from, she would put it up on the marquee: "The Inner Change proudly welcomes Sony Records." She was so excited for me I thought she would burst. My whole crowd was. We felt like one big family: over that last year we had all cried and laughed and grown together and suddenly here were labels that thought I had something. Two women execs came in one night, which was a nice break from all the males. They introduced themselves as Inga Vainshtein and Jenny Price. Inga managed a local band on Atlantic Records and Jenny was the secretary for the band's A&R. They had heard about me and driven down from L.A. The next week they brought a big music lawyer named Eric Greenspan. He fell asleep halfway through my show and was woken to the chuckles of fans who were enjoying my improvisational song about his head on the table and his little snores. Eric is still my lawyer today and I have never let the poor guy forget about falling asleep the first time he saw me sing. Inga became my manager and Jenny brought the legendary Danny Goldberg down, who would end up signing me to Atlantic. Jenny would be promoted to be my A&R.

Before I made a decision about which label to sign with, I was flown all over the country to meet with RCA, Sony, and Warner Bros., in addition to Atlantic. It was surreal. Right before it came time to sign my contract, I hesitated. I went to the beach and tried to really think it all through. My mom and I had often taken walks by the ocean, talking about the dream that my music might one day be discovered. On one hand, I was so excited by the opportunity. On the other, I felt there were two significant things that could potentially be damaging for me. I had just begun to turn my internal life around. I was getting happy and finding peace. I was worried the pressure of the business might not help me in this area. I knew I was deeply flawed, and as I studied what I thought fame was, it looked like kerosene that accelerates or ignites the natural insecurities you already have. I had many. I also feared for my art. My favorite novelists wrote their best work in their fifties, but most songwriters wrote well only into their twenties. I felt lifestyle had a lot to do with that. Fame is a path that many people lose their footing on. I had already lost my footing, and what ground I was gaining I was not eager to give up for the long shot that I might be able to make it one day. That day I decided to sign, but also to develop a plan to help me avoid losing what was so important to me.

Someone gave me a book called *All You Need to Know About the Music Business* by Donald Passman. I learned about mechanicals and royalties and that an advance is really money you borrow and have to pay back. There was a bidding war over me and I wound up being the biggest signing of the year. I was told I could have gotten a million-dollar signing bonus, but remembering that hard wood grows slowly, I turned it down, opting instead for the largest back end any artist had gotten at the time. I knew what music was played on the radio and that I sounded nothing like it. I knew my music was a long shot, and that if I cost the label a lot, it would drop me if I didn't make that money back quickly. By turning down the advance I was betting on myself, and taking the pressure off my music. I hoped to have a cult following like John Prine or Tom Waits. With hard work and touring, maybe I could make this my livelihood, and if my record ever did break and sell big, then I would have earned whatever money was coming to me. I only asked for the label to pay rent on a small house that my mother, younger brother, and I could live in, and for the money to buy my mom and I each a used car. They both had come back to San Diego after I had called home to share the news.

I had told Danny I was a simple singer-songwriter and he believed in me and was very respectful in suggesting producers to help me make my first album. I met with about twenty different producers but none seemed quite right. Many of them heard my six-minute songs and wanted to shorten them. I was not interested in this. I knew nothing of radio, genre, or rules, and I did not want to learn. I wanted to be myself. One day Inga and I were listening to Neil Young's *Harvest* and we turned the CD over to see who had produced it. Neil Young and Ben Keith. Let's call him, Inga said. I met with Ben and knew within five minutes he was my guy. He never once asked to edit, shorten, or change me. He never mentioned radio, singles, or genre. He talked about my lyrics and the story and then about musicians he thought would be a good fit for me. He wanted to use the Stray Gators as my band, who had all played on *Harvest* and *Harvest Moon*. Kenny Buttry on drums, who had played with Dylan. Tim Drummond, who had played bass with James Brown. Spooner Oldham, a legendary Muscle Shoals player. We recorded much of it at Neil Young's ranch in Northern California. Being able to record there was not a favor to me even remotely, but to Ben, for Neil loved him dearly. I arrived to stay in a guesthouse at the ranch and was absolutely on cloud nine. Neil's studio was in a log cabin and was a museum of artifacts and gear: Elton John's rhinestone boots sitting on an organ, Hank William Sr.'s acoustic guitar on a stand in the corner. I had just died and gone to musician heaven. I was extremely nervous, however, as I had never played guitar with a band. My rhythm was not that even, and so I asked Steve Poltz to come up with me to play guitar, as he could mimic my style well on songs like "You Were Meant for Me." I had less than zero confidence, and when I would ask Ben if a take was good, he would always ask me how I felt. Everyone seemed to be from the old-school tradition of being there to support and rally around the songwriter and the songs. They kept asking me what I heard, what I wanted, but it seemed so backward. They had more experience between them than I would ever have. Tim is the one who came up with the cool groove for "Who Will Save Your Soul," and the natural country swing on "You Were Meant for Me" thrilled me. Neil's wife, Pegi, came and sang backup for me on some tracks as well. But overall I got very few songs with the band that I felt really let what I did shine. I just didn't know how to sing and be as emotional with a band, so I made the decision to record most of the album live back in San Diego at the coffee shop where it all began for me. Before we left, we had a big dinner at the ranch and the band came over. Afterward I went to sit in the living room and was surprised to hear the piano behind me being played. I turned around to see it was Neil. I was starstruck. I had no idea what to say to him, but felt compelled to say something. I had always regretted that I did not play piano, and so reaching for some conversation I asked, "Is that a C chord?" Neil said nothing. He simply stood up, closed the piano cover, and walked out of the room. His daughter, Amber, about eight years old then, happened to be in the room and she came up to me and said, "Don't worry. He always ignores you when he thinks what you say is stupid."

It FELT GOOD to be back in San Diego. How quickly my life was changing in such a few short months. My local fan family came out and I recorded two shows. It was an amazing feeling to have the support of that room. Those folks gave me all their heart and all their love and I swear it can be felt in that recording. I sang more like myself when I was live in front of an audience. In the studio my throat tightened to the point I almost sounded like someone else. Someone else famous. Someone else green. Yes, on tracks like "Who Will Save Your Soul" and "You Were Meant for Me," I sound like Kermit the Frog. You need to set this book down and go listen. I'm proud that the label and Ben allowed me to be myself. *Pieces of You* is a perfect time capsule of exactly who I was. It's imperfect, full of mistakes and guitar flubs, but it is honest.

eighteen

will she fix her teeth?

I f you're a young, unknown artist in a highly competitive field, you have to find an edge, not only in the larger scope of the business among literally thousands vying for the few slots on the charts but also at your own label. There are hundreds of artists at any given time fighting for a piece of the same budget. The label can't invest in every artist at the same level, and like horse races, executives begin to bet on their favorite to win. They might prioritize someone they've signed personally. They might favor someone who seems easy to work because they are radio-friendly. At this point, Danny Goldberg had left Atlantic, and I needed a new champion to protect me and fight for me. The person who stepped in was Ron Shapiro. He had seen me sing at a showcase in L.A. He believed unwaveringly in my talent and our careers became inextricably entwined. Although having an ally was not everything. I still had to work the system, within the label and outside it.

I took on a tremendous workload, as my only real secret weapon was live performances and my ability to outwork anyone. Because media didn't really care about me yet, I couldn't get on TV. Atlantic thought up crazy schemes to get me in front of people. I swallowed my pride and made it my job to make the best of any situation, to make people listen, and to make them remember me. And I tasked myself with making sure I didn't compromise on integrity or artistry. No excuse. Never once did I phone one performance in, or accept being treated as background music, no matter how hard the gig was to conquer. I was frustrated a lot, and it wasn't a lot of fun, but my competitiveness was rewarding. I was one gritty, mean, lean working machine. Fear of ending up on the street again was a powerful motivator. Danny Buch in the radio department came to me at one point with the idea to circumvent national radio. He was an excitable and passionate person, and he nearly spit whenever he talked, his enthusiasm spilling out of him. "Hey! Jewel! I can buy an hour on shortwave radio, channel 540 AM, and we can go down to Broadway and we'll have a mile radius we can broadcast to! Do you know how many people there are in one mile of Manhattan?!" Me: "But how will people know to tune in?" Danny: "I'll have interns walk around during rush hour wearing signs that say, 'Hear new Atlantic recording artist Jewel on 540 AM,' and we'll have you stand on top of a van with a speaker system singing live for folks on the street, and we can broadcast the whole show out to the cars around you!" It sounded like a long shot, and like zero fun. There was no way to sing louder than the honking horns of New York City traffic, but I sang my little heart out standing on a white van, taking in the sights when I had the courage to open my eyes, interns walking around the block with their cardboard signs. Earlier that same day I'd sung at the opening of a shoe store in Times Square. In these in-stances and others I learned more about how to make people stand still and pay attention to the fact that I was an actual living, breathing person in the room, not a soundtrack pumped in. I would hold notes. I would yodel. I would say shocking things or make up songs about people as they walked by. Whatever it took to make eye contact, to make them stand still and listen. If I could get them to listen, I could get them to care.

I also participated in something called Earth Jam in the morning because they helped fund the tour. They had a rental van and sound gear and the sound guys, so I had free transportation to my own gigs, but I had to perform in the morning at high schools where they first did an environmental educational component and then I'd sing. On one occasion I was in Detroit, and there was a rapper named Jewell trying to break around the same time. I remember using the restroom, and as I was in the stall, I could hear one girl saying, "I'm so excited! Jew-ell rocks. I love the way that girl raps." Insert record screeching to a halt. *What? The way she raps?* I had a bad feeling. I had long hippie hair and was wearing a Pink Panther T-shirt and baggy jeans. I walked out, the whole gymnasium chanting, "Jew-ell!"—and the hands stopped in midair. Silence rang with deafening weight. I took it one step further, as I was already a flop, and started with "Pieces of You." *She's an ugly girl, does it make you want to kill her? She's an ugly girl, do you want to kick in her face? She's an ugly girl, she doesn't pose a threat. She's an ugly girl, does that make you feel safe?* rang out and emptied the place in half a song, the teachers actually exiting students row by row exactly like in a fire drill. The principal was spitting mad.

I did an insane amount of traveling and tons of shows. I remember trying to count: Between radio station visits where I played for listeners who'd won a chance to come in, local record stores (remember those?), opening for someone in the evening, doing my own coffee shop show at midnight, and then one more at a high school at 9 a.m., I probably averaged six shows and often two cities a day, driving zigzag through a state to cover as much territory as I could. I never took breaks. There were many comical moments where I locked my guitar in the car, or my stoner surfer driver-friend drove us to the wrong city while I slept, but boy did

I learn the ropes. I had to settle out for myself, which means getting paid by the promoter and getting my piece of any merch sales. I was cheap, cheap, cheap, and every time someone at the label said, Hey, my artist is more important than Jewel, let's drop her, my supporters could say, She costs us nothing and works hard. That took the fight out of the equation. There was no risk in letting me work my brains out.

Around this time, in 1995, I got my first TV break. Conan O'Brien and his team always had a fondness for new music and I found myself booked on the show. I remember I was exhausted and wearing the same outfit I sang in every night. I had no money for clothes and wore the same thrift store outfits I'd put together in San Diego. I knew nothing about glam squads and my label was in no hurry to tell me about the miracle of hair and makeup and clothing stylists. I think I was wearing purple polyester pants with a black T-shirt and a tacky belt with a rainbow buckle that I loved. The performance was a huge break for me. For some reason, when people saw me sing, they had a stronger reaction than when they just heard me sing.

Soon after this performance I went home to Alaska for a short rest. It felt so good to sink my toes in the dirt and smell the cottonwood trees and ride my horse and recalibrate. I'd gone from being a strong, tan outdoorsy kid to a pale anemic musician who never drew a breath of fresh unregulated air. To sleep, stare at the sea, and just write all felt good.

My dad was building another cabin and so I stayed in its unfinished cinder-block basement, but it was dry and free. I helped haul water up from the creek for the garden and for washing. There was no running water, but there was electricity and a phone line. One day my dad came to find me, saying, "Jewel, you must be getting some kooky fans out there in the Lower 48. Some guy just prank-called and said he was Sean Penn." "No shit," I said, chuckling. "What did you do?" "I hung up on the weirdo," my dad said. I knew I was making some die-hard fans out there, and had a few stalkers even though I wasn't famous. There were people in need of help who seemed to cling to my lyrics and music thinking I would save them somehow. Maybe prank calls were par for the course. Dad walked back up to the cabin to find the phone ringing again. The person on the other end managed to convince him before he hung up a second time that he was indeed Sean Penn, and he had seen me on *Conan* and wanted me to write a song for a movie he was directing. My dad set the phone down, put his boots back on, walked over, and told me to come to the phone. I pulled on my own boots, walked several hundred yards across the meadow, taking in the beautiful light as it reflected off Kachemak Bay, and made my way to the other cabin, where the phone was sitting on the counter. It must have been ten minutes of waiting for whoever was on the line. The voice was unmistakably Sean Penn's. He had seen me on *Conan* and was working on a movie he'd written called *The Crossing Guard*. He wanted me to compose a song for it. I told him I would and he said he would meet me anywhere to screen the movie, I could name the day. I gave him my cell number and figured I would never hear from him again.

When I was in L.A. shortly after that, he saw a show of mine at the Wiltern. He screened the film for me the next day. The movie was intense and dark and interesting. Sean was the same, and also charming, witty, and bright, and our instant verbal sparring characterized our friendship for the next year. I was headed back to San Diego for a long-overdue surf session, and we agreed to talk creative soon.

Several weeks later I was in a salon, getting a cut from my gay hairdresser and friend, when Sean called, saying he was in San Diego and asking where we could meet. I gave him the address of the salon, and the next thing I knew, a town car had dropped him off and my car was all we had left. My hairdresser asked if he could come along—although I have no recollection where we were headed. Sean was friendly and unpretentious and said sure. My car was a total mess. Like a holy mess. Clothes and food wrappers everywhere. There was so much crammed in there that the only open space was the front passenger seat. So Sean let my hairdresser sit on his lap. Who got no small thrill out of it.

I wrote a song called "Emily" for the movie while out on the road. I cut it in a radio station on the station mic and Sean put it in the film. In the meantime, we spoke on the phone a lot and he was a fantastic flirt and I did not mind one bit. But I intended to give him no such conquest. I put that man through his paces and he took it in stride. He began to court me in earnest, following me around on tour, acting as my de facto roadie. I was nowhere near famous, opening for Peter Murphy of Bauhaus in small clubs. Goth fans in makeup, fangs and scars, and black clothes. I'd play earnest folk songs and inevitably stop mid-song to ask someone to be quiet or kick someone out. Sean stood side stage. We talked about art and books and had a great time. I moved very slowly with him but he was a persistent and inventive suitor, and I enjoyed it immensely. He sincerely believed in my music, and this felt as good as anything. He was a talented artist and took my songs and lyrics seriously, and I was starving for any-one who believed in me. I kept our burgeoning relationship very quiet. I was determined not to be "discovered" because I was dating someone in the public eye. I liked his mind, and had fun sparring with him. When I told him this in all seriousness, in a dive bar after a sound check, he re-sponded with a melancholy stare and then a canary-eating grin and said that it would be impossible not to fall in love with me. I looked at him to see if he was serious. It seemed he was.

When the movie was finished, he asked me to go to the Venice Film Festival with him to debut it. I was nervous and excited—so far my expe-rience in the music biz had been decidedly not glamorous. My time with Sean wasn't spent at Hollywood parties, but on the road with me at Red Roof Inns, where he would get his own room and carry my guitar back after my humiliating gigs. No tabloid had yet picked up on us, so I was anxious about a trip like this. At the same time, I couldn't turn it down. It was the first time I'd ever been out of the country apart from Mexico. I told him I didn't have the money for a ticket. He said I could fly on the private plane with him.

Sean said there would be a red carpet and lots of press and I would need to bring something to wear. I didn't want to walk down a carpet with him, and he said I could walk it on my own as songwriter for the film, which seemed okay. It was my first time getting gussied up with a professional stylist. The very fashionable woman eyed my polyester en-semble and began to pull dresses—as I tried them on I felt like a dog someone had dressed in sunglasses and a ball cap and a sweater. I also felt a little like Cinderella going to the ball. But I was not a girly princess and not used to standing out unless I was standing behind a guitar. I finally decided on a pair of satin pants and a beaded asymmetrical top that showed a bit of midriff. I had no idea how to do makeup or hair, and had no idea there were teams of people to do it for me. At a TV taping before leaving for Venice, I confided to the union hair and makeup lady, and she was kind enough to spend an hour with me and teach me how to put on eyeliner and shadow. I showed her a Polaroid of my outfit, and when she found out I owned no makeup, she gave me a lip liner, a blush, and shadow from her kit. She then drew pictures and step-by-step instruc-tions on a piece of paper that I could refer to when the time came to get ready. I thanked her profusely and then kept busy with work so I wouldn't have time to be too nervous. My manager Inga took me shopping at a Nordstrom Rack store for cute shorts, coats, and sweaters, and I was ready to go.

The day arrived for the flight and there I was walking onto a private jet and finding myself face-to-face with several other Hollywood types. I tried not to make a fool of myself, but I fear I may have asked to feel people's noses when a good one came around. When I studied sculpture in school I'd become obsessed with feeling faces so I could better feel the shape I had to re-create. Particularly feeling the tips of people's noses. The curve and spring of each was so idiosyncratic that when I saw a good nose, I'd ask complete strangers if I could feel it.

First we went to Paris. We stayed in beautiful hotels and ate with Roman Polanski. Of course I had to be told who he was. I had shocking gaps in my knowledge of pop culture and knew no one, nor who anyone was. Sean would whisper in my ear and explain everyone's backstory to me. It was not my world and I was pretty sure it never would be. Sean took me to see the sights in Montmartre and wrote me sweet notes that he hid in my pockets. Next was Venice, and while Sean was in meetings, I took water taxis around and explored canals and cathedrals. Heaven. It felt exotic and luxurious to be so free. I'd never been on this side of travel—"this" meaning not staying in youth hostels and hitchhiking with knives. This was the Cipriani and private drivers and all the food I could eat, like fresh figs and prosciutto. Interesting people to talk with, some well educated, some well read, some simply vain and drunk on their power, but altogether an especially rarified, fascinating breed I had not come across before. I recorded each moment in my mind to write about later. One day I went to lunch with several women and Jack Nicholson. He was gregarious and entertaining. He struck me as very bright and possibly bored with most people, able to cope with the help of a mild combination of recreational drugs and a curiosity for watching interesting circumstances unfold. I liked him. I can only imagine what he thought of me—I looked like I was twelve. None of it was lost on me, but it was all a game and I was enjoying myself. I trusted myself to be me. I enjoyed Sean and would eventually fall in love, but I did not go around holding hands or trying to be seen or noticed. At the end of lunch Jack said in his classic way, "Ladies, who wants to go lingerie shopping?" I declined.

The morning of the film premiere, I nervously pulled out my crinkled paper with the makeup instructions for a little review. I looked at the drawings and then at my face, and after about five minutes of frustration, abandoned the mirror and notes and went to find some food in the sun. When I came back, Sean's assistant, a friendly and outgoing Australian girl, had been tidying the suite and walked out of the bathroom with my makeup crib sheets in her hand. "Jesus Christ in hell, is this yours?" I froze for a second and just stared at her. She looked at me with a broad smile and said, "You poor kid. You don't know how to put makeup on?" She didn't seem mean-spirited, but she was getting a kick out of it. She seemed to understand that this was nowhere near my world. She handed me my notes and left me alone with my thoughts, which felt like fish that had gotten spooked and swam away.

I did my best with the plum lip liner and the sheer nude lipstick, to highlight my brow bone and the lid of my eye, and worked the mascara wand into the lash line like I had been shown. I pulled my hair back simply and got dressed. I think Sean sensed how out of my element I was, and he was kind and careful to give me my space. When I walked out, he said I looked beautiful.

It was really cool to hear my song on the big screen. The next day the producers and industry folks got together for some big lunch, and Sean asked me to sing. He seemed to love watching people's reaction to me, and I'm sure he was also trying in his way to get the word out about my music. Someone handed me a guitar and I sat up at the banquet table, the whole room staring at me. No mic. Just a giant ballroom full of jaded execs. It was broad daylight and the room was busy talking until Jack spoke up and asked me to sing "Angel Standing By." I obliged, not knowing where the hell else to start. I shut my eyes, blocked the room out, and focused on the message of the song and then on my heart and on the particular feeling of needing to feel peace when unsettled. Of needing to be told you are loved when you are scared. That small concentrated feeling expands outward like heat from a flame. I get goose bumps and my eyes tear and my voice shakes just slightly when I harness emotion and force it through my throat and out of me like a warm wave. No vibrato for this song. Straight falsetto tone. Tone and vibrato have different effects, and for this a straight clean tone can cut you like a divine knife. When I wrote that song I was seventeen, and it was only the singing that would help me get through the nights when my anxiety would rise to almost insufferable levels. I experimented on myself and found that a widespread vibrato distracted me but that a straight tone was pleasing and calming. I learned to let passion and angst spill out occasionally in riffs like *I'll be right there baby, holding your hand, telling you everything's going to be alright*, and then go back to a straight tone, creating a vocal map of my own longing. When I opened my eyes, the room was quiet and no one clapped for a moment. I suddenly worried that I was just another part of the long day they had to endure when the whole room erupted at the same time. Sean requested "Nicotine Love," about a woman who had been raped as a child and so damaged that she became a monster who wanted to harm men the same way she had been hurt. The performance was intense and cinematic. When I finished, the room was quiet again. Then applause. Folks came up to me afterward who'd ignored me previously. Sean stood back and watched their reaction. An agent came over and Sean told him that if he had any sense he would sign me to some acting jobs. "Will she fix her teeth?" the agent asked. I remember the look of total amazement on Sean's face. He shook his head. The agent looked at me, unconvinced.

Sean seemed to think I was talented and smart, which was nice, because no one had ever told me I was smart before. He enjoyed putting me in situations that brought out the best in me, and he never ridiculed what was still so half-wild and messy about me.

One day at lunch in L.A. Warren Beatty walked in and sat down. I knew Warren from the movies, but mainly I knew he had been with Joni Mitchell. That made him some sort of a god to me. Sean asked me to sing for him. "Would you?" Warren asked. I sang something with my guitar and Warren rested his head on his hands, looking up at me with a dreamy look on his face, like he was watching a kitten knit mittens. When I finished, he tilted his head toward Sean and after a dreamy sigh said, "Where did you find her?" as if I were a puppy or something that could be acquired. I laughed at the absurdity of it all.

arriving

I got another cool break that same year. I had been singing on NPR and talking about my life, and a director heard the interview and cast me as Dorothy in an all-star production of *The Wizard of Oz* that would be performed at Lincoln Center and broadcast on TV. He took a big risk in casting me, as I was the only unknown, and yet he was certain I was his Dorothy. I had never acted before but was excited to dig in. When I first showed up at rehearsal, the all-star talent was pretty intimidating. Roger Daltrey, Jackson Browne, Natalie Cole, Debra Winger, Nathan Lane, Joel Grey . . . and yours truly, who had no clue what she was doing in the lead role. Holy shit. Deep breath. I dove in and studied and worked hard.

Jackson would come over to my hotel with his girlfriend and listen to my songs, mentoring me along. He taught me to play a bit of slide guitar and gave me a lug nut to practice with. He was paternal and protective of me, and it showed one day when we had a comical misunderstanding. One day in the rehearsal studios I borrowed his shirt because I was cold. The next day he pulled me aside and said, "Jewel. I found what you left in my pocket." I waited for him to tell me what it was. I had no idea. "Jewel. I found it. Do you want to talk about it?" I could not imagine what he was talking about. He kept staring at me like I should come clean and I was getting nervous. Finally he said, "Look, I can't make you talk about it. All I can say is, if you ever want to come clean, I'm here," and walked away. I was perplexed but had no idea what I should feel guilty about. I walked over to my mom, who was waiting in the wings, and told her the weirdest thing had happened. Later that day I had another bout of the miserable headache I'd had for a week and went to my mom for some BC, a powdered aspirin that comes in wax paper. Suddenly it dawned on me. I ran over to Jackson and looked around as if to make sure we weren't being watched, then pulled the sachet of powder out of my pocket and said, "Hey, you want any?" He looked at me with such shock and disappointment until I told him it was just aspirin. He was so relieved he laughed out loud and hugged me. "Jewel! I'm so relieved! I was so worried you were doing drugs! I quit years ago, but I had a friend come over and test it when I found it. He actually snorted it and said whatever it was, it wasn't very quality shit!" "Did it get rid of his head-ache?" I asked, laughing.

The show went well, apart from a minor snafu when I lost track of where we were in the story and jumped ahead in the wrong costume, luck-ily realizing it just in time (when I heard my cue) to run out onstage with the wrong outfit on and my boots unlaced, but able to deliver the correct lines. Roger Daltrey as the Tin Man and Jackson Browne as the Scarecrow were unbelievable. The whole cast was encouraging and kind to me and I worked hard not to let anyone down and to make the director proud, as well as myself. I have never been competitive with other people, but I am highly competitive with myself. It's pointless to focus on others, as we can only control ourselves. I set a high bar and then it is my own private race. No one knows I'm winning or losing but me. I try to make the hard parts look easy, especially in my music. Whether it's seeing if I can elicit a visceral reaction from an audience, hit a particular note, or get a song on the radio, it has been a wholly internal process that, as it grew and spilled over, eventually led me to awards and money and chart positions. I am convinced that if I had started out with an eye on the prizes, I would have failed. For me, success was finding the courage to be true to myself, and holding on to a sense of humor along the way while refining my craft.

Sean surprised me by flying my dad in from Alaska for opening night. It was such a welcome surprise. My dad and I didn't talk often, although he had been sober, in therapy, and working on his own healing. And while I would not say our relationship was close at this point, it also wasn't hostile or angry. I was working hard myself on figuring things out, dating someone who believed in me, acting with a cast of people I never dared to dream would be peers. And there my dad was to see it!

I don't know if any of you were raised on a ranch, but my dad showed up in his "town clothes." In Alaska we had two sets of clothes: work clothes we did chores in and played in, and town clothes we touched only when we were going to school or to sing. My dad wore his creased jeans and good boots and a clean new cowboy hat and his largest, sharpest, shiniest animal necklace. Did I mention my dad makes jewelry out of animal parts? Roadkill is an accessory where I come from. His pieces are actually very beautiful, made of eagle talons, bear claws, wolf teeth, and bird bones. As a thank-you to Sean for flying him in, Dad made him a grizzly claw necklace in the shape of an anchor, because he'd heard Sean had a tattoo of the same. He also wrote Sean a song. He was so excited about both that he previewed them for me before presenting them to Sean, and all I can say is I was so touched by the gesture that I could only hope Sean would be too. My dad is a very authentic and earnest person, and the song he wrote was his way of trying to understand and pay homage to Sean's world, which was so different from his own. My grandmother Ruth, who was living in Tennessee at this point, had kept every headline printed about Sean, and my dad had strung them together into a song. At the time, some of the lines were so uncomfortable that I was sure they would be seared into my mind forever, but as I write this now I can recall only a few. Sean sat through the song with a smile, seeing through to the heart and spirit of my dad's intentions.

At the party after the *Oz* performance, someone came up to Dad, in all his glory, candlelight glinting off his shiny animal-carcass necklace, and said, You must be very proud of your daughter, she did very well. For some reason everyone in the room turned to hear his response. Jackson Browne, Debra Winger, Natalie Cole, all waited to hear what he would say. The room was hushed just as my dad slapped the guy on the shoulder jovially and said, "Well, I guess I put my best sperm into that one!" Awesome. The crowd was kind enough not to gasp collectively in horror, and I had to admit that as embarrassing as it was, it was touching. He did not change because he was around other people. And I knew that it was his way of acknowledging that he was not the best parent, but that he was proud of who I was becoming and the work I had done to get there. What seemed like an awkward and seemingly tacky moment to everyone else spoke volumes to me. He was growing and changing. We were a long way from healing but there was hope.

I had taken a general acting lesson in high school but there hadn't been much theory or technique involved. There was one line in particular in the show that I had no idea how to deliver sincerely because it was so unlike anything I would say. I think it was something very simple, like "Oh golly." I visited with Sean about my conundrum. He asked what I would say instead. "Um, I'm not sure, but probably something like 'Holy shit!'" He said, fine, say that with my body and my voice but use the words in the script. He explained that what gets communicated has very little to do with what we say. Simple but profound acting advice. Life is full of body language and subtext and people rarely say what is actually on their minds, but it all gets communicated anyway. I loved this about acting. When I wrote songs, the subtext and psychology of the characters were limited by the fact that songs are so short. Acting, I quickly saw, was all about subtext, and I was hooked.

As I stepped onto the stage to sing "Over the Rainbow" with Ry Cooder playing guitar and a full orchestra and the Harlem Boys Choir backing me up, and as I looked out into the beautiful auditorium of Lincoln Center and all the people sitting there, I was so overcome I could hardly sing. The recording reveals my voice cracking at the high note because I was choking back tears. When I said that famous line—"Toto, I've a feeling we're not in Kansas anymore"—I meant every word. It felt like a tornado was carrying me along and delivering me to a strange and magical new world. I had no way of knowing then how many other parallels there were, and that the all-powerful wizard was not real in my life either. There would be lions and tigers and bears, *oh my!* and the way home was not in someone else's hands, but in my own. Behind the curtain there was a drama that would take years to unfold. But for now I was Dorothy, literally and figuratively. And I was just arriving.

twenty

the long shot

While I would like to have done some things better, I was proud of myself and of the whole *Oz* cast. The standing ovation at the end was overwhelming and felt good. Afterward there was a party, champagne was sipped in fancy glasses with pinkies extended, and everyone was dressed in expensive clothes. Apparently black was all that was available in New York City stores, and people let you know how important they were by the way they stood and how they treated the people who served them. My dad had been a good influence on me—he talked to taxi drivers the same way he did famous actors, and I loved this about him and still follow his example to this day.

My mom was in all her glory, and was eating up the attention and culture. You would never have known she was raised in a tiny cabin in Alaska; you would have thought she came from money and power. I noticed that when people congratulated her on my performance, her reaction just seemed a bit off. I didn't know how to put my finger on it except to say that while my dad was eager to let people know how hard I'd worked, my mom gave the impression somehow that she was responsible for my performance. It was just a sense that I got. Like she was envious. It was a strange feeling to have a talent and an opportunity that somehow she wanted to claim as her own.

Things with my mom had become increasingly complicated. At first she was just looking out for me in my career. I trusted her because she was my mom, after all, and her interest and caring had been so hard to come by. I was desperate to feel safe and loved, and it seemed that since I'd been signed to a record label, my mom had really stepped it up, wanting to be sure I was not taken advantage of. It wasn't long before she brought up the question of compensation for her time and dedication and her unique wisdom and so I had a talk with Inga about sharing the management role. Inga was commissioning 15 percent—of nothing, as I wasn't making anything yet, but 15 percent at any rate. My mom wanted an additional 15 percent. I felt that was too much, but it was hard to argue with either of them, so I asked them each to take 10 percent, and we would all eat the cost of having two managers. An artist is responsible for all costs, so managers can charge back hotels, flights, food—anything related to managing the act. Plus they commission the gross of any income, taking their share before the cost of doing business. So theoretically if I make five hundred dollars for a gig, the managers get 20 percent of it. Then I have to cover the costs of touring, which are most likely higher than five hundred dollars because I have to pay a tour manager, a sound guy, and for a vehicle to get around in (assuming I don't also have a band to pay), and so I borrow money from the label that I will owe back to them. Then the managers charge me for their plane tickets and hotel if they came out and helped on a show. Then a video costs about five hundred thousand dollars, and a marketing budget is way more expensive—and the costs stack up against the artist. An artist is about one million in the hole just to see if a record even has a shot at working, and then that money needs to be paid back to the label before it starts splitting the profit with you once you have recouped. The odds of recouping and making money before you are dropped from the label are very slim. Then you pay your agency 10 percent of the gross of all touring, your lawyer fees, then pay all your costs of doing business out of what's left over, then pay taxes . . . and that's how a lot of artists are signed to a big record deal and may even sell a million records and not be recouped and are dropped without ever making a cent. If an artist has taken a big advance on signing a record deal, that will have to be repaid as well.

Needless to say I didn't feel good about giving up more percentage points for my mom to manage me, but I desperately loved her and believed she was the only person looking out for me. She went with me everywhere. It was the closest we had ever been and it made my child's heart so happy to have her with me. But she also had incredibly specific views on things, and she always seemed to set herself up as the wisest person in the room. Increasingly I found my own self-esteem shrinking as her magnanimous spirit permeated every aspect of our lives. I began to believe she knew more than I did about everything and that I would be nothing if she weren't looking out for me. Having my mom around simply felt good. She said she was my soul mate, and we were meant to do great things together. If I listened to her, everything would be just fine. My lack of confidence, my fear, and my need to be loved created a perfect breeding ground for doubt and dependence—she was the only person I needed to listen to.

Sean and I parted ways before I ever became famous. The breakup was hard for me. My self-worth came from outside myself, from the approval of others. After Sean, I turned to my mom with more resolve. She was more than happy to be my source of self-worth. It seemed she gave or withheld tenderness depending on how I behaved, and I could be trained the way dogs are trained with treats. I would do anything for love.

WHEN I WAS SIXTEEN I had a dream that I got to open for Bob Dylan. I had just started writing songs and of course he was an idol of mine. I had no intentions then of becoming a professional musician, but I suppose my submersion in Dylan's music could not help causing my subconscious to dream even if I dared not dream that big during waking hours.

I studied my favorite writers for years prior to writing songs. Pablo Neruda and Octavio Paz fired my passion for revolutionary writing that honored nature and the courage of the common man, giving a voice to the voiceless. Bukowski and Anaïs Nin taught me to be brave and honest as a writer, and not to use art as propaganda to sell yourself as more perfect than you actually are. Steinbeck and Flannery O'Connor taught me about character development and about the nobility in working-class heroes. Nabokov and Dostoevsky brought color, psychology, and intensity to fiction. Plato and Pascal taught me about economy and potency. I studied writers more intently than I did musicians. I studied singers, which led me to Sarah Vaughan and Ella Fitzgerald and to great trumpet players like Miles Davis, who used tone and phrasing to convey emotion—which is what pure singing should do, when words don't get in the way.

But at sixteen I began to get into singer-songwriters, ones who embodied all the traits I admired in my authors. I loved Loretta Lynn's honesty and pride and authenticity—her song "The Pill" blew my mind with her frankness in saying that she no longer had to feel like a hen in a coup laying eggs, that she didn't have to keep having babies every time her husband got a hankering for sex. Joni Mitchell, of course, blew me away with her originality and her poet's voice and complex chord and melody structure. Neil Young with his grit and tension, which was married to a softness that could be heard on *Harvest* and *Harvest Moon*. Merle Haggard, who was so prolific and willing to say what was on his mind, and to also pay unabashed tribute to his heroes. I suspect he also listened to jazz, as I could hear strains of elegant melody and passing chords amid his everyman's topics. I loved Tracy Chapman and saw her as a modern troubadour whose heart was full of a soulful need to give a voice to the underrepresented. Rickie Lee Jones with her whimsy and her bite, her unique harmony layers and her funky rhythmic beats. And then there was Dylan, of course. Whose intelligence and beatnik New York City background and whose fascination with the great folk heroes before him all combined in a revolutionary way that still leaves a footprint so large it takes several of us to fill any one step.

As a new songwriter, I found that all these influences, along with my own hurt, my own longing to give a voice to the voiceless, my own need to make sense of the world around me, made their way into my songs. I did not write love songs as a sixteen-year-old. I did not write about crushes or about mean girls. I wrote about my life—about the injustices and inequities and the search for answers and self-responsibility. Songwriting lit me up because for the first time I was able to combine many of my passions: poetry, storytelling, character development, melody, shape, and singing. I was in heaven. I had no idea that a mere five years later my dream of opening for Dylan would come true, or that many of my heroes would actually mentor me.

When I got the call to open for Dylan, my first record was considered a failure. I had received critical praise—the London *Times* said I was the most glittering singer-songwriter since Joni Mitchell. The *New York Times* said I was bursting with talents. But many others called me naive, overly optimistic, and completely off-trend in a country gripped with a fascination for grunge and obsessed with apathy and cynicism. While I was living in my car I had learned to let go of cynicism in order to survive. True cynics all kill themselves. The rest are posers, trying to use clever sarcasm and snarky remarks to hide insecurity and the fear that if they put themselves out there they will fail. I learned that inner safety exists only in vulnerability, in having the courage to admit that the glass is half full and half empty, and to choose to live your life within the part that is half full. To have faith. Anyone can try to beat life to the punch, lower their expectations, and feel smart because they predicted disappointment, even braced and hardened their hearts for its impact. But to look at life with an open heart, take it on the chin and say *I am more yielding, I am more open*, takes real courage. This is where I was in my life and in my writing. I wanted to document my yearning to not be a victim in my life, but to affect its outcome.

And I was on fire. I didn't mind if I was called naive. The critics and journalists who responded with acrimony to my music betrayed their own sense of fear and their unrealized dreams, as far as I was concerned. I learned to toughen my skin and ignore them while at the same time remaining soft enough to create and to feel the people I actually sang for. I saw a different response to my music in my fans—people like me, out there struggling every day who were desperate for a way to feel empowered and more hopeful. They weren't concerned with being cool, they were earnest and eclectic, and they wanted a sense of camaraderie and support. We found a way to connect to each other online, in the early days of the Internet. Fans began to call themselves EDAs—Every Day Angels—a term coined from a lyric in "I'm Sensitive." They shared bootlegs of live shows and lyrics to unreleased songs and built a community.

Still, after a long year of playing for fifteen people in each town I visited, the record had gained no real traction. Atlantic Records had tried all year to get me played on the radio at the height of grunge, and I was beginning to fear that I would be dropped and wind up in my car again. I played my guts out that year, opening for the Ramones, Belly, Catherine Wheel, and grunge audiences. The difficulty of playing for the audiences, along with being called worthless by the press, would make anyone lose some heart.

I began to doubt that the small groundswell I'd somehow inspired would ever become more than a ripple. I started to feel silly and awkward and like maybe I should just try to write stuff that sounded like what was on the radio. I could do that. I could change, if that's what it would take to stay out of my car.

The decision not to take a huge advance bought me a lot of time at the label, because I was affordable. I didn't cost a lot to support on the road—I toured in a rental car with a friend driving. No tour manager. No fancy bus. Hard wood grows slowly, and I was trying to live by that idea.

It ended up being the best thing I did because it continued to ensure that I was the cheapest act to support, even if I had the most difficult music to break. I wrote letters to every secretary at the label, the ones who did a lot of the real work, as well as the department heads who were fighting for me. I sent postcards from the road to thank them for what they were willing to do to help me live my dream. I tried to make sure people knew what this meant to me, how deeply I cared about it, and how thankful I was. I hoped everyone would feel gratified and energized to keep fighting for a long shot like me. I learned that a lot of the artists and mangers were brats. They beat the label up, they complained, felt cheated, were suspicious, ranted and raved. I worked hard, and if they said jump, I said, how high? Every artist on the label was talented—the only competitive edge I had was to be the person they would rather pick up the phone to call. It was so humbling to have a team of people fighting to help me achieve a dream.

We first tried to get "Who Will Save Your Soul" onto the radio, but after a year we gave up and tried with "You Were Meant for Me." But it was too simple, everyone felt—a country shuffle and four minutes long, a full minute longer than songs on the radio were supposed to be. We decided to revamp it to make it sound more "radio," and hired Juan Patiño, who had produced Lisa Loeb's "Stay." I gutted sections of the song to make it shorter, we cut it faster and with more of a pop sound. I was enthusiastic about trying to make it work, but when all was said and done, I was too embarrassed to tell Atlantic I hated it. It cost about forty grand to recut, and I deeply feared that if it became a hit, it would be my only one.

To my amazement, Danny in the radio department caught me in the hallway of the New York office one day and said he didn't want me to change for radio. He wanted radio to change for me. He and Andrea Ganis redoubled their efforts to gain traction on "Who Will Save Your Soul," and we came up with a strategy for college radio. I began touring college campuses and building another small groundswell with students. Enough to get a little more notice.

Enter Bob Dylan. He was looking for an opening act for an East Coast run and somehow my name came up and I was asked to do it. I was ecstatic. I never expected to meet him—I assumed I was some promoter's idea. At the first show, his tour manager came out and said, "Welcome to the road. You have thirty minutes—don't get offstage late. If anything, get off early. And just wanted to let you know, Dylan will not see your show or meet you. He doesn't really do that, and I've found it's better to let the opening act know that upfront." "No problem," I said.

Four nights later he came up to me again, and said, "Well, you're not going to believe this. Dylan heard your stuff and he's been watching your show. He wants to meet you downstairs in his dressing room." I was stunned. I walked downstairs and knocked gingerly on his door. I heard that iconic nasal voice say, "Yeah. Come in."

I opened the door and there I was face-to-face with my hero. I tried to take it in stride. Or at least to not trip awkwardly before I even said hello. I sat down immediately just to be sure I wouldn't, and then had no idea what to say. Luckily I didn't have to. He was full of questions. "Hey, uh, I like your song 'Who Will Save Your Soul.' How did you write that?" I'm sorry? Was Bob Dylan asking me how I wrote a song? My mind was spinning and my mouth would not open to speak. I sat staring at him like a deaf mute. Maybe fearing I was a bit slower than he anticipated, he approached it from another angle. Quoting my own lyrics to me. Again. Flabbergasted. I must have managed to stammer out some kind of response.

"I see you reading side stage before you go on—what are you reading?" he asked. Proust, I told him sheepishly. "Oh yeah, I learned French to read him." Of course Bob Dylan learned French to read Proust.

Dylan invited me to his dressing room after every show. He went over lyrics with me, talked about books, asked me what I was listening to. Far from the stories I'd heard about how eccentric he was, in our conversations he was curious, humble, engaging, sweet even. He seemed to believe in me and later I heard that he liked the fact I was touring without a band, just my guitar. It's harder if you can reach someone else's audience like that, it means something. He liked my yodeling and asked if I'd heard of the Blue Yodeler. No, I said, he sounds like a superhero. "Oh, he is," Bob said, clearly a fan. He asked for my address and said he was going to send me some CDs.

One night I worked up the courage to ask Bob a question in return. I sat there night after night looking at Dylan's nose and tried to resist the urge to reach out and give it a squeeze. Finally I blurted out, "Can I feel your nose?" Much to my surprise he simply shut his eyes and leaned forward and presented it to me. I squeezed it firmly but politely. As I'd imagined, the curve at the tip had a springy cartilage-y feel that was very satisfying. I filed it away mentally in my data bank and we resumed our conversation without ever referencing it again.

The last night of the tour Bob invited me onstage to sing with him. I was shocked and his tour manager seemed to be as well. Bob asked if I knew "I Shall Be Released." I knew it well. He gave me a verse to sing on my own. I waited in the wings as he played his show. He gave me a very flattering introduction and I walked out and over to a backup singer's mic. He waved me over to come sing with him. On his mic. I felt my knees get weak. There I was, sharing a mic with my hero. Our lips nearly touching. His pale blue eyes inches from mine. Singing one of the classic songs of all time. I guess I sang my verse, though I have no recollection of it. I might have been hyperventilating. At the end of the song, he put his arm around my shoulder and said, "Isn't she wonderful? She reminds me of a young Joan Baez." Then he gave my hair a sort of fond little tussle, like a kid sister he was proud of. I nearly fainted. My CD may not have been selling. Radio didn't want my music. The world might not ever discover my music, but Bob Dylan liked my lyrics and my chutzpah, and that was all I needed to stay my path. I left that tour reinspired to be true to myself.

A few years later, once I was selling out large venues, Bob asked me to open for him at the El Rey Theatre in L.A. I showed up with bells on. I got done with my set and Bob had me up to his dressing room. "Congrats on all your success. You've sold like a bazillion records." "Thanks," I said. He continued: "Hey, you didn't play 'Who Will Save Your Soul' tonight." "Yes, I did," I replied. "I ended on it." "Huh," he said. "It must have been in a different key." Well, he had me there. I had dropped it a whole step to accommodate a tired voice that night. He said, "Hey, did you ever get the CDs I sent you?" He had sent me the Jimmie Rogers anthology, and I said, "Yes, thank you—I loved them." "You never called," he said. I could not tell if he was kidding or sincere. "Well, I didn't have your number and

I didn't think you were in the phone book." He took out a piece of paper and wrote his number down for me and said, "If you ever want someone to write with, let me know." I was floored. Surely he must be joking. I left the room and was whisked away to do some interviews. Afterward, about halfway through his set, I reached in my pocket for the number, only to find it gone.

My grandfather Yule, photographed by my grandmother Ruth.
(Courtesy Kilcher Family Trust)

My grandmother Ruth and Yule. I look a lot like her. *(Courtesy Kilcher Family Trust)*

Ruth, holding Sunrise, and Yule with (left to right) Fay; my dad, Atz; Wurtilla; and Mairiis (who we call Mossy). *(Courtesy Kilcher Family Trust)*

Ruth and Yule, the poet and the philosopher, both cut from the same pioneering fabric. (© *William Wakeland, Courtesy Kilcher Family Trust*)

My dad, Atz, and his sister Fay.
(*Courtesy Kilcher Family Trust*)

My mother, Nedra,
at about age seventeen.

My dad's portrait from
the army, age twenty.

Me, at the piano early.
I didn't get the hang
of playing instruments
until much later, but it
didn't keep me from
trying.

My parents.

Top to bottom:

Atz Lee,

Shane,

Dad,

and me.

Shane, Dad, Atz Lee, and me. Yule is standing in the doorway, playing a homestead flute, which he made from various materials.

Shane, me, and Atz Lee.

One of my early performances in my
Swiss yodeling outfit with Dad.

Rehearsing, with Dad at my right, at a friend's house in Anchorage.

At about age twelve I loved to escape by myself and ride in solitude, here with my aunt Mossy's horse named Enchantress and her foal, Souldance.

(© *Mairiis Kilcher*)

With Dad, playing the cafeteria at University of Anchorage when he was a student there.

Even after I got my driver's license, my horse Clearwater was my trusty form of transportation. (© *Mairiis Kilcher*)

Performing at the Inner Change in 1993, where I was discovered and, more important, where I found the love and support of fans who are with me to this day.

Steve Poltz and I were inadvertently part of a drug bust in Mexico, in 1993. We'd made the trip to do some songwriting, crashed in an abandoned house overnight, and tagged along with some federales to go whale watching on their skiff. We found drug smugglers instead—after a high-speed chase on the Bahia de Gonzaga, they led us to their enormous stash of marijuana, which we hauled back to the camp and loaded in a government vehicle, pictured behind us.

Performing at the Inner Change after I was signed, July 1994.

Making my first album at Neil Young's ranch
in Northern California.

In Neil's studio with bass
player Tim Drummond.

Drummer Kenny Buttrey, Steve Poltz, and me in Neil's studio.

Making the video for "Who Will Save Your Soul." Director Geoff Moore is behind me as we shoot in the women's bathroom at City Hall in Los Angeles, March 1995.

With Sean Penn in Venice for the festival premiere
of *The Crossing Guard*, 1995.

With Jack Nicholson at
the Venice Film Festival.

Me, in costume as Dorothy. I was
the one relative unknown in an
all-star performance of *The Wizard
of Oz* at Lincoln Center, November
1995. *(© Photofest, Inc.)*

I opened for Johnny and June Carter Cash at The Royal Albert Hall in London, in April 1997. Backstage, with the legend himself. Little did I know I'd get to play June in a movie about her life years later. (© *West Kennerly*)

With my friend Lee Greene, who I met when I was fifteen and who is still my dearest friend today, on the set of *Ride with the Devil*, 1999.

Going back to Interlochen to perform, 2002. The power went out, so I just sat and talked to the crowd. (© *West Kennerly*)

Performing at the Coors Theater in San Diego, for a much bigger crowd . . . (© *West Kennerly*)

Performing with my dad in Alaska in 2008.
(© Joe Hardwick)

Showing off my roping skills during a cattle branding in Texas.

Visiting the homestead in 2008. I'm standing on the hill where as a child
I would sit beneath the Pegas Tree to daydream. (© *Joe Hardwick*)

With Ty.
(© *Joe Hardwick*)

My dad and me.
(© Joe Hardwick)

A Kilcher family reunion, including a few Murrays, 2008. *(© Joe Hardwick)*

My beautiful son, Kase.

(© West Kennerly)

Performing at the State Theatre in New Brunswick,
New Jersey, in 2013. (© *Chris Owyoung*)

I tell my son, Kase, that my first job is to be his mom, and my second job is to be a singer. (*© Chris Owyoung*)

My first job is my favorite.

Recording a song that I wrote called "My Father's Daughter" with
Dolly Parton in Nashville. Kase was impressed. (© *Philip Macias*)

Lee and Kase making a new friend, on the ranch in Texas.

With Kase and my old friend Lee, who has become part of our family.

twenty-one

every day angels

W ho Will Save Your Soul" had its day on the charts and the label
felt that we would not get traction on any other songs, and so I
went back into the studio to record a second record. The lack of success
and sales vexed me and I found myself listening to the critics. In Wood-
stock, New York, I began production on a reactionary record that was
edgier, with more angst. Flea came to be my bass player, and related his
own tales of being in the public eye, which helped give me some perspective on just what being a professional musician was all about. My mom
told me that some die-hard fans had asked if I would do a free show for
them, which we said yes to, if they'd organize it. The date was set and I
showed up to a small theater for what fans had dubbed Jewelstock. They
had driven and flown in from all over the country and camped out, and
they knew every obscure song of mine that had never been recorded.
They circulated bootlegs, and I put on a five-hour show. They were amazing fans and really gave me heart at a time when I needed a lift.

I went back to the studio questioning my new direction when I got a call asking whether I would open for Neil Young. So I left the studio and went out on the road. Meanwhile, Atlantic decided to take another run at "You Were Meant for Me" for radio one more time—with the original version. Neil was intimidating to open for, as he was playing large outdoor sheds with Crazy Horse. It was usually still daylight when I took the stage, and I had to work hard to get the fans to notice me. Ten stops into the tour, at Jones Beach with the flu, I had to keep giving my guitar player long solos so I could run offstage, and Neil watched me throw up in a potted plant standing in the open-air courtyard.

Neil did pull me aside early on in the tour and asked me how I was. With little more than that invitation, I let the floodgates open and told him about all the pressure I felt to get on the radio, how my first record was considered dead, and how I was trying to write songs that would get played or sounded like what was happening elsewhere in music. He listened quietly, and then became quite serious and said, "Do not ever write for radio. Ever." All that mattered was staying true to myself, and touring and singing for the people. No one else mattered. Not the press. Not radio. It was advice I sorely needed. Midway through our tour, we were playing Madison Square Garden, and I must have looked nervous, because Neil stopped me as I walked past a common area and asked what was wrong. Was I nervous? I looked him in the eye and said, "Yes! I am nervous! You are Neil Young and you have Crazy Horse with you, and a stack of Marshall amps up to the ceiling, and we are at the Garden, and they are gonna murder me out there!" He got very stern and pointed his finger in my face, and said, "Look. This is just another hash house on the road to success. You go out there and show them no respect." I had gotten my marching orders: Don't be intimidated by anyone. I went out there solo acoustic, walked past my mic and out onto the keyhole stage reserved for the middle of Neil's show. It took a while for the spotlight to find me, and a mic to be run out. The crowd talked noisily. I decided to switch things up, and instead of rocking with my band, began a stripped-down version of the classic "Summertime." I sang in the quietest tone I could, almost in a whisper. Gradually everyone began to wonder what I was doing and saying. I could see them all begin to shush one another until the room was so quiet you could hear a pin drop. I had them. And they would stay with me for the whole set.

On a day off I filmed a video for "You Were Meant for Me" with the director Lawrence Carroll, featuring Steve Poltz, and finally the song started to get some traction on radio. A full two years after *Pieces of You* came out, it picked up momentum. It had been a long road to get there—what the press was calling an overnight success had been a lifetime of bar singing, writing, and two years of grinding it out in dives and clubs and being told folk music was out and I would never break through. And now, I had somehow made my voice heard amid the angst of grunge, boy bands, and the shiny super-girl groups like the Spice Girls, and gotten a simple country waltz played on pop radio. I went from selling several thousand copies over twelve months to selling five hundred thousand every single month. It was staggering. A tiny snowball in hell had caught enough momentum to create a tide change. It was wild to read the very same critics who'd praised the CD when it came out now saying it was self-absorbed navel-gazing. Critics who were still clinging to cynicism and grunge like a badge of honor. I learned to turn a deaf ear to them.

I had fans to talk to now, to share what I was learning about hope and what I called informed optimism. The critics seemed to think it was somehow cooler to be cynical, but I saw that as a lack of discipline and a weakness. Informed optimism is different from a willful ignorance that simply wishes not to see bad in the world. Seeing the truth and choosing every day to see it, letting life break your heart but doing something about it, took courage. It was not about hiding your head in the sand, but rather digging in, accepting the challenges, and doing the hard work it takes not just to complain about a problem but to be the solution. I handed out flyers and used the Internet (social media in its infancy!) to let my fans know who I was and what I stood for. It was the fans who really changed the mainstream acceptance of me, and artists like me, and the music industry eventually came around too. People wanted to feel better. They didn't only want feel-good songs, and they didn't want to numb out either. They wanted to earn happiness in their lives just like I did. I was working harder than ever, although it no longer felt like I was pushing water uphill but rather like I was being swept along in the current. The most surreal moment came when I was in an airport on the way to tour in Europe and there was my face on *Time* magazine in every newsstand with the headline that summed up everything: "Macho music is out. Empathy is in."

I knew what my mom's reaction would be. She had told me I was but the tip of an iceberg, the part above water that people could see, but that she was the greater body that existed beneath. She was the reason any of my success existed. And she wanted more because of it. She wanted my manager Inga out. She wanted control of the money and she wanted a salary of half of everything I made. I looked at the magazine cover, and while part of me was excited and proud, the other part saw my face as just the tip of the iceberg.

Looking back now I can see that as a child I was street-smart and savvy. No one had taken advantage of me as a destitute homeless kid, but when it came to my mom I had a massive blind spot. I wanted her love more than I wanted the truth. I thought she was a god, and thought myself insignificant compared with her. I was born with the instinct to love my mom. I don't believe she loved me like I love my son. The imbalance made me vulnerable, as my love worked against me like a weapon. As a child, the pain of my relationship with my father made me place her in a role of mythical proportion. Dad was the dragon who hurt me and took us from our innocent mom. My mom was a distant martyred queen pin-ing for her children. She wrote me letters on holidays that I saved as proof of her goodness and love. She taught me about the power of my mind and made me believe I could do everything. As time went on, her views be-came even more appealing to my natural senses: *Surely you don't think all this is just for you. Abundance is for the greater good of the community. It is a river that flows through you. If you dam it up, it will dry up.* If these tac-tics didn't work, she would shame me and I would feel so badly about myself that I would do anything to earn back her affection. It was a slow and gradual transformation as I emptied myself of my own instincts and replaced them with her wants and her needs, until eventually I was basi-cally incapable of making any decision without her counsel. I heard a story once. If you place a lobster in boiling water it will scream. If you place it in cold water and then turn up the heat gradually it will not pro-test as it goes to its death.

At the beginning of the album's success, my mom decided to bring Jacque, the woman who channeled Zarathustra, into our circle. When I'd moved back to California at eighteen, I'd seen no harm in going with my mom to the gatherings. It was informal and supportive, and it felt good to have a group you felt seen by and loved by. We all sought to know our-selves better and to be of service in the world. I also hoped it would help to heal my kidneys. If I could just raise my frequency enough as I was taught, I would quit being ill. I felt like such a failure every time I got an infection. I resolved each time to pray harder. To be better . . . more pure . . . more full of light.

When my mom had left San Diego, I'd quit going, and discovered that when I relied on myself and my own feelings and instincts, I did so much better. But as she lobbied for greater income or power over my career, and as I resisted, she would now say, "Don't take my word for it. Ask Zarathustra." As her influence grew, so did my dependency on Z. And

Jacque. Jacque had become a de facto mother to me. She was warm and loving and when I struggled with my weight or binge eating it was her I called for love and support. I loved her and I believe she loved me. As my fame and popularity grew, my personal life became increasingly strained and difficult—suppressing your own thoughts and instincts takes great effort. I tasked myself unrelentingly to be more spiritual and less selfish and to give back and to know nothing was mine—it belonged to my mom and her vision for the future. I never did care if I had millions; I just wanted enough to be taken care of. If my mom wanted it that badly she could have more—though I could never agree to half. It just didn't seem fair. So her campaign continued.

I remember the day Eric Greenspan came to a show of mine at the Wiltern in L.A. and handed me a one-million-dollar check. He was so excited and proud to surprise me with it. I think my reaction disappointed him. I had already been conditioned enough to have no sense of joy, pride, or accomplishment when he presented it to me. I already knew it wasn't really me who'd earned it. It also scared me to get a check like this—I was afraid that much money would jinx me somehow. I smiled and was shy about it and had no idea how to take it all in. It was incomprehensible to me. Later it was handed over to my business manager. I knew nothing about money. Less than nothing. I had never had a bank account, and I did not know how to open one. I had never paid a bill other than rent and utilities. I went from being destitute to having Atlantic Records pay bills for me to hiring a business manager to do it for me—finances were complex and there were lots of folks to pay. All I cared about was paying for medication and insurance if I got sick, and that if I wanted to go to a movie or fly somewhere I had the money to do it. Those were real luxuries for me. Not the glitz or the fancy cars.

My mom never shared my conservative tendencies but I loved for her to have what she wanted. I bought a home for both of us to live in, located in an orange grove in Rancho Santa Fe, an upper-class area of San Diego. It was a heady time in many ways. I was working constantly, but I was becoming successful and I had my best friend with me every step of the way. My mom and I were close. We stayed up late talking, and I finally had a maternal shoulder to rest my head on and watch movies with. It felt good. It felt right. She meditated constantly and was always connecting to the "source" to guide me in my career and inspire me to work harder. We held hands and giggled a lot and I was so happy to have my mom finally to myself. Two souls in the same body came to mean I was an extension of her, and it gave me a sense of belonging. In hindsight I wish I'd believed in myself enough to just go my own way.

One day my mom came to me when I was home between tours and accused my business manager of stealing from me—not a lot, just a little—but that she felt why trust anyone else? I got all fired up and said, heck yeah. We agreed she would handle all the money and she got the forms for me to sign. I was so busy being angry about the accusation that it never dawned on me to ask for proof, or to talk to the guy. To this day I have never seen proof. I just felt lucky my mom was my best friend and there to look out for me. I confided everything in her, and when I heard horror stories about other kids with parent-managers I felt so sorry for them. Everyone at the label knew to deal with my mom, and increasingly it seemed like a waste, she said, to be paying Inga to do something she was basically doing already on her own. Soon Inga was fired and my mom was in total control and managing me, and I was so grateful she was taking the time out of her life to help me with such care. She reminded me how lucky I was every day and of the unique gifts that only she could bring to the table. Looking back I remember making decisions about my career. I dealt with videos, treatments, timelines, release dates, tours . . .

and my mom and I had a huge staff who executed them all. But still I saw her as some integral part of myself that I could not do without. I would be lost without her.

As time passed and I started touring in larger venues, the money must have been pouring in, but I had no idea what I made from a show. Once my mom was in charge of it, I just let go of looking at any of it. I trusted her implicitly. If she had not been in the picture I know I would have been on top of every detail, but because she was looking out for me I relaxed about it and focused on work. And I worked a lot.

She steadily built an empire. A publishing arm. A screenwriting arm. A charitable arm (which I was excited about, the opportunity to give back and fulfill a promise I had made to myself years earlier on the street), an accounting division. I think by the end of it there were around twelve different business entities. All the salaries were being paid by me. And I was kept on the road working so much that I had no idea what was going on at home. My mom believed herself to be the reincarnation of a famous entrepreneur, though the problem was she had no business training. I was aware of all this in a vague way. There were aspects of the company that were exciting as well, like the nationwide talent search called Soul City Café that discovered singer-songwriters and gave them the opportunity to open for me across the country. My mom said she was building something that would help support me later, and that seemed like a good idea. All I knew at the time was I was working a lot and my mom lived like a rock star. She flew in yoga instructors from Hawaii and took jets everywhere, and if I was too tired to work she said I needed to be more disciplined about my meditation and to focus more. To connect to the source for more energy. God forbid I stop touring and rest for a second.

twenty-two

let your light shine

I had little time for or interest in dating. My career was my mistress and the effort it took to keep the ball rolling and capitalize on that momentum was dizzying. I had flown a million miles by my early twenties. I went around the globe without going home more than a handful of times in a year. When I wasn't touring the States, I was trying to break Europe—a market that escaped me no matter how often I toured there. I had looked at Europe as a retirement policy. Europeans had a reputation for being less fickle, and when musicians could no longer sell a lot of tickets in the States, they could go to Europe and sell out. But my music was so different from what was happening there and it never took hold on radio. In some markets I was able to play large venues like the Royal Albert Hall in London, while in others I would open for Willy DeVille in five-hundred-seat clubs. Australia and Asia were better markets for me.

A band was a big adjustment for me, as I had been solo my whole career, but the venues got big enough that it was a necessity. My first real foray was Lilith Fair, in the large outdoor sheds that begged for a band to fill the space. I hadn't played guitar with a band much, and my pocket (where you land on the groove) wasn't that tight; my tempo sped up and slowed down depending on how I sang. There are drummers who are used to listening to the singer for cues more so than memorizing a chart. Because I was self-taught, I often left whole bars out. I was famous for spacing out on my own lyrics and making others up. There were never the same number of bars in any given verse. I had a drummer who was professionally trained, a great drummer, just not great for me. Bands made me feel like I was wearing a wet wool suit. I was used to calling audibles and changing songs midstream depending on how I read the crowd. I never did set lists because I liked to be wherever the crowd was and choose songs in real time. When I needed to pick up the energy to keep the crowd interested, or drop into something slow and emotional, I felt my band lagging behind. I had no idea how to lead or guide them. I would get so frustrated that I couldn't keep the crowd's attention the way I did solo. I would stop mid-song and tell them I was going to finish the set on my own. It took me a couple of years to understand there was a certain type of musician I needed to play with—they had to be "feel" players more than technical virtuosos. Playing with drummers who were famous for their feel, like Jim Keltner, felt suddenly effortless. He always seemed to be right where I was. I asked him how he did it, and he said he had me and my guitar up in his mix. When I listened in on my own drummer's mix, he didn't have me up at all. It was the bass and electric guitar he had up, which is typical, but makes it hard to follow the singer. With time I learned that there were drummers who focused on the singer-songwriter and I set about finding one. While I was a folk singer, I approached music like a jazz player. I improvised and felt my way and altered arrangements on the spot. Everyone had to be listening with no preconceived plan. If a solo was great and building, we let it go longer. If we discovered a different beat or feel, we went for it as it happened. If I felt like holding a note longer, I did. I learned to lead the band and communicate in real time to them about where I was headed if they weren't yet feeling me head there. The band learned forty or fifty songs I might choose from on the spot. Over time my band shows started to feel as spontaneous and edgy as my solo acoustic shows had. Almost. And having the muscle of a band for large venues was worth whatever small compromise was made in not being up there by myself.

When I sing I don't think about what I'm singing—I think about the effect I want to have on the audience, then I use the tools I have at my disposal to do it. I don't care about how I sound while I sing, or how I look. I care about delivering a transfusion of the feeling in my vein to the vein of the listener, hitting their heart with gravity and force, undiluted by ego or pretense. It's my job to get out of the way of the emotion, to be a good vessel, and to bring attention not necessarily to myself but to the emotion in the story. Music and art are a potent medicine if the artist will get out of the way. This is the craft and art of live singing to me. It takes learning to get out of the way so that a pureness can travel through you to the audience.

I feel that I do my job most effectively when I'm alone onstage. I prefer to sing in theaters, where I've noticed the shape of the room affects the psychology of the crowd. Square rooms have a deadness you have to work harder to overcome. Round rooms allow feelings to circulate. My favorite room is a fan shape, or semicircle, with the stage as focal point, widening out so that each seat has an equal view. Energy flows easily back and forth and audiences are effortlessly attentive. The worst is a long rectangular space, as the views aren't equally clear and I have to work hard to get people to focus in and settle.

The first thing I do when I walk onstage is read the temperature of the crowd. I listen with my whole being. You can feel the spirit of the city—some cities are rowdy, some consider themselves more intellectual, more blue-collar, more arts-oriented. The East Coast is always more vocal and rowdy. The West Coast is more reserved. The middle of the country has a sincerity and earnestness. The South is intelligent, and resents anything that seems pretentious to them. New York City prefers musicians to have a little pretense. Each city has a feel, and each crowd has a unique feel on any night. Some nights the crowd comes in exhausted, like everyone just came from work. They need to be unwound a little first before we dig into deeper material. I can't start with material that is too poetic. I'll start with some humor to loosen them up and then warm into something more intense. Other crowds make it clear they want to be impressed: arms are folded, they want to be wowed before they will open up. I have to lead with headier lyrics and more intellectual story lines. Some crowds just feel ready to be moved and if I start with an emotional set, they all open up. When I start a show, I can feel two thousand separate people in the room. My goal is to choose songs and stories that bring us closer together, until the whole room clicks and it feels like one partner I am dancing with out there, instead of two thousand separate ones. Once that shift happens I can really have fun, we can cry and laugh and reflect together. You can feel everyone let go of their individual worries and explore their hearts in the safety of like-minded people from different walks of life. I've sat side stage many times and watched the room fill up before the lights went down, and it has occurred to me on more than one occasion that my audience has an eerie resemblance to every phase of my life. There are ranchers, surfers, fine arts aficionados, kids who feel estranged and want an emotional escape, '60s dreamers, and Gen Exers, and I love that they each set aside their identity once we get into the set and they open up. We really become one—we might wear different clothes or have different sexual preferences or lifestyles than the person next to us, but really those are just details. The person inside is looking for the same thing as their neighbor—freedom, expression, acceptance, love. They are not looking at each other's cowboy hats or dreadlocks; they are seeing the person inside and seeing that they are all on the same journey.

Building that connection was most important to me. My fans had really become an army of their own and organized themselves in a profound way. They are responsible for helping break my career, via the Internet and bootlegs—I recently found out I'd been included in several textbooks as a pioneer of grassroots marketing online, but I have to credit my fans for this mostly. I was able to talk to them directly about who I was, inviting them not to idolize me but to join me on my journey of self-discovery. We created a culture without the filter of the media. They supported one another and created a family who lived by the values we all shared: individuality, community, tolerance, and learning. And my music became the soundtrack for the movement—the Every Day Angels believed, as I did, in our ability to affect our own lives and those around us in a positive way. They continue to be an amazing group who still rally around me and who have helped me sustain a career twenty years in, founded on little else than being genuine. Through folk, rock, pop, country, and children's music, we have been exploring hand in hand.

I THINK OVER THOSE FIRST two years I toured, I dated two guys for a year each, though I'm sure the days we actually saw each other would add up to only a few months. I just didn't have the time. It was awkward to have a guy on tour with me, and off the road I didn't feel like going out or being social. Apparently I was not immune to certain rock and roll clichés, because both of the people I dated were male models. It hadn't occurred to me until I was at dinner one night in New York. Flea invited me out for sushi with the Peppers and some other friends. I was sitting at the end of the table, looking around, and noticed all the funny-looking rock stars and the stunning Amazonian women sitting next to them. As I leaned over to my boyfriend to comment, it dawned on me—I was a funny-looking snaggletoothed musician with a model on my arm! These men were beautiful and sweet and kind to me, but when they came on the road I felt like a trapped coyote that wanted to chew its arm off. I just was not in the headspace to be dating. It took all my energy to keep building my career. I also began to notice the shift in power as I went from being a destitute woman to one with her own means. It was hard on the male ego to date a woman who was more successful. These men waited for me to come off the road, and when I did, they wanted to go out. I, of course, wanted to stay in. I did not feel my age. I felt old.

Pieces of You went on to sell twelve million copies. It was one of the best-selling debut records of all time. It blew my mind that a simple folk record could go so far. I watched MTV and saw all the other videos, with the cool kids and the shiny, pretty perfect people full of bravado and hip heroin-chic ways, and I could not believe my earnest style had found a place in modern pop culture. The video for "Who Will Save Your Soul" was up for an MTV award, and the amazing late, great Kevyn Aucoin did my makeup, hair, and styling for the event. I still had not caught on to fancy glam teams, and had only met the famous makeup artist because he basically stalked me. I'd been walking into David Letterman's studio and my label publicist recognized a giant six-foot-five man standing with fans behind a rope watching me go in. Kevyn was a big deal, the first makeup artist who was a celebrity in his own right. My publicist said, "Kevyn?! What are you doing here?!" He said he was a big fan of mine and was dying to work with me. She pulled him from behind the rope and he came in with me. I was going to do my makeup myself as usual, but here was this larger-than-life gay man who was fabulous in a way I loved instantly. He had fingers the size of bratwurst and promptly set up the kit he had brought. He talked away as he got me ready. He began by plucking my eyebrows, which apparently were from another decade and no longer in fashion. I did not watch while he did this. He moved on to foundation, then eyes, and by the time I put on the little gray dress and black cardigan I'd picked out, I felt like Dorothy all over again. I looked like myself, but a version seen through Kevyn's eyes. It was the first time I'd had fun being dolled up.

It was my first award show and I had no idea what I was supposed to do or how to behave. Kevyn asked who was doing my hair and I gave him a blank look. "Okay," he said, "do you have any baby oil? I have no idea how to do hair, but we can make it look shiny if nothing else." I must have been touring and still had no official stylist. I think I wore a pencil skirt and a cardigan. I remember never having the right kind of undergarments. The bra made the outfit, Kevyn said, but I had never paid much attention to this sort of thing and had only whatever Walmart number I'd been wearing since God knows when. He assured me that he would make me fabulous anyway. I started to get nervous and asked if he would walk me down the red carpet.

The limo pulled up and I could see a dizzying array of flashbulbs and hear the screams of photographers yelling out orders to young starlets in frenzied tones. Suddenly I could hear them screaming my name. This was nothing like Venice, where I'd been anonymous. This was for real. They knew who I was. The limo stopped and the driver got out and made the long walk back to open my door and I had an absolute panic attack and slammed the lock down. Through the tinted window I could see a confused look on the driver's face. He walked back to the front seat to click the unlock button again, while Kevyn and my label rep looked at me sort of stunned. They didn't say a word. Neither did I. The driver walked back to my unlocked door and I took a deep breath as he reached for the handle. Again a terror seized me, and just as the driver pulled the handle, I pushed the button down again. Confused, the driver took a brisk walk to his door, and very deliberately and forcefully hit the unlock button.

Without saying anything, Kevyn took my hand firmly in his own as the driver walked back to my door. He squeezed it affectionately and with his other hand opened the door a crack. My eyes welled with tears as I was overtaken by the terror of being stared at on a catwalk. This couldn't be my life. I know this sounds odd from a famous person who has made a living being watched, but being onstage always felt different. It was vulnerable and honest somehow, and people could see me for who I felt I was. But the press and media scared me. They looked at your body for fat and flaws. They listened to your music for things to pick apart. The idea of stepping into the spotlight in this way was nerve-racking. A relieved limo driver held the door open as Kevyn guided me out. He said, "You are beautiful. Let your light shine," and with that I was swallowed into the maelstrom of screams and flashing bulbs. "JEWEL! Look this way! Jewel! Top center, top center! Jewel, look over your shoulder!" I looked at the other girls ahead of me and behind me and saw I was underdressed. I felt awkward and shy and my poses for the camera said as much.

After the photos I politely went to answer the silly questions from red carpet TV anchors as best as I could (What's your favorite nail color? What's your one beauty must?) and especially appreciated the ones about music. I was next in line for a major outlet and saw Shakira, whom I admired, ahead of me. It was crowded and chaotic and everyone was elbow-to-elbow. I saw a space open and as I was stepping in to speak to her, I suddenly felt a pain in my ribs. Someone's publicist had elbowed me sharply. I looked up, stunned. The publicist would not make eye contact and shuffled their artist in ahead of me to take my TV slot. The Alaskan in me came out, and I elbowed that woman so hard in the ribs I hoped she choked up a kidney. She looked at me in shock and I smiled at her and stood back to let her artist have my spot anyway. I would have waited an extra five minutes if she had just asked. Kevyn was nearly dying with laughter. He'd caught the whole thing and hugged me and said, "Oh my god, I love you. You're like a little Barbie hillbilly and I love you!"

Inside it was wild to see all the musicians I had watched on TV. We are rarely in the same place at the same time. In that way fame was nothing like I thought it would be, like France in the '30s when painters and authors and poets and muses all hung together sharing and creating. When everything was over I was walking to the after-party when Tupac came across my path. I, of course, knew who he was but had never met him. He was apparently taken with me because he stopped in his tracks and gave me an electric stare that was hard to mistake. I felt like a deer caught in the headlights, and then just as suddenly I moved on and the electricity dissipated. It was so visceral and undeniable that my boyfriend whispered in my ear, "Holy shit. He was looking at you like a piece of meat and he looks hungry. I know I should be mad but it honestly sort of scared the shit out of me." At the party, I was surprised by the musicians who came up to talk to me. Marilyn Manson was huge at the time, and was in full Goth drag. He said, "I love your song 'I'm Sensitive.' It's sincere but also ironic at the same time. I bet the press doesn't get that." Not a song choice I expected from a man wearing white contact lenses and plastic pants.

I was about ready to wind it down and head home, and was momentarily standing by myself, waiting for my date to return from visiting with a photographer friend he'd spotted. Stealthy and silent, Tupac was again suddenly standing next to me. He spoke softly and looked at me directly with soulful eyes. He said he was headed to Vegas with a whole crew and thought I might have fun if I came. He had a hypnotic but vulnerable quality that was fascinating. I told him I was there with someone but hoped he had fun. He was shot three days later in Vegas. When it hit the news I couldn't help but think of all the forks in the roads of life and how we never know where they will lead. I heard he had a fiancée and wondered why the hell he had invited me to Vegas. I will never know. I was sorry about his passing. He was a great talent with undeniable star appeal.

With time the red carpets got easier, and I got used to the culture. I never got used to rudeness, however, and in the aftermath of the shock-jock craze that the amazing Howard Stern started, I found myself dealing with a few radio DJs who lacked his intelligence and talent, and tried to make up for it with a willingness to be just plain shocking instead. Everything from my tooth to my weight to my being raised with an outhouse was fair game for them. I remember being in the Midwest somewhere at 7 a.m. and a local DJ said something like, "Jewel, you're beautiful but Jesus Christ that snaggletooth of yours is disgusting. Do you scare men off with that thing? I mean, who would want you to go down on them with those chompers?" In response to these kinds of questions, I would look at them and say playfully, "Well, I can fix my teeth. You can't fix stupid." Or "I can fix my teeth. You'll always be bald." Another time I was down south and the DJ seemed nice as we made small talk until it was time to go on air. I was tuning up my guitar as the red light came on indicating we'd just gone live. The DJ's voice changed from the normal tone he had been speaking to me with, to an almost comical imitation of a radio host. In a booming and highly energetic voice, he said, "Hi! You may have heard me describe my next guest as a large-breasted woman from Alaska—it's JEWEL! Jewel, how are ya?" Without blinking, I adopted my own radio voice and said, "I'm doing great! You must be that small-penised man I heard so much about!" I thought he would laugh and we would carry on our conversation, but instead his face went flat and he pushed the button and the red light went dark and I was escorted out of the station without another word from the DJ. My label begged me to just cool it on the back talk, but I felt that if DJs were going to be shocking and rude, that it should at least be a two-way street. Verbal sparring was fun even, I thought, and fair was fair.

It always stunned me in group interviews and at press junkets for shows where multiple artists played to see how journalists at the time treated the women songwriters differently from the men. They would ask Beck about the meaning behind the lyric *I'm a loser baby, so why don't you kill me*, and then turn to me and say, What's your favorite color for spring? There was an incredible women's movement in music that had happened, and I felt blessed to be surrounded by talented peers such as Sheryl Crow, Sarah McLachlan, Natalie Merchant, and the Indigo Girls. I felt we all stood on the shoulders of our predecessors and owed so much to Joni Mitchell, Joan Baez, Rickie Lee Jones, Carole King, Carly Simon and so many other greats. I was only on my first CD and felt I still had much to prove to earn my place next to them.

I LIVED LIKE AN EXILE on the road, exhausted and in desperate need of a break. Then I met a cowboy. And I decided to take one.

Early into 1999, I did a fund-raising concert in Aspen for my charity, Project Clean Water. I had a day to kill in Denver before my next show and I heard the rodeo was in town. I grew up rodeoing a little—just a barrel or keyhole race, or pole bending when there was one in town. They were outdoors, muddy, and small by any standard, but fun. My dad had been the all-around local champ on a horse he'd trained himself as a kid. I asked my label if they could get me tickets to the sold-out show and it turned out they used a car company that sponsored a rodeo cowboy and they were able to get me tickets through him. I showed up and got to my seat and enjoyed the show. The event organizers asked if I would ride the stagecoach and let them announce that I was there. I felt embarrassed but conceded. When the coach did its lap and exited into the backstage area where all the rough stock was kept, I was greeted by a quiet but enigmatic cowboy who introduced himself as Ty Murray. He had helped get the tickets and wanted to be sure I was being looked after. I had heard of Ty Murray. He was known as the Michael Jordan of rodeo, though I had never seen him ride. I asked if he would send an autograph to my dad, who, I knew, would flip. We exchanged numbers so we could work out the details. No sparks flew. I was headed to New York City the next morning and on to a world tour from there.

I toured Europe, Asia, and Australia for the next year. I was single the whole time and very lonely. My fame had grown to heights I had never imagined. My single "Hands" from my second album, *Spirit*, did well for me, which I was very happy about, but still I was unprepared for the life-style of success. It wasn't the fantasy some people imagine, at least not for a sober female. I was unable to have casual sex with groupies or fans the way my male counterparts seemed to be able to enjoy. I found fame fantastically isolating. You wake up in a hotel, your tour manager shuttles you to an airport, you travel all day, you get to a new hotel room, try to catch a nap if you have time, though I usually had just enough time to shower and put on makeup for back-to-back interviews that backed right up to show time. I would hang with the band to try to unwind from the interviews and assault of questions as people tried to find the "real" you or get a scoop or a rise out of you for a story. Then I would walk onstage where I could let everything go. I would be absolutely spent by the time I walked off. I rarely got out to sightsee like the band did. I was cut off from nature, with no friends other than my band.

I felt like an astronaut drifting in space, able to see people only from the darkness of the stage, like looking at Earth from a great and beautiful distance. I began to carry Tupperware containers of Alaskan dirt and cottonwood balm my aunt would send me, so I could smell something natural and familiar that reminded me of home. I had no opportunity to even make friends, as I never went anywhere like normal people did and I wasn't a partier. When I did go out in public I was shocked to be recognized by so many people. While I could see my album sales on paper and I was playing larger venues, my experience of day-to-day life hadn't changed. I did not drive fancy cars or go on fancy vacations or hang out with fancy people. My mom did those things. I traveled and worked in a very insulated world with a band and crew that did not change. It wasn't until I went home to San Diego after the first few tours and went to the store to get groceries that I was suddenly confronted with just how surreal my life had become. I would wait in line and someone next to me would start crying. People would watch to see what I put in my basket and I would see them whisper to a friend immediately to tell them I ate Grape-Nuts, I supposed. I was followed to my car by shy fans who wanted to see what I drove. It was the same used Volvo I'd gotten when I was signed. I had no need for a new car as I was never home to drive it. One man came up to me at a taco stand and said, "I have no idea who you are, but I can see everyone is staring at you, so you must be somebody. I just wanted to be the one to tell you that you are not that special. You're no more special than me." I looked at him with a mouth full of food and managed to say, "Thanks. I agree," and promptly asked the waitress for a to-go box.

I had been a voyeur my whole life, studying and watching people, but now people were watching me. I often felt like an exotic animal in a zoo. People would walk by, gawk, and sometimes even reach out to touch me as if they could not believe I was there. I would run a commentary in my head like a narrator from a nature channel. *Look, here is the folk singer in her natural habitat, eating a taco. Here is the elusive folk singer blowing her nose. Look at how she turns her head slightly to shade her eyes from the sun.* Being that famous felt like being screamed at all the time, even when no one was talking to you. You could feel the focus even when they said nothing. Being idolized and being torn down felt oddly similar. They both made me feel alone. Friendship and trust should be earned, and when you're famous, people seem to want to give them to you whether you've earned them or not, and it felt dishonest to me. Fame was not real. It was all a projection—fame made me a blank canvas that people projected their love, lust, troubles, self-worth, and desire upon. Fame and power do not change us; they amplify us. If we are insecure, we grow more so. If we are addictive, we become a greater addict and insatiable. If we are desirous of truth, we seek it more. If we are generous, we become more so. If we seek to fill holes through dishonest means, we have greater access to do so. Fame and power are masterful teachers. This made me double down on my commitment to be sure I was creating a genuine and honest connection to my fan base. It helped me feel I could show up authentically in the spotlight.

Ty and I spoke a few times as I traveled. When I came back from Australia, I left him a voicemail. He called while I was in Asia. A year after our first meeting we decided to try to meet up on the road somewhere. I had a day off near a rodeo he would be riding at in Livermore, California. We lived parallel lives, in vehicles and on the road performing for large crowds. I would sing in the same stadium that he would ride in a week later. Cowboys and rock stars both starve for the chance to do what they love, and a very few make it big. Ty was one of the few who made it big, and he revolutionized the business of rodeo. When he was in third grade he said his goal in life was to break Larry Mahan's record of six all-around wins. He went on to break the record with seven. He broke the all-around record on the rough stock events, which are considered much harder than the timed events like calf and team roping and steer wrestling. He also won two world championships in bull riding.

Ty was a perfect fit for me because he loved the outdoors and had values we shared. He was down-to-earth. He was not a fame-monger. He was passionate about his craft and liked to challenge himself. He was raised poor and was self-made. He knew what it took to build a career and what it meant to work hard. He knew what it meant to be in the public eye.

We were both at the height of our careers. Ty had just broken the all-around record and was the darling of the rodeo industry and western culture. *Pieces of You* had won a diamond award for selling more than ten million copies and my current record was burning up the airwaves. We were young, rich, and at the top of our game. I flew to Livermore and watched him ride broncs. I never traveled with an entourage or friends, so I sat in the outdoor stands by myself, mostly unrecognized. The first event Ty was up in was the saddle bronc. The horse reared wildly in the chute. Ty nodded his head for the gate to open, and the animal pivoted on its hind legs and surged out of the chute in a cresting wave of muscle. Once the animal got out of the gate and into the arena, Ty's free arm moved forward and back in time with the bronc's bucking, as his feet whipped from flank to neck with crisp, precise movements. Chin tucked in, hat never moving an inch. When the whistle blew he timed his exit and, capitalizing on the momentum and force of the animal, let go of the rein on the next buck and catapulted into the air, landing on his feet like a cat. He stared down at the dirt and walked out of the arena in his trademark baby blue and tan chaps with a determined gate, without so much as looking up. He was all business.

Next up was the bareback event. Ty combed his horse with what I would learn was perfect form. He wore the customary foam neck brace to prevent whiplash, and his legs fanned open, bending back by his ears, then snapped closed, the dull spurs neatly grazing high on the horse's neck. When the whistle blew, he used his free arm to pull himself up to sitting position and waited for the pick-up man while the horse continued to buck. He jumped from his horse to the pick-up man's and then slid to the ground. Again he walked out of the arena looking down at his feet, almost as if he were angry with himself. Already thinking about his next ride. All business.

The final event was bull riding. When Ty's turn came around, he crawled over the fencing in the back of the chute, straddled the bull, and prepared his rope. The bull lay down in the chute but Ty nodded anyway. When the bull saw the gate open, there was a blur of spinning and kicking in the blink of an eye. Ty's body bent forward at the hips, waiting for the bull to leap forward and buck before he started his series of countermoves like playing a game of chess with body and life. Each move the bull made, Ty had to have an exact countermove. He had to absorb the bull's momentum by putting his body in a position to neutralize the force of the bull. He could not anticipate what the bull would do, nor could he be late in responding. Everything had to be in perfect time.

Hearing Ty describe riding bulls later sounded almost Zen, though he had never read any Buddhist texts. When he rode, time slowed down enough so that he could turn what would feel like a car crash to the average person into a slow-motion give-and-take, where he responded in perfect time with the animal, feeling for every move it would make. He was entirely in the moment, focused only on the now. Living with fear and danger, but being able to remain fluid within it. He liked the stakes to be that high. He liked having to perform with that kind of pressure and consequence. It was truly beautiful to watch. When the whistle blew, he made sure not to get off in the well (the inside of the bull's spinning, where he could be trapped), and walked stoically back to the locker room, but this time he nodded to the crowd, without really lifting his head, only giving them his eyes as he looked up at the audience. The place erupted.

We rode in his limo back to San Francisco and talked about life. Hours passed before we knew it. I would stay the night in San Francisco then fly to a show the next day. He wasn't even spending a night before leaving for another show elsewhere. When it was time for his flight he hugged me goodbye. It was a sober and conservative hug. We were standing by the door, my unpacked bag holding it open. He wore a loose T-shirt and my hand accidentally landed on bare skin. There was an electrical charge and transference of energy that's hard to explain. I had met guys on the road and never so much as a spark flew. When I hugged Ty, I suddenly felt I knew everything about him. I sensed that beneath his tough persona he was boyish and naive in a way, that his body had been battered and beaten and educated, but that he had made it through his life without his heart ever being hurt.

twenty-three

so. she can ride.

Our next date spanned a four-day break we found in our schedules. We went camping in the mountains of Northern California with an old cowboy friend of Ty's named Pat Russell. I met Ty in Reno, where he was up that night in all three events again. I went to find Pat's truck after being given some vague directions via text like, *gray flatbed diesel with ball hitch and dent on left fender, back right of parking lot.* I found the truck and with it Pat, whom I had never met until that moment. He was in his sixties with gray stubble on his unshaved face and a grimace that must have been the original Clint Eastwood aspired to. We stood beneath the hum of fluorescent bulbs in the parking lot taking each other in. Other than removing his hat briefly when I arrived, he kept busy packing the truck and asked me nothing about myself, choosing instead to bark orders at me. "Grab that rope, would ya? Throw it over here. You need a bedroll, I suppose. I don't see that you have one on you. Here, roll this one up."

I had flown in on a private plane right after my show and had not taken the time to change. I wore black leather pants, biker boots, a white T-shirt, and a jean jacket, and I was beginning to feel a chill as night closed in, leaving visible only the pinprick formation of stars.

The silence was unceremoniously broken as Pat was attacked from behind. A figure leapt through the air and put him in a choke hold, knocking off both their hats. Pat stood his ground and without so much as moving swatted Ty off as if he were no more bothersome than a gnat. "'Bout time you showed up, Pud." Cowboys have a habit of nicknaming each other with handles that summarize their worst fear or trait. There was a cowboy named Jim Sharp, who, while a world-champ bull rider, was not known to be the sharpest of guys, so they called him Razor. Another had teeth with such wide gaps between them that they called him Rake. To Ty, the worst insult was to call him a Puss. In cowboy terms, if you pussed out on a ride, that meant you hunted for the ground instead of hanging tough and gutting it out to the whistle. Ty despised cowboys who did this. He'd heard that Walt Garrison would call other players Pudding when in front of the press, since he could not use the other word in public. Ty decided to try it out on a cowboy the next day, and told everyone that when he was calling them "pudding," he really was calling them a puss. It backfired on him and he was stuck with the nickname for life.

At the truck, Ty said, "Pat, you old bastard, how the hell are you? Did you meet Jewel?" At this, Pat looked over and considered me directly for the first time. He looked back at his bag and said, "Yeah. A bit lean in the flank and poorly dressed for the task at hand. I guess there is no accounting for taste." Pat had a rare talent for saying something mean and making you feel liked. He threw a thick coat at me as we got in the truck, saying, "She didn't even have the good sense to bring a proper coat."

We drove without talking for a ways, watching the road open up beneath our headlights and fly by into darkness again. Pat broke the silence to keep himself awake as much as anything, I suppose: "Ty tells me you got a book of poems out. Recite us something."

A Night Without Armor had recently come out and was exceeding everyone's expectations—poetry was finding a mass audience in spite of an industry's skepticism. I was unprepared to recite some, though, and had none committed to memory except one called "Wild Horse." Pat would accept no excuses, and suddenly I found myself reciting for a crowd of two. It was a love poem I had written years earlier.

I'd like to call you my wild horse
and feed you silver sage

I'd like to paint my poems
With desert tongued clay
across
your back
and ride you savagely
as the sweet and southern wind
through a green and wild Kentucky.

Pat interrupted. "Goddamn. This isn't poetry. This is horny prose!" he exclaimed, and we all fell into laughter. It turned out Pat was fluent in Latin and he spent the rest of the ride reciting to me his favorite rhymes, limericks, and sonnets while Ty slept.

We arrived at Pat's ranch in the middle of the night. He showed us to a single room. I was mortified. Ty could tell I was uncomfortable and we both went to bed fully clothed and he promised not to touch me. And true to his word, he slept. Instantly. I lay awake, unable to relax. It was strange to be sleeping next to a strange man, in a strange house. Around 3 a.m. I finally had to pee. I stumbled to the bathroom only to realize there was no bathroom door. In bare feet I felt my way downstairs and outside with tissue in hand. It was about that time the dogs began barking. All of them. A chorus of bird dogs let loose a mournful wail and the whole place *had* to wake up. I cursed under my breath and headed back upstairs to see Ty was undisturbed. I would lie awake, thankful to finally see daylight slowly blush on the horizon.

I hadn't told Ty much about how I was raised, other than mentioning I'd lived on a homestead as a child. He knew I had ridden horses, but I was not eager to overshare, because as a kid giving tourists rides, I had learned that when dealing with novice riders, they always seemed to brag about what great riders they were. The next morning I could see they had set aside the oldest, slowest gelding for me. That did not stop Pat from telling Ty to grab an ear on the old horse, while he mugged down his neck like one would to keep a bronc still enough for a good hand to climb on. "Very funny," I said, and waited for the games to be over before I put a foot in the stirrup and swung a leg over.

"So. She can ride," Pat said, unimpressed. Enjoying razzing me still. Those men razzed me the entire trip. "We need a fire. This is how you build one. It will be hot." They "taught" me how to catch a fish, clean it, and cook it. They showed me how to find water and warned me I would have to use the facilities outdoors at night. I kept wondering what kind of person they thought I was, and more important, what kind of girls they had been hanging around with. I resigned myself to nod along, knowing that if Ty ever came to Alaska, the last laugh would be on him. (This eventually did happen, and my patience was rewarded. After seeing the place where I was raised, he said, "Do you remember when we first met? And how I assumed you knew nothing about camping? Your childhood *was* camping!")

Ty showed off some fancy roping for me—he had competed in a phenomenal six events in college rodeo before he decided to focus on rough stock events as a professional. He did ocean waves and hoolihans and figure eights and other fancy tricks. He had a makeshift roping dummy and when he set the rope down I picked it up and daubed it on the dummy, clean around the horns. I wasn't sure I would nail it, but once I had, I was pretty cool about it. He sat up and said, "Well, where did you learn that?" "On a movie set, actually," I confessed. "Here," he offered, "Let me show you how to turn your wrist over so the loop won't change planes when you release." He came behind me and stood close. His body fitting the form of mine as he bent down and helped twirl my arm, both of us standing under the spinning canopy of the lariat loop. I was sure it was a tactic he'd used before but I didn't mind. The closeness of his body felt electric. And my roping improved significantly. He taught me about heeling calves, walking in front of me so I could practice roping his feet. Eventually we sat in the shade of a tall pine and sipped fresh spring water. "So, you shot a film? Is it out yet? Was it a western, I guess, if you learned to rope for it?"

It was not out yet nor a western per se. It was a Civil War–era drama called *Ride with the Devil*, directed by Ang Lee. Acting had been a goal for me since the beginning of my career, though I rarely had time to go out on auditions. I happened to be in L.A. when Ang Lee's office asked to meet with me. Thankfully there was no script yet or sides, so I did not have to read lines (a practice I was not particularly good at). Instead Ang asked me about how I was raised. To my surprise he asked me to walk for him. I walked across the room. "Again," he said, in his quiet but assertive way. I walked back across the room. "Okay," he said, "This time be heavier. You are too light on your feet. Don't be graceful. Be determined." I was caught off guard but obliged, and put more weight in my heels and let my arms feel the gravity of the room. He stood watching with his arms crossed, his hand holding up his chin, his head tilted slightly to the side. He stared at my feet and my fingers. Abruptly he looked up at my face and said, "Thanks for coming." That was it. I called my agent and recounted the odd experience. I expected I would never hear from him again. Every great actress in Hollywood was trying out for the part.

I was shocked to be offered the female lead a few weeks later. I had less than zero experience other than theater classes in high school, and was very intimidated by the cast of talented young male costars. Ang assured me that we would get together for weekly acting lessons. He began our next meeting by handing me his watch. "Pretend you are not from this planet. Pretend you don't know what this is. Go." I felt utterly ridiculous, but when he handed me the watch I dropped it immediately. It fell to the floor with a thud. I hoped I hadn't broken it but didn't pick it up. I felt if I had no idea what something was, I wouldn't want to touch it before I'd figured out whether it was safe or not. I studied it there on the floor. Once assured it did not have legs or teeth, I touched it cautiously with my toe. When nothing bad happened I reached down to touch it quickly. I studied it like a child would. Was it soft? Edible? After I went as far as touching my tongue to the man's watch he stopped me and I handed it back to him a bit sheepishly. He put it on his wrist. "Let's do some tai chi." After that the lesson was over.

For weeks I had lessons that consisted of nothing more than tai chi and walking. Ang gave me glimpses into my character. She was a Civil War bride, widowed. She would have a baby at a young age and need someone to protect her. She would learn to be tough and survive. As the filming date neared I began to panic. I needed to learn to act, not walk!

On the day of our last lesson, Ang and I shared a car back to a hotel in New York. It dawned on me that this was it—time was up! I felt utterly unprepared and massively underqualified. In tears, I looked at him and whimpered, "Why did you hire me? You could have any actress you want. Why *me*?" He looked at me, his face as calm and smooth as the moon, and said, "You have period teeth." And that was it. No pep talk. I turned back to the window. I was the only actress who had not fixed her teeth. That's what had gotten me the role. Awesome. He got out and left me with my low feelings of self-worth and doubt. Looking back I think he was counting on these feelings, and also on my willingness to look inside myself and dig deep for solutions. It mirrored the journey of my character, I would find out. If I hadn't been blinded by sheer terror, I would have laughed at the irony.

I showed up on set in Missouri to find a cast who, for the most part, were less than pleased that a pop star had been hired on their credible film. Many felt I was going to ruin it. I silently feared the same. I didn't want to disappoint Ang, much less make a fool of myself in front of millions who were going to buy tickets just to see if I could pull it off. One actor in particular was quite mean to me, which was just the kick in the butt I needed. The more he hated, the harder I dug in.

I got into character using the tools I already had—writing. I was able to connect with her fear, her longing, and her strength when I wrote from her perspective. I wrote a song about her loss and her isolation and sang it before I filmed my scenes, to get into the emotional framework. By the time we finished rehearsing and began filming I felt mildly courageous, and for better or for worse was as ready as I would ever be.

I don't think even Ang was prepared for how little I actually knew about filmmaking. In one scene early on, I was to walk into a cave where some soldiers were and deliver a line. Action was called. At the end of the shot, Ang came up to me and said, "Jewel, you're not hitting your mark." I thought he meant metaphorically—an emotional point I was not getting to. I vowed to act harder, to bring more emotion. Action was again called, again I walked into the cave, and again I said my line, and again Ang came up to me afterward and said, "Jewel, you need to hit your mark." He was perturbed, I assumed, by my lack of ability. I had a talk with myself and I went *big* the next time action was called. But still I fell short of the mark. Ang came out from behind the camera and said, "Jewel, you have got to hit your mark!" This time he pointed downward and I followed his gesture with my eyes to see a beanbag on the floor. The actors saw the light go on for me and some snickered. I never missed a mark after that.

I had no idea there were close-ups to save emotional intensity for, or long shots in which I could be less dramatic. I was spent every day before we got to my close-ups. Ang took me aside and pointed out that I was approaching acting like a theater artist. This was not in real time. I had to conserve my energy over a twelve-hour day, not blow it in the first two hours as if it were a live concert. This was most helpful. I began to get the hang of the technical aspects, and with time I gave myself permission to just assume I knew what I needed to know about acting emotionally. I remembered what Sean had told me. He said I was a natural, and to stay out of my own way.

Voices in my head would say things like, *You don't know what you are doing. You are going to make a fool of yourself. You are alone. You are afraid.* I stayed up nights worrying about the next day's scenes. Fear was once again ruling my life. To which I told myself, *I am capable. I can figure anything out. Half measures dictated by fear are the only thing that can make me look foolish. I will show my heart and try my hardest. I am joyful.*

I bought a tape recorder and taped my antidote sayings, listening to them on a loop all night. It sounds silly, but it really helped. I would wake less exhausted, less anxious, and able to access my courage and some joy for the day rather than doubt and fear. Even if my costar still hated me, I didn't. I might not be the best, but I would try my best. That's all I could do.

The best part of filming was the head wrangler named Rusty Hendricks. He was older, kind, familiar, more like the people I had come from—rural, in a word. On days off he would let me ride the horses to unwind. He taught me to rope, and I practiced on a roping dummy every day waiting for my scenes.

Halfway through filming I got the news that Jacque was losing her battle with cancer. She had been sick for some time, but we always thought God would spare her. We thought she could raise her frequency to the point cancer could not exist in her. We thought she could pray and meditate it away. She was in hospice and her family was told to come say their goodbyes. I was devastated. She had become my rock, my source of unconditional love.

Ang was kind enough to film around me and let me go back to San Diego to see her. I had paid her hospice and her medical bills, and gathered with her family and my mom, and we stayed with her until she passed. It was the Fourth of July. To this day conjuring the memory of her emaciated frame brings such a sadness to my heart and tears to my eyes. I loved that woman, and as odd as it sounds, I loved Zarathustra. I would never get to speak to either of them again. I would no longer be able to call Jacque when I lost faith in myself and hear her sweet pep talks or have her there to encourage me when I felt small. Dusk settled in as we stood around her bed, and she drew her last breath just as fireworks began to explode outside. We cried and we laughed, sure that she was orchestrating such a grand and dramatic departure. We held hands around her body and watched the beautiful display of color explode across the sky through the window.

I returned to filming but felt utterly alone. My friend and guru was gone. I was so convinced I was not strong or capable of knowing answers for myself. I still could not see my own strengths, and felt I needed my mom or someone else to tell me what to do.

jewel

Making the film and writing the book of poetry helped me deal with the grief, and my saving grace was that my dear friend Lee was there with me every step of the way. He had worked with me for several years, and he was my only friend and connection to Alaska. He cooked for me on busy days, went on tour, and came with me to the set. We lived in the same house together in Missouri where we filmed. When I was exhausted he rubbed my back and soothed me to sleep. He was aware of my mom's influence over me, though for the most part I kept my spirituality, and my mom's, to myself. And I kept it from Ty as I told stories of my life. I felt no one would understand other than those of us who were followers of Z.

BENEATH THAT PINE TREE, Ty listened as I carried on about the movie and myself. When I finally paused, he asked if I wanted to go fishing. We walked with a clear fishing line, no pole, to the spring. I watched his thick hands deftly puncture a bright orange fish egg on a small silver hook. He dropped it in and guided the line to a quiet eddy, where the water calmed. He spoke quietly, letting go of the cocky bravado he had led with. A fish bit and he lifted it out of the water. It had a silver and pink belly and brown spots, a brookie. Ty strung the line through its gills and tethered the stringer in the water to keep it cool while he caught others. At the end of an hour five small fish hung from a clear line, glittering in the sun. We would fry them later and eat them. I watched him handle the tiny fish, cleaning each one. The air took on a magical quality as the light turned golden and specks of dust were illuminated in the sun's final rays. I was falling in love. I walked behind him as he took the fish to the camp and began to wonder what was beneath his shirt.

That night beneath a full moon we kissed for the first time, the water sang and babbled and the dry fingers of the pines rubbing together in the wind serenaded us. I could see his muscles working beneath the translucent sheath of his skin. We glowed. I felt as if the brightness of the moon was illuminating our hearts and lighting us both from the inside. The passion and our connection were so visceral it was hard to move. "If I pass out," he whispered, "don't leave." I smiled and lifted the white sheet over me like wings.

twenty-four

do you love me
like i love you

Ty was still rodeoing and was traveling with the Professional Bull Riders, an organization he and nineteen other riders founded in order to make bull riding a stand-alone event, a trackable sports property, and to make their salaries comparable to those of other pro athletes. The top athletes of rodeo hardly made enough to retire. Promoters and the Professional Rodeo Cowboys Association made most of the money.

He had not had the chance to see me perform yet, so I kept him on the phone one night as I walked out in front of a crowd. I held the phone up and asked all eighteen thousand people to say hello. Then I put the phone in my bra strap and put my guitar over my shoulder, while Ty stayed on the line for the first several songs, in a front-row seat from hundreds of miles away.

The next night he handed his cell to a cowboy behind the chute and climbed on a bronc. I could hear his breathing intensify, and the announcer say, "And now, the great Ty Murray is up on the great bucking mare Spring Fling." I heard Ty call for the gate, the grunt of the animal, the whistle eight seconds later, and the announcer again saying, "That was Ty Murray, ladies and gentleman, putting in a score of eighty-one." He returned to the phone shortly after, breathless.

Eventually we would spend every day off with each other, either on the road or at the rodeo or bullring. I fell in love with the culture, studied the ins and outs of each event, and had the opportunity to partake in brandings on ranches that were hundreds of years old. I was usually the only female who wasn't in the kitchen cooking or watching kids but instead out with the guys.

I'd grown up working cattle, but Alaskans did not do things the way they did here in the Lower 48. Ty was a fifth-generation cowboy and there was a way of doing things that had been passed down from generation to generation. On one particular day we were at the Muleshoe Ranch in Gail, Texas, and a cowboy named Gary had given me a colt. It was customary to name a colt after the person who had given it to you. Gary was called Nanner because they said his nose was longer and more hook-shaped than a banana. He was nice but prone to sudden moods, from what I had been told. The guys asked what I would name my new colt, but before I had the chance to respond, Nanner turned on me and said something quite mean in front of everyone. Everyone turned quietly to me to see what I would say. His remark hit me hard and stung, though thanks to years of barrooms and touring, I turned to a cowboy next to me and said in a bright tone, "Hey, Kleet, I think I'm gonna name my colt after the guy who gave him to me after all." "You're gonna call 'em Gary? Nanner?" Kleet asked. Many of these guys did not know me. All they knew is I was some pop singer and they wondered what the heck I was doing there anyway with the King of the Cowboys. Everyone was curious to see how I'd handle myself. "No," I said. "I'm gonna call him Cock-sucker." At this the guys broke up laughing. Gary was less amused but knew he had no ground to stand on and he looked down and grumbled and fiddled with some rope in his hand. No hard feelings though. We went on to be good friends. Cowboys tease hard and test each other and move on. I didn't mind holding my own.

Later that day the owner of the ranch asked Ty if I knew how to rope. He invited me to get up and heel a few calves. Everyone's favorite job at brandings is to heel calves, but all I'd ever heeled were Ty's feet as he walked in front of me. I mounted one of Ty's horses and headed into the pen with Chris Shivers, a world champion bull rider. I was nervous, but knew enough to go in slow so as to not stir the herd. I pulled my hat down hard so it wouldn't blow off—the cowboy equivalent of toilet paper on your shoe. I remembered what Ty told me, that I had to change the plane of my rope depending on the angle I approached the calf. Chris got one before me and I was so nervous I wouldn't hold my own. I swung my rope and pantyhosed one (when you catch the calf around the hip instead of the ankle). "Bring 'em!" the pit boss called, and I dallied quick and turned my horse toward the fire, where the guys mugged the calf down and took my rope off so I could drag another. After the first one, I got into a groove. Chris and I went one for one, and eventually there was only a single calf left. Chris swung and missed. This perked the gang up. I walked in and took my shot, and missed. "Woooooo!" one hand called, razzing us both. Everyone gathered around yelling, "Chris, you better not let some singer out-rope you!" "Don't you worry," he answered, "No way she will!" He swung and missed. Finally I swung and got that last calf clean around the ankles. I was so proud I could have burst. But I remained stoic. Just another day in the office, boys. I took my dally and with my free hand tipped my hat at Chris as I headed out of the pen. To this day, when all the cowboys get together at the bullring they love to tease him about it. He still turns bright red. All those men teased me so much that I am not too proud to say that having the chance to rub it in his face in this book brings no small pleasure. It brings a large one.

Ty was wild in those days. He drank whiskey and carried on. Many nights were spent in honky-tonks, me dead sober, but enjoying the fun everyone was having. When Ty was with me on the road, his presence usually inspired all my band and crew to be a bit braver and a bit wilder. He and Steve Poltz were fast friends. There were many a drunken night when clothes were switched and Steve would be wearing a cowboy getup and Ty his baggy faded 501s and vintage tuxedo shirts, his hat tipped up and cocked to the side at what I called "drunk o'clock." Hotel rooms were trashed in Vegas during the National Finals Rodeo, and once my drummer Trey jumped off the balcony yelling, "I'm a cow-fucking-boy!" after imbibing with Ty. To be fair, he had asked my permission first. I said sure, as long as he knew that no matter what, he had to play the next day. He played the next day with me at Royal Albert Hall with a severely sprained ankle. I remember having him play the kick drum intro to "Everybody Needs Somebody Sometime" extra long to torture him a little. They were fun times.

Those were my last tours overseas, as it was too hard to be gone six months at a time. I realized why so few musicians had serious family lives—they were gone too long to sustain a meaningful connection. I was tired and I was in love and I wanted to give my relationship with Ty a chance. I figured love is a garden, and if you want something else besides daisies to grow, you need to tend to the roses. Despite my critical acclaim for *Ride with the Devil*, I realized I would have to live in Hollywood and go out on auditions on what few days off I had if I wanted a second entertainment career. I enjoyed acting, but I didn't need to be any more rich or famous. I moved instead to Texas with Ty and took a break after *Spirit*.

I just wasn't sure I liked what my career had become. It had gotten bigger and bigger until it was a machine that consumed me. And the machine my mom ran at home exhausted me. It was hard to ever find balance. I wanted to step away and see if I would choose it again. I had sold so many records by this time that I would never have to work again. I wanted to fall back in love with music, and if I didn't, I wanted to fall in love with something else, maybe photography, or visual arts. I spent a lot of time drawing and working with pastels.

My mom appeared to be supportive, and it was nice to get a break from her. She had taken over the house I bought, and when I was there on days off it was full of employees, decorators, and other people. She had business meetings at the house even though she had a second house down the road for an office. I felt pushed out, and every time I tried to voice an opinion it just didn't seem to matter. I didn't matter. She would tell me I needed to be more open-minded and meditate more to bring stillness and silence inside myself. She continued to build an empire and hire more employees, and when I tried to say it made me uncomfortable, she would spend hours talking me into feeling more comfortable. I missed Jacque and Z, and having someone else to consult and talk to. Enter Dean, David, and Solano. Dean channeled an entity named Solano. David was Dean's life partner. Soon they were my mom's best friends, and soon I was sitting alone face-to-face with our new guru Solano. David was an aspiring scriptwriter and my mom gave them their own company to develop scripts, none of which were likely ever made. Thinking about it short-circuited me. My mom was bent on her vision and I was worked on daily to keep it going.

Solano was altogether different from Z. There was no group, no followers. Just me and my mom with our own private channeler. It is very hard to sit here and say that I was involved in something so cultlike. It honestly never dawned on me that I was. Before this I felt lucky to have a spiritual teacher like Z in my life. It was much like church. Z taught love, tolerance, and basic spiritual beliefs like in any other religion. It certainly began to take some bizarre turns near the end, as Jacque channeled Jesus and even an alien at one point. Yeah. It sounds weird to me now as I write about it.

All I can say is it's hard for me to adequately describe the scared girl I was then, how deeply compartmentalized and disassociated I'd become emotionally. What an extension of my mother I had become. How eager I was to believe her, how desperate I was for her love at any price. I was told I would get cancer if I dared decrease my frequency by thinking "low" thoughts. I saw my mom as a visionary and great leader. She had the charisma and influence to draw an army of believers around her, though inevitably there were a few detractors who may have had their doubts and they moved on. I believed Solano was a free and clear third party with no skin in the game who I could use as a neutral sounding board. How dumb I was. I never told a soul about Solano. I never told Ty, although slowly he began to suspect that something was not quite right about my business and my life.

It was around this time that my former manager Inga filed a lawsuit against me for being cut out of future earnings, one that would take years to resolve. All this stress and pressure were making me want to hide, and I thought at least thank God I had millions in the bank to make these problems go away. And that I could afford to take a break and regroup. I wasn't aware that I didn't have the money to do this. My mom played it cool and let me take the time off. Everyone remained on the payroll. It would be a year until I felt ready to work again.

Ty's ranch was beautiful and full of large, wide-open spaces. I wrote and drew, but over time I could see Ty wasn't ready for me to be there full-time. He became uptight and withdrawn. He was a self-professed commitment-phobe, and without asking him about it or making a big deal, I decided to move out after the year. He had been clear from the start that he didn't ever want to be married, and I knew my mom wanted me to be with someone she deemed a spiritual match of some sort. I went back to making records. The single off *This Way* was "Standing Still," about my inability to see where Ty was and what his feelings were with me.

Cutting through the darkest night are my two headlights
Trying to keep it clear, but I'm losing it here
To the twilight
There's a dead end to my left
There's a burning bush to my right
You aren't in sight
You aren't in sight
Do you want me
Like I want you?
Or am I standing still
Beneath the darkened sky
Or am I standing still
With the scenery flying by
Or am I standing still
Out of the corner of my eye
Was that you
Passing me by

Work was always easy for me. When I worked there was no onus from my mom, no programming kicking in—I was free of guilt, shame, and controllers. I thrived on making music and I knew the business inside and out, and called the shots. I took my music in directions I felt it needed to go, following my instincts without doubt. It was a stark contrast to dealing with my mom and money and the things that became crippling, as I was asked again and again to forget myself and my instincts, forgoing my needs for hers.

I lived in a bubble. I had no close friends other than Ty. I never spoke to my lawyer Eric anymore because my mom laced comments into each conversation about him that made me doubt his ability and made me thankful she was there to do the work for me. There was no business manager and I had no other talent manager. One day Ty asked me whether I ever saw bank statements. I said I didn't even know what one was. Everyone else did those things. And the beauty of having your own family involved is that you can trust them. I could just be an artist. Ty said it seemed like something was wrong. A lot of money was going out—did any business *make* money? I didn't know the answer. Ty asked me if I knew how much money I had. I said no. He said I should see bank statements and see what my monthly bills actually were. I sat down with my mom to have a talk.

It was the beginning of a long, slow slide into heartbreak as I unraveled the truth about my finances. It's not that my mom was intentionally trying to ruin me. My perception is that in her mind, I was an extension of her to do with as she pleased. I felt like a sweater she put on and took off. I truly was in the land of Oz. And it wasn't until Ty came along that I was able to see a bit more clearly.

She began waging war against Ty. I was told he was spiritual heroin and that he was lowering my frequency. Solano was gravely concerned for my welfare and my health. I was sure to get cancer. My stress levels were off the charts. I was very much in love with Ty, and he continued to lovingly help me ask questions about my finances. When I showed him the financial documents I'd been given, he looked at me dumbfounded. "These aren't official documents, Jewel. This is a printout from a computer, a document an accountant made. You need to ask to see actual bank statements." He cared and was deeply concerned for me.

I went back and insisted on real bank statements. My mom's team met with me. I saw what I spent per month in bills and salaries and it shocked me. I did not think it was sustainable. We were hemorrhaging money. I told her we had to cut back. Instead, she said, you should go look at ranches for yourself, I know you have been wanting one, it's time. And I had been wanting one. I never spent money on myself. My mom booked private jets for me to go look at ranches with a real estate agent. I had no idea that in reality there was no money for a ranch. I made all my music decisions never caring whether I had a hit because I knew that I personally never spent what I'd already made. And I believed whatever my mom was spending was easily made back because eventually her empire would pay off.

As I looked at ranches, Ty came with me and advised on whether a place was worthwhile or not. But in the end I decided to put off the search for a while. I wanted to see where it went with Ty, plus I had to get back on tour and back to dealing with the lawsuit with Inga. We filed a countersuit and the battle went on for years. It had finally come to a head and it was time for me to get in a room with her. In the judge's chambers in Los Angeles I saw Inga for the first time since we'd fired her in my house in San Diego. She looked exactly the same as the day we'd met, when I was a homeless kid singing in a coffee shop. I remembered first seeing her show up with Jenny Price. Inga had long, thick hair and deep, dark brown eyes. She was of Russian Jewish descent and had traces of an accent left. She was young, bright, a go-getter. I remembered how she'd sat with her mouth open as I'd sang. As that night wore on, she and Jenny both had their heads propped up on their hands, looking like they had fallen in love with me. And now here we were, sitting next to each other in a judge's chambers. The judge had asked to see us alone, no lawyers. No momager. Life was a funny thing.

"What do you guys want?" the judge started. I studied his hands as they moved like the wings of an exasperated bird, fluttering open and closed as he spoke. I was quiet. So was Inga. It didn't seem like he was really asking us. "Look. You guys can take this case to court. You can fight it out. And honestly I have no idea who will win. Except I know one thing for sure—no one wins." I looked at Inga, who had a habit of clearing her nose just before she spoke and did so, but must have thought the better of speaking. She looked down at her lap. The judge said, "What would it take for you to just settle this?" I can't remember how it happened, but we agreed to settle. I was tired of fighting.

I felt relief as we walked out of the chambers. I was just happy to be over with it. The judge communicated our agreement to our lawyers. Out of the corner of my eye, I saw my mom walk up to the lawyers and judge. She asked to speak with me and my lawyer privately. I was gathered and we went into a small windowless room off to the side. We were standing in a triangle, facing one another. My mom spoke, but the words seemed unreal. "Jewel doesn't have the money to pay her."

I stared at her dumbfounded. She chose this moment to tell us that I was broke. She was one hell of a poker player but her hand had been called and she had to show her cards. The next thing I knew I was back in the judge's chambers with Inga and her lawyer, my mom, my lawyer. I could only hear the blood in my head and my breath straining to remain even. The judge said I was broke and asked what we would do about it. Would Inga accept less, would I make a payment plan? Inga charged in, incredulous. "How can she be broke? She sold seventeen million albums! She wrote every song!" We both looked at my mom. "Where did it all go?" Inga said. My mom sat still as a desert day. Her hands peacefully folded in her lap. A Buddha's smile on her face. Calm. Tranquil. A payment plan was devised. I don't remember leaving. I don't remember the payment plan. I do remember going back to work.

Many fights with my mom ensued. I demanded to see every bill, to sign every check. There were hundreds. Long talks over the phone when I called from backstage before going on, after approving a packet of bills I was sent. The overhead was not going down quickly enough. She told me I was like a fire alarm that would not turn off. She said it took time. My heartache and disbelief were staggering. My need to keep up the illusion of my mom's love kept costing me dearly. It was a confusing web to untangle. My mom was unwavering in her vision and I was still trying so hard to see what she saw.

Ty stood by me through all this. He was sweet and we continued to be in love, but there was a wall there. He was pretty emotionally unavailable and still made it clear he would never marry me. My mom stepped in with extra love, extra doting, extra care. She said she would fix everything. My mom hated Ty. Ty hated my mom. I loved them both. There was a great tug-of-war and I felt like the rope. I knew my mom would love me forever. I reasoned Ty probably would not. He was not kin. He did not want me like I wanted him. Finally, to relieve some of the enormous strain and pressure, I gave in to my mom and Solano and did the right thing. I chose life. I chose being cancer-free. I chose my family. I left Ty.

It broke my heart into a million pieces, and all I can say is it took a hell of a sales job by my mom and Solano to get me to do it. Hours had been spent talking me into it. They said Ty was a fun dalliance but that it was time to return to my position and duty, as if we were royalty and I had to return to the castle and take my rightful place. They said all Ty wanted was for me to cook and clean and fall asleep on his kitchen floor. It's true Ty was traditional, but he liked that I worked and was a modern woman, I thought. They said again that he was deadening my frequency. Frequency was everything. I deeply feared being sick, and still struggled with bladder and kidney infections. Maybe if I left Ty, everything would go back to normal. I would focus on work. I would be loyal to my mom. We would go back to getting along. I would earn my money back.

But first I wanted to fully understand my finances, and so I hired an independent auditor to show me what the heck was going on and how to fix it. I was sure my mom and I would then put our heads together and we would come out of this intact. I believed I could still fix it.

twenty-five

truth over fantasy

The last time I saw my mom's face or spoke with her was in 2003. We were in a conference room at my new manager Irving Azoff's office building. I hired Irving just after I released my pop record *0304*.

Irving is a living legend in the music business. He had come recommended, but with a few warnings. I Googled him and discovered an enigmatic and intriguing figure. He came to see me in New York, where I was working. Several things were immediately evident: He was smart. He was funny—playful and mischievous, really. He was loyal. Irving had a keen ability to get to the heart of any matter. A half hour into our discussion I confessed I had read a lot of confusing things about him—one article went so far as to call him the devil. He chuckled and said, "Well, let me tell you how Don Henley responded when he was asked about that. He said, 'Irving may be the devil, but he's my devil.'" Irving would not shy from doing something controversial if he felt it was right for his artist. He proved this to me again and again once we began working together. Irving feared no one and nothing if he believed in your talent. He trusted my instincts at any cost. He was also a wonderful partner in crime. I remember Irving saying, "I have tried to be nice modern Irving, but I am about to get seventies on his ass!" I almost cried laughing as he told me about the styles of whoop ass he has handed out over the decades. I never saw Irving start a fight, but I have seen him be very creative in ending them. He told me once that he sent someone who had wronged him and his artist a never-ending fax for days that said, "Fuck You," over and over on the page. He always had my back, and if I needed to make a left turn musically, he simply asked how sharp a turn I'd like to make.

I'd spent the year leading up to this trying to fix things with my mom, but instead of my finances making more sense, the more I looked into them, the more convoluted and bizarre things had become for me. It was like living in a nightmare. Forget Oz—I felt like Alice in Wonderland waking up from a bad trip. I had fallen down a rabbit hole, and now all the pretty colors and cartoon candy faces had revealed themselves to be far less pretty. The auditor I hired discovered I had gone broke several times in my career. Not only was I broke but as we dug deeper I also found out I was in significant debt. My mom had published a book called *The Architecture of All Abundance*, under her new spiritual name, Lenedra. I had helped her promote it. It was about creating abundance in one's life. In it I felt she made herself sound noble, almighty, all-knowing, responsible for all my abundance, now gone. It made me look like a bumbling, scared kid who knew nothing and needed her.

I tried not to think about it, and focused on the fact I was in debt. I hated debt. My worst fear was being homeless again. I looked at the assets I had that could be sold. There was my house in San Diego, filled with expensive art. There was an office in San Diego.

I was in shock but tried to keep my attention on what I could do. I have always been at my best when all the chips are down. Plus, I could live with nothing. I was not attached to anything. I just wanted to be out of the hole. I could tolerate the intolerable, as many children of abuse learn to do. Selling everything off would get me out of debt, and as I put the finishing touches on my pop record, I knew it had to be a success so I could get back on my feet.

Most normal people at this point would tell their parent to shove off, but I couldn't go that far. I couldn't cut the cord entirely, or envision life without my mom in it. But I did work up the courage to tell her we should consider not working together anymore—I wanted to just be her daughter, and I wanted her to just be my mom. This was very hard for me to do. I was scared and lonely, and deep down I sensed that if my mom quit being my manager, she would also quit being my mother. Solano's words kept ringing in my ears: "If you leave your mom, what is yours will decline and what is your mom's will continue to rise." I also couldn't help thinking of what Nedra had told me about one of our friends. He had worked for us, and after he quit, my mom told me he had developed cancer. I felt terrible for him. Separation equaled sickness. But I had to separate our business and family lives, so I carried on.

I got back to work. I was given a tall order on the first single off *0304*, because my mom had arranged a deal with Schick. They had paid me and the label to name my next single after their new razor. When the deal was coming together, Val Azzoli, the head of my label, took me aside and said he was concerned that it was not in my best interest. But my mom had prepared for this and had already planted the likelihood in my head that the label would try to stop us, but that it was best for me. I signed the deal. I set about trying to write a hit single called "Intuition." I wrote about twelve different incarnations and hated all of them. It was nearly impossible to write a single with a hook that revolved around intuition, and it couldn't sound like a sellout or a TV commercial. It had to sound like a song I'd written and that a company later heard and wanted to license. That's what I wanted at least. And it had to be in line with my new musical vision as well. I had wanted to make a pop record for some time, but starting it this way took a lot of focus and skill to pull off.

I began working with Lester Mendez, a young producer and song-writer. We had music chemistry and wrote feverishly together. I wanted a dance record that had soul. I wanted pop music with poetic lyrics. I wanted to re-create my version of postwar big band music. I wanted to write clever pop songs like Cole Porter did. The country was at war, Bush was president, everyone was scared of terrorists in a post-9/11 world. I wanted to be free. I wanted to dance. I wanted to feel young and like everything was okay. I loved writing *0304*, even as my life fell down around my ears. Once again writing saved me. My mom's voice began to fade, and I could hear my soul speak to me. I wrote "Becoming," eerily full of portent, though still I didn't know the extent of what I was dealing with. A deep part of me was screaming at myself to wake up.

Listen, heart
Listen close—listen
to the melancholy
Melody of your own voice
I am weary of my own dreaming
I am tired of waiting
So this time, I'm leaping

I am hurting
Oh, I am not yet born
I am the mother and the father
Of what is not yet known
Darkness surrounds me
I scratch, I struggle, I breathe
I'm witnessing my own becoming

The beginning of the album was the beginning of the end for my mom and me. I told no one what was going on. I quit talking to Solano, though Dean called often. I would not give up and just fall in line again, although I held out an impossible hope that I would see it was all just an honest mistake and my mom and I would get to live happily ever after. I was desperately alone. No Ty, my relationship with my mom strained even as she kept managing me. There were many days I cried in the vocal booth, where no one could see me, trying to keep my throat relaxed enough to let the song escape and lift me. I would walk out of the booth, a smile painted on my face, and get back to dealing.

I was in my room at the Sunset Tower the day I finally saw who my mom really was. I had been trying to get her to sign off on selling her vacation house. I needed the money, as I was unable to tour or work while I made the record. She kept stalling. I had invited her over, thinking we could resolve this once and for all. She always had that calm Buddha's smile on her face. She had never once apologized for all that had happened. It just "was." The prevailing wisdom around me was that there was nothing that was truly real. Not the way most people thought of things as real. It was all a projection of our spirit's wanting. Life itself was only what we chose it to be, and if a person chose pain or illness, it was what their soul wanted. If I was broke, then it was an experience I must have wanted. I sat in that hotel room and pleaded with her. She needed to sign it over to me so I could sell it. Finally she cracked. I had never seen her speak above practically a whisper my whole life, and suddenly the mask fell away. She screamed at the top of her lungs, "*I will give you the fucking house!*" Spittle flew from her mouth. Her face was twisted with such sudden rage and anger that I sat back in my seat. She scared the daylights out of me. I knew then that she would not give it to me. She would not let it go. She never did.

When I hired Irving, he helped me find a good and reputable business manager, Lester Knispel. Irving and Lester spent countless hours helping me dismantle all the organizations that had been built around me. In a bizarre turn I still can't explain, the auditor I had been working with disappeared. We could find no trace of her. It was completely strange. So I had to start from the beginning again, and Lester had to sort through all the books. I had to pay severance to every employee. A bitter pill does not begin to describe it. Money I did not have. My mom and I had quit talking. I kept working on the album and moving that ball forward. It was my only hope and it was my joy. My salvation in more than one way yet again.

I would never get to sell her vacation home. I was on my own and it was up to me to clean up the mess. I did not want more fighting. We would never have a coming together of the minds. I would never get an apology. I would never get a hug. And I would have killed for just a hug. I was alone, a scared little girl.

I decided to walk away and be done with it. Let go. Forgive. Rebuild. I didn't want to let her ruin me this way, or ruin my legacy. I didn't want to be known as the girl who was broke. The girl who once believed she and her mom were the same soul in two bodies. I was deeply ashamed and embarrassed. I wanted her gone and that was all I wanted. We had to have a legal parting of ways. I needed her to absolve herself of my career and all future earnings. I needed her to sign an agreement saying so, and I needed my lawyer for this, so he could draft up the paperwork. I would have to tell him everything. Well, almost.

I remember calling Eric—the same Eric who had come to my show in San Diego years earlier before I was signed. He had been with me ever since, though we rarely talked once my mom took over. He was surprised to hear my voice. I had no idea how to start, so I just blurted it out. "Eric. I'm broke. I'm in debt. I need my mom out of my life and I need you to draft something that she can sign." He was dumbfounded. It took him a while to catch up with my words. Everyone in the business knew my mom and I were best friends. We held hands everywhere we went. The first thing he asked was whether I was okay. I was so surprised by the tenderness it brought tears to my eyes. It was hard to be seen like this, even just a little, and I was unprepared for empathy. Tears began to flood down my cheeks. "Not really," I said weakly. "But I'm dealing."

A few weeks later I sat across from my mom in the conference room of Irving's office. Irving, Lester, Eric, and I sat on one side of an impossibly long wooden table. On the other, my mom and her lawyer. I shook with adrenaline and fear. She sat still. Her hair freshly dyed blonde. Her capped teeth pearly white. The same Buddha smile. Hands folded in her lap. This was my mother. This was the woman I had known my whole life and loved dearly as life itself, and yet never knew. And this was how it was all to end. As the lawyers spoke, my mind drifted back to the days in San Diego. Her bedroom was painted in a pearlescent white that shimmered. Her bed was white and ghostly, and sheer drapes fluttered in the breeze when the patio door was open. It felt like the inner sanctum of a palace. We would lie on her bed, that warm wind playing with our hair, laughing like schoolgirls. Sharing secrets. She would hold me and pet my hair and it felt like the sun was shining down on me. God how I loved that woman with my whole heart and being. And it almost killed me. And still there is such a sad and tender girl in me who tears up thinking back on this same image. I would always be a child. I would always love my mom.

When it was all done and decided, she looked at me for the first time that day, and said, "I look forward to just being your mom now." I knew better. I never saw her again.

I think about my son reading this one day. I think about what I tell him every night: Mommies always love their babies. I will always be your mommy. I love you when you are angry or happy or sad or silly. I love you all the time.

This is not always true. Some mommies don't love their babies like that. I can't tell you the tears I've cried to see who my mom really is. I can't tell you about the pain, and how my heart to this day screams to have a mom in my life. But I know that it is not safe with her. Every day I miss having a mom. But I don't miss Nedra. I will always want a mom, the concept of what a mom is. But I don't have that. I never did, no matter how hard I tried to fool myself. Nedra is not that. Reality wins, and I'd rather see the truth than stay in love with a fantasy.

THE INFINITE ACHE

disoriented
standing in the shadow
of what yesterday
was a great brightness
in my life
so sure the brightness was forever
that I'm confused now
by the feeling
that shadow is all
there is left

how could this be?

yesterday I knew the sun
it was so present in my life
that I was sure
I could never be unsure again
so happy that I just knew
there could never be
sorrow again

worst of all
ashamed

feeling like a bad child
cast from heaven
by some deed I did in my
    unknowing
I search for my badness
so that I may expunge it
so I might feel the grace of
    sunlight on
my face again
shame robbing me of the
true gift

often I have been gripped
by the terrifying fist
of a sadness so complete
it shut out the sun entirely
like an eclipse
I had landed
on the other side
of myself
a stranger to me

. . .

this sadness has come and gone
since childhood and so
ever a student of nature
here is what I learned:
there is nothing wrong with me.
    nothing.
in fact, my sadness
is the result of something right

I am not just body but also spirit
and so it is true in reverse
I am not just spirit but body
and my body has the same salt
in its cells as the ocean does
and is under the same influence
as all living things
the physics of being an organic
    being
on earth mean I cannot escape
the natural rhythm and order
    of things
by praying it away
and shame only locks me out
of my experiencing the gift
paralyzing me with fear instead
of reaping the benefits of the cycle

sometimes the tide is just out
but it always comes back in
sometimes hibernation is required
to build and prepare for a new
    season of awakening
sometimes there is devastation
fire burns it all down cleansing
    allowing rebirth

there is a wisdom in death
and we experience a shedding of
    our skin
many many times in life
and in fact the more committed
we are to living
the more deaths we experience
along the way

loss of friends who no longer
    feel like
who we have become over time

loss of self, even
loss of "girl" as we redefine
ourselves as woman and mother
loss of fertility as we redefine
    ourselves
as matriarch and goddess
wisdom keepers and doers
free of small children and able
to focus on self after so long

. . .

loss of boy as eros consumes
loss of eros as husband emerges
death of child ego as manhood
must take root
redefined by the need to no longer
be the center of the family
but the supporter of wife
    and child
rediscovery and redefinition of self
as husband and father die within
    giving way
so that
the next phase where self must be
attended by self and self alone
may come fully into realization
when elderly

and so many deaths in between
as we re-create who and how we
    want to be in the world

I have learned to treasure the
eclipse of my soul
to let myself explore fully the
    infinite
ache the sorrow when it washes
    over me
for to resist is to miss it
and to miss it is to not fully grasp
what is next in my life because I

struggle so hard to keep what was
and this is truly painful

hanging on is much more painful
than listening in the darkness
for my future calling to me

let all else fade away for a few
    moments
spend some time with sorrow
see what it is asking for
there is a deep wisdom in you
tapping yourself on the shoulder
asking for some attention
it asks quietly at first, but if ignored
it will demand you listen
by creating so much discord
    you must
finally pay attention
it will not be denied
for to deny it is to
be buried alive
inside your own flesh
as your inner life and outer life
become so out of sync
drastic changes must be made
to rectify them

make them!
live!

give yourself permission!
write so you may see
the snakeskin of your soul
as it sheds
read the scales so you may see
who you have been
and honor it

then get excited

even in this time of mourning

for something new your way comes
nothing is wrong with you
you are alive and living and growing

if we are truly pushing ourselves
    to learn
we are reborn
many times in one life

have the courage
right now
to sit in your sorrow
in your silence and know

something is right with you

your body is working beautifully
it is experiencing a longing
from your soul

and making room for something
    new
in your life
it is emptying its self out
getting rid of what no longer serves
tune your ear to what is next
trust your body to do its work
nature knows its job
trust it knowing soon
you will be full again
(never doubt this—it's a
    mathematical certainty—the
only mystery is the quality you will
    be filled with, which will
be determined by the quality and
    creativity and the thoroughness
of your grieving)
turn your ear toward it
so you may calibrate
to the level to which you want
    to rise
bring your consciousness
to the moment
don't numb out
don't escape
don't rob yourself of the gift
so that you may better choose
    and guide
and inform what should be next
    for you
get to know the exact nature

of your discontent
for only in becoming intimate
with what we lack
may we know what to replace
    it with
be vulnerable enough
to want without knowing if you
    will receive it
dare this much
engage your creativity
let your mind daydream about

how you wish it to be
imagine the face of what is unborn
and have the courage to name it
don't rush

for you are pregnant with yourself
a new you
and it has its own gestation period
because you cannot
force nature
only nurture it

twenty-six

brilliant resilience

It was a huge risk to make *0304*. When I'd originally come up with the concept I thought I had all the money in the world, and had never before let money govern my decision about what direction to go. With "Intuition," I made a song I loved even though it was manipulated into being. It was still an authentic part of my soul and I was proud of it and believed in what it said. Knowing how much I needed the money made it surreal. So much was on the line, though I never doubted my direction. It was a risk in terms of the media or those who did not follow my career closely. My real fans saw it coming. I had experimented with loops on my third album, *This Way*, with tracks like "Jupiter" and "Serve the Ego." I began doing dance remixes. I was pushing myself. I felt if an artist was put in a box, it was their own fault for not being willing to break out of it. Now was not the time to safety up. I had to define what being a sellout meant to me. Being a sellout was doing what everyone expected of you, if it went against your own instincts or heart. I could have done *You Were Meant for Me 2* and the press would have loved it and said I was being true to my roots, but I would have felt like a sellout. Only we know when we are being true to the small and quiet voice that whispers from our soul. Very few on the outside of our skin are in a position to know. Bob Dylan and Neil Young taught me that. The fans will know the difference between changes made of contrivance versus authenticity. And if they didn't, I would. I knew it would be controversial but I was tired of being controlled, of being told as a woman that I had to hide my sexuality to be considered smart. I doubled down on my instincts.

As usual my label heard nothing until I turned it in. Ron Shapiro was still my champion at Atlantic, along with Craig Kallman, Judy Greenwald, and Andrea Ganis. They all believed in it and my vision, and we went for it. I went to Europe to tour, and while I was there my label called me to say "Intuition" was at the top of the charts. My video, which I thought clearly articulated my satirical comments on pop culture, was widely viewed but also wildly misunderstood, which tickled me to no end. It infuriated people to see me dolled up. It was polarizing, although I felt it was in line with my values—to question, to seek, to explore. Regardless, it became a performance piece, illustrating the mindlessness in culture and the fight for irony alongside the fight for truth alongside the right for sexuality alongside the right to just have fun. I remember talking with Clive Davis about writing for an artist of his, and even he said no one wants to see this generation's Joni Mitchell wear a miniskirt. It created a huge debate, and that was all I could have hoped for. I never hoped to tell people what to think with my music; I hoped to start a conversation so they could think about it for themselves. My experiences at this point made me more determined to never be dogmatic in my music. I was so relieved my single was doing well. God knows I needed it to be. I had done it against impossible odds, and I would slowly get back on my feet. I would never get back what I had lost, but I would be okay.

After my European tour I went back to the States. And I went back to Ty.

It was hard to come to terms with the fact that I had let go of a man who loved me and stayed with a mom who did not. I chose so wrongly. I told Ty as much. We rekindled our relationship, though he was hurt by our parting and I had to earn back his trust. He was an absolute knight in shining armor. He stood by me and held me when I cried. He stayed up nights talking with me as I tried to make sense of it all. And when there were no words, he stayed close as I tried to heal a broken heart. I confided all the things I had never told him before. All the things I never told anyone. I told him about how Jacque was not just a dear friend but about Z as well. I told him about Dean and Solano. Telling this to a true-blue cowboy was quite an experience. He turned to me and said, "Jewel, I think you were in a goddamned cult!"

I told him about all the things I'd been raised believing. That I could control the lights with my mind if I focused hard enough. That when I failed it meant I didn't have enough focus. That life was a web of inter-connectedness, and that if I didn't anticipate something in my life it was because I was not connected enough. That if we could harness and fully grasp our true genius and spirituality we would be able to absorb the frequency of any object around us, even be able to walk through walls. Again, I'd always failed. That I would be sick if I lowered my frequency too much. There were some legitimate spiritual beliefs and practices, es-pecially in the beginning, but with time the net effect made me feel insig-nificant, subservient, obedient.

Ty was the opposite of all this, it seemed, and it felt good. There was nothing touchy-feely about this man. No gray area. It was all black and white and real in his world, and I needed that. He felt like rock-solid earth that I could fall the hell apart on. I began to research cults and how they worked and came across the word *programming* a lot. I don't know if what I was involved in was a cult in the classic sense, but I did know I had ideas and thoughts in my head that didn't belong to me. It was hard to tell where I ended and my mom began. My mind felt as if someone had shattered it with a hammer. There was a lot of guilt and shame, and I trusted no one, especially when it came to my mind. My God, I could spend years in therapy and never get over this. I wanted to look back over my life and think of everything my mom had ever told me, to try to see whether any of it was real. I called my dad.

My dad told me that he didn't blackmail my mom into letting him keep us. She told him she was tired of being a mom. He told me that she did not have cancer that year we lived in Anchorage. She had told him that she had one year to live and that he needed to give her the money to have us for one year. Every single thing I thought I knew about her no longer seemed real. Nothing about my life seemed real. I found out our former employee had never had cancer. Suddenly the grief and stress of everything I had gone through, it all caught up with me, and I could not just go back out on the road like nothing had happened. I had been juggling all this while I worked. I was smiling on the cover of every magazine. I did all the interviews and all the TV shows. My album was a hit. But I needed to stop. I needed to be with Ty. I called Irving and said I needed to cancel my American tour. He didn't bat an eye. He asked if I was okay. I said I would be. He said okay, he would take care of it. I would make no money.

I was on my way to the bathroom one day—where all eureka moments happen, right?—when I caught a glimpse of myself in the mirror. I knew something in a flash. It was like a revelation. I see thoughts visually. I saw an image of light that had layers upon layers of sediment covering it up. But the light was under there, intact. I said to myself, *A soul is not a teacup. It is not a chair. It cannot be broken.* I knew I was alive in there. I was just covered in layers of shit that did not belong to me. That idea would be my key to deprogramming. The idea of therapy was depressing to me, and I didn't trust a therapist or a support group at this point. I was terrified to give anyone influence over my mind again. But I saw that I had been operating on the premise that I was ruined and needed to fix myself. I knew in that instant that I was not broken and I did not need to be fixed. I needed to go on an archaeological dig back to myself, where I was still there. Whole. Unspoiled. I had a memory of myself as whole, before all the heartbreak. I remember being a child and lying on my back in a green field and I felt free. I could shut my eyes, go inward to this part of myself, and tell when a thought or a feeling was not part of my genuine self, and I could gently push it away. I could lovingly remove all that had been put on me. It would lead me back to myself.

I called this exercise "self and other." Thoughts that stemmed from me had a distinctly calming feeling, a warmth and a soothing effect. Thoughts and fears that stemmed from programming had a completely separate feel—anxious, metallic, colder. They left me feeling tense and frightened. When I felt triggered—if something made me suddenly highly emotional—I used the phrase *if it's hysterical, it's historical* as a rule of thumb, to acknowledge that whatever was affecting me in the present was probably reminding me of something more damaging from my past. I learned to go off by myself, sit, close my eyes, and focus inward. I would breathe into my body and ask what had set me off. Something angered me once, and someone who was with me said, "Don't be angry, it will just make you sick." For most people this is a kind and caring thing to say. For me it triggered memories of never feeling allowed to express anger or any emotion contrary to my mom's needs and wishes. There was still a part of me that believed it and a part of me that became incensed when I heard those words, and neither reaction actually had anything to do with the person in front of me or the current situation. The disconnect between my fear and emotion and the conversational stimulus was my first clue that a "hysterical" reaction was "historical." It took me a minute to calm down enough to access my own thoughts and ask myself whether this was my self or other. I could not come up with an answer until I asked myself specifically, "Do you think feelings like anger can make you sick?" Suddenly I said aloud, "I think stress is harmful, and has negative effects on your health. I think our thoughts affect us. But I think expressing anger and darker feelings allows the energy to move out of your body, and that is better than holding them in and denying them." This sounded more like me!

I noticed while examining my thoughts and reclaiming my beliefs that there was a grain of truth in things my mom told me. She appealed to a part of me that was altruistic and ideal, playing to my genuine nature and then slowly using my own strengths against me, to the point where I was not allowed to take even the smallest pride or pleasure in what I built, nor to feel entitled to the fruits of my own hard work. My mom is not all good or all bad. Like each of us she is comprised of a million variances of gray. I don't think she set out to ruin me, or us. She is not Evil. I believe she was doing what she felt was in accordance to a higher calling she believed in and that, in her mind, justified the means.

how our natural gifts get exploited

I can handle anything was another natural gift that had served me well many times in my life but that started working against me. I could handle a lot. But at what point was I allowed to say it's not about how much I can handle—it's about whether I should be handling it? So much of my self-worth was tied to the belief that I could handle anything that I never stopped to wonder—should I? I just felt like a good dog when someone piled more on for me to deal with. If they patted me on the head, I did anything gladly. It took learning to love myself on a whole new level to let go of this as a source of self-worth and to say, If you were loved, you would not be asked to do this, no matter how capable you are.

Another natural gift I had was an inclination toward philosophical thinking—the concept that our thoughts form our reality and thus our lives, and health. This idea was perverted for me at a young age and made me solely responsible for every time I got sick (and eventually for any bad thing that might ever happen to me), and closed my mind from wondering whether it was just a physiological problem with my kidneys. I began to let go of the notion that I alone was responsible for *it all*. I learned to take a truth I came by naturally or when I was young and to update it to complement who and what I was—expanding on philosophy with real experience and knowledge from where I stood now.

Reality is dualistic by nature, because there is the subject we look at and the person looking at the subject. Before we can decide how to interpret reality we must first make sure we are seeing reality. Really seeing it. Not fooling ourselves. Not letting wishes or wants or wounds become the filter through which we perceive reality. If we can give up the myth that we can control facts and truth, thus distorting them through our willfulness and need, then we can use our mind and spirit to *choose* what we do with those facts and how we continue to experience them. We must practice seeing with clear eyes before we can exercise our power to effect meaningful change.

innocence is not lost—it is
traded for wisdom

Betrayal converts our innocence to wisdom if we can let go of pain, bitterness, and fear and create enough self-love and safety for ourselves to allow it to do so. I kept my original feelings and built on them until I was rid of the part that did not belong to me.

The truth was I could never make my mom love me or be tender toward me without giving her something in return. No amount of wishful thinking or good deed or compliance would change that. I had tried for years not to see that truth and to will a different reality. It was a myth and I had to face that now. But how I allowed her treatment to affect me, how I allowed her betrayal to affect me, was up to me. That was the only power I had.

I WENT THROUGH SEVERAL PHASES that helped me confront my feelings of betrayal and discovered that each of them had to be experienced fully in order to heal. I learned to see them as distinct stages in reading psychotherapist Melanie Brown Kroon's valuable insights on aplacetoheal.com.

Shock, which comes in many forms. It can cause an urge to run (flight) or an incapacity to move (fright). It can feel like numbness or chaos. Your mind swirls in anger, disbelief, humiliation, sadness, as it tries to grapple with an old reality being shattered by a new one. In a crisis it is so important to talk about it, if you can, to help understand your feelings and lessen the impact. I wish I had found a support group, a twelve-step program like Al-Anon or one specifically for those who had been in a situation like mine. I want to tell anyone who feels isolated and alone that you are not going through something that no one has ever gone through. You are not alone. Reach out to support groups if you don't have friends. Don't let shame keep you from finding connection and healing. After being isolated for so long, I had to work hard at finding friends who loved me and were a safe place to turn to when I needed help. I was terrified to be seen as less than perfect or to be myself, especially if I sensed it was not what people needed me to be. Twelve years later I have three friends who hold a place for me in their hearts and who remind me of my worth in moments I can't feel it for myself. I consider myself rich for their love and friendship.

Grieving the loss of a person whom I loved. I had to see my mom for who she was and let her go. I had to accept that missing having a mom was less painful than having the one I had in my life. No one will ever replace what she should have been, but I'm okay with that. I know now I am strong enough to love myself enough for the both of us on those inevitable days I wish I had a soft shoulder or a warm place to land.

Grieving the loss of the person I thought I knew. This step is unique to betrayal. I was in a relationship with a person who did not actually exist. I had to grieve the loss of the person I thought I knew first. There are lots of questions in this phase: Why? Why did it happen? Why me? Why did they do this to me? A need to understand it and how you could have been so wrong is very painful. It's hard not to let your self-esteem become wrapped up in the equation. You must remember betrayal is not about you—it's about the other person. It's a crime to let their betrayal cause you to doubt your own goodness and worth. Piercing the veil of this fantasy, and grieving for its loss, was the impetus for my next album, *Goodbye Alice in Wonderland*. We trade in fantasy, it is a currency, and I wanted nothing to do with it anymore. I wanted truth. The title track distinguishes between dreaming as a positive act that helps us create and envision a new world for ourselves versus dreaming as a tool we use to fool ourselves about the truth.

Forgiving the person who betrayed me. People often confuse forgiveness with condonation. Forgiving someone doesn't mean you condone or approve of what they did. Forgiveness is not for the other person at all. It has nothing to do with whether they deserve it or not. Forgiveness is an act of self-love. The best revenge really is a life well lived. While fantasizing about all kinds of revenge was fun for a while, I realized it would only perpetuate what I wanted to be free of, and it would keep me from healing. My advice to anyone struggling with betrayal is don't let yourself be abused twice. First by the act committed against you, and second by believing it has ruined your ability to experience happiness, trust, or love. Forgive someone who has hurt you so they may receive that gift, and more important because you know it is the scissor that cuts the cord that binds you together. Remember that betrayal doesn't happen *to* you so much as it happens *by* someone else. Forgiveness allows you to release anger. Carrying anger with you is like lighting your own house on fire to get rid of rats. The rats run to safety while you burn yourself down. Forgive. Let go. Heal.

Self-forgiveness has been the hardest for me. Shame and humiliation kept me from speaking out for a long time. It has been very, very hard to forgive myself for having been fooled. For not watching the money when I should have known better, and because I was capable of learning to do it for myself. For adopting beliefs that ran so counter to my own instincts. Me, who set out on a journey at age fifteen to avoid being a statistic and landed right in the biggest cliché. Me, who read books about reason and science and fell for the biggest bunch of malarkey a person could. I felt like a failure, and I can't tell you how many nights I have lain awake shaking my head, sick to my stomach with humiliation, guilt, and shame.

Irving (who never knew the details of my life with my mother) told me that he was sure I knew what was happening with the money and that I let my mom do it because I loved her. He said, "You're too bright not to have known what was happening, Jewel." I was flattered that he thought I was bright, and yet it felt hopeless to try to explain how I could not have known. I actually believed I should be able to slow time down enough to catch a missed flight! I felt like a liar and a phony. It took a long time to have enough self-love to see what I'd been up against, to see my part in everything, and to see the part of it that was simply a young child's innate trust in her mom that could not be guarded against. I had wounds that made me vulnerable. That was my part in it, but there is no shame in that.

The difference between guilt and shame is best described for me in Brené Brown's book *Daring Greatly*. She wrote separately on her blog, "There is a profound difference between shame and guilt. I believe that guilt is adaptive and helpful—it's holding something we've done or failed to do up against our values and feeling psychological discomfort. I define shame as the intensely painful feeling or experience of believing that we are flawed and therefore unworthy of love and belonging—something we've experienced, done, or failed to do makes us unworthy of connection. I don't believe shame is helpful or productive. In fact, I think shame is much more likely to be the source of destructive, hurtful behavior than the solution or cure. I think the fear of disconnection can make us dangerous." There is another book I read many years after this time in my life called *Focusing*, by a philosopher and psychotherapist named Eugene Gendlin. He and a group of colleagues discovered that internal transformation in a person was not contingent on the type of therapy received, but rather that it was dependent on a process the patient engaged in inwardly. With practice, the natural tendency to engage in this self-reflection is teachable even to those who may not naturally do it. I highly recommend this book if you are interested to know more. It can be practiced on one's own or with a trusted friend. I like this method because it does not require money and can be done on its own, yet it also helps if you are already in traditional therapy. It goes beyond an intellectual understanding of a problem and helps engage your whole being in healing, affording real breakthroughs. When I read the book I recognized instantly that it was a process my writing led me to naturally since I was quite young, helping me get beyond merely my mind and into what I call my greater sense of intelligence. Our minds are wonderful tools but can also create a lot of interference or circular thoughts and chatter, which do not let us access our real intuition and truth.

I do believe in therapy, and recently have started going for the first time in my life. But it is important to find a therapist who works for you. I found it can be helpful to go in with a goal and that you use your therapist to help you effect change in that area. Therapy is like a road trip—it's important to look in the rearview mirror and see where you have been, but you also need to know where you want to end up. Without knowing your goal, and developing a plan to get there, and spending time imagining and creating new neural pathways to support it, you will find yourself looping back to where you have already been because the roads are so familiar. It takes years to embrace a new emotional habit. A good therapist can help you look at the motivations and wounds from the past, and then help you make decisions about where you would like to be so you have an opportunity to actuate change.

It's also important to look at different types of therapy. A breakthrough experience for me came just recently at a wonderful place called Onsite in Tennessee. They use some different modalities and do retreats that can create a real life-changer for participants. The Living Centered Program is my particular favorite, and their new facility for those suffering from trauma is very good. It was very useful in helping me process and find tools to deal with things that trigger trauma in me. I like to call it human school. Therapy is expensive, and often the best facilities and practitioners are not covered by insurance, and so mental health becomes a luxury. I think that's a shame, but there are still resources for anyone unwilling to accept unhappiness or emotional pain. No one in need of help deserves to feel like the answers exist solely beyond their own skin. Our happiness and fulfillment can be achieved with or without traditional therapy, with or without a supportive spouse, money, or a family we feel safe with. It is our birthright.

It has been important for me each time I faced betrayal to spend as much time visualizing my new happiness and new life as I have spent replaying and mourning the loss of the happiness and life I thought I had. It's important to examine our hurt, our loss. It's natural to feel rage and anger and to fantasize our perpetrators coming to a perfectly devised end, but it is very important to also spend as much creative energy imagining a life for yourself beyond your current pain. New neural pathways need to be built. Let the addictive nature of our brains work for us— spend time visualizing what you want, instead of what has caused pain. Taste it. Smell it. Imagine the love you want. Get specific about how you want to be treated. Imagine your life in a new house or at a new job. This is the groundwork required for creating a place of happiness. It begins in believing it's possible. Then we take steps to bring it into our lives. Do the things that lead to the happiness you want. Make sure your hands carry those thoughts out into the world and do not serve your negative thoughts. Discipline is key. Change one thing about your life when you wake up. To have a different life, you have to behave differently.

Brilliant resilience. We have all heard of coping mechanisms. When we hear the phrase, we think of negative ways of coping with difficult times, like turning to a medicator to help numb our feelings—be that work, drugs, sex. Medicators can take the form of compartmentalization, or disassociation. I can see now that many of us also find brilliant ways to cope—ways that don't harm, but serve us. With time, however, they can also limit our ability to feel and experience fullness and joy. Our greatest strength can become our greatest weakness. This happens when we harness one of our natural gifts to get us through hard times, but after time it becomes an armor we use to protect ourselves, and ultimately it can cut us off from our ability to feel joy. We need to examine where that gift stopped working, and then ask it to kindly step aside where it has calcified and hardened us a bit. Peel it back to where it is in balance and working for you again.

I will give a few of mine as an example. Independence. From a very young age, I made it work for me. It made me feel safe, and in many ways it kept me safe. But after a time, I didn't learn how to accept help. After a while it was isolating. My independence got me to safety but it didn't teach me to connect once I was there. Once I identified it as an area I wanted to improve on, I chose small, safe ways to let myself accept help from those who genuinely offered it. I don't recommend diving right into the most intimate parts of our lives where there is a big emotional risk by reaching out in a new way. I started with letting a door be opened for me when someone offered. I started with letting a friend bring me soup when I was sick.

I realized that often we get into relationships we are historically familiar with. I wanted to be self-reliant, and so I ended up in a relationship with someone who needed me to be also. This felt comfortable. I didn't know the side effect of this meant that intimacy was impossible. For it to be possible, two people have to be willing to be vulnerable in order to connect. Renegotiating midstream in a relationship is tricky. Both partners have to be willing to change the script. You have to start inside yourself. To start saying, I am worthy of being cared for. I'd like to be cared for. Start taking baby steps to build your courage and comfort with the concept of changing your emotional language.

Another bit of brilliant resilience that served me for a long time was the notion of being a fixer, and that I was not a quitter. I have grit. I have never looked at short-term solutions and commit to whatever I do for the long haul. As a young woman, much of my self-worth was derived from this notion of being capable of fixing things. I was rewarded for it. I would dig in, examine a situation, make a plan, execute it. This can be an act of self-love and love for others, but unless it is informed by a genuine and deep sense of self-worth, it can be a mechanism you use to try to prop up your own ego and to get love for. It helped me to cover up a deep fear that I was not lovable just for existing, that I had to do things to earn love. And this set me up to be the fixer in every relationship I was in. It took decades for me to realize it was not all mine to fix, especially in a relation-ship, where it's up to the other person to decide how much work they are willing to put in. Sometimes we have to step back and stop fixing, be-cause being engaged in constant fixing limits our ability to say, This is not all mine to fix. I love you enough to let you fix what is yours, and I love myself enough to leave if you are not willing or able to meet my needs. Sometimes fixing is a desperate attempt to resuscitate something that should die. I did not want to feel the grief and pain of the truth about my mom, and so I "fixed" everything I could right up to the bitter end. Say-ing I was done and that there was no more fixing to do was a frightening prospect indeed. I am learning to believe I am worthy of love just for being alive, whether I am perfect or not. I am saying this at age forty. This is not something I understood at thirty when I left my mom.

My assumption that I don't have all the answers has also served me at times. I believe this is common for many. We do not believe we know it all, and so we are often in a great position to learn. We will buy books, and we will accept we might need help. It's a natural humility that is genuine, and no one grows unless they begin with the premise that there is room for it. Where it quit working for me is when I lost touch with my sense of knowing *anything*. This was a very lonely place to operate from and it got me in a lot of trouble. I let my mother be my moral compass and assumed she knew what was best for me. I did not see it at the time, but I would do this to myself again. I would make Ty my new moral compass instead of reclaiming my own. I was so ashamed and embarrassed that I could be so thoroughly subjugated by my mom that I lost what little trust I had for myself. I asked Ty to be my eyes and ears for a while, not realizing that was the same thing I'd trusted my mom to do. No other person can replace our own sense of right and wrong.

At fifteen I set out on this journey, trying to find happiness and avoid becoming a statistic. I thought diligence would help me avoid the pitfalls of life. I avoided some while finding others. The one thing that kept me safe was not my hypervigilance, it was the attitude with which I faced my trials. The point is not to avoid pain, it's to learn and let go.

Another exercise that worked for me was learning to recognize and dismiss my internal critic. One of the most pernicious aftereffects of abuse is that our abuser's ghost lingers and speaks to us still. We can hear them run us down in our minds as if they were there watching over our shoulder. We often internalize them so thoroughly that we become the critic, inflicting self-abuse once they are gone. I cannot stress enough how important it is to listen to those voices and make distinctions between self and other here. We would never be so unkind to a child as to call them stupid, fat, an idiot, or worthless, and yet we find it entirely permissible to say these things to ourselves. I really had to slow down and pay attention to what I was saying to myself, and when I noticed that critical voice, I would tell myself, *I can practice self-love and still effect the change I need in my actions without running myself down. I don't need to be cruel to myself to give me the motivation to change. Shame only paralyzes me.*

People often talk of regrets. It's tempting to bravely say, "I have none. Each thing has shaped me into the human I am." I feel that way about most hardships in my life, but not all of them. I have one regret that haunts me. It happened at a fork in the road I did not see at the time. If I had a time machine and could change one single moment, it would be the day I went to a pay phone and made a collect call to Homer, to tell my mom that record labels had come to see me. If she had never come back down, if she had never been involved with my career, I am confident I would have been better off. I would have continued to build my inner compass, my relationship with myself, and learned to make my own mind work for me. I would have built on what I learned while living in my car. Instead I took one hell of a detour. I climbed to great heights anyway. But I can't help wondering sometimes how much higher I may have gone, or how much happier I might have been along the way. Spilled milk.

Goodbye Alice in Wonderland

It's four in the afternoon
I'm on a flight leaving L.A.
Trying to figure out my life
My youth scattered along the highway

Hotel rooms and headlights
I've made a living with a song
Guitar as my companion
Wanting desperately to belong

Fame is filled with spoiled children
They grow fat on fantasy
I guess that's why I'm leaving
I crave reality

So goodbye Alice in Wonderland
Goodbye yellow brick road
There is a difference between dreaming and pretending
I did not find paradise
It was only a reflection of my lonely mind wanting
What's been missing in my life

I'm embarrassed to say the rest is a rock and roll cliché
I hit the bottom when I reached the top
But I never knew it was you who was breaking my heart
I thought you had to love me
But you did not

Yes a heart can hallucinate
If it's completely starved for love
Can even turn monsters into
Angels from above

You forged my love just like a weapon
And turned it against me like a knife
You broke my last heartstring
But you opened up my eyes

So goodbye Alice in Wonderland
Goodbye yellow brick road
There is a difference between dreaming and pretending
That was not love in your eyes
It was only a reflection of my lonely mind searching
for what was missing in my life

Growing up is not an absence of dreaming
It's being able to understand the difference between the ones you
  can hold
And the ones that you've been sold
And dreaming is a good thing cause it brings new things to life
But pretending is an ending that perpetuates a lie
Forgetting what you are seeing
For what you've been told

Ohh truth is stranger than fiction
This is my chance to get it right
Life is much better without all of those pretty lies

So Goodbye Alice in Wonderland
And you can keep your yellow brick road
There is a difference between dreaming and pretending
These are not tears in my eyes
They are only a reflection of my lonely mind finding
They are only a reflection of my lonely mind finding
I found what's missing in my life

twenty-seven

life as a country song

The years 2004 and 2005 were spent deprogramming, reclaiming my mind, practicing self and other. I recorded *Goodbye Alice in Wonderland* with producer Rob Cavallo at Eldorado in the Valley. Everyone in the business said I had to stay pop, but my inspiration took its own turn, and I couldn't contrive something to capitalize on the momentum of *0304*. I'm sure that would have been smarter but my music was coming out the way it came out. I loved giving birth to songs like the title track, the dulcimer "Where You Are," which I wrote for Ty, and "Long Slow Slide," which was about the strange place I was climbing out of. "Good Day" was about the hurt I was dealing with, but also my sheer determination to wake up and say I was going to have just that. They were all laced with a need to believe I was going to make it a better day.

It was my last record under my Atlantic contract. I loved Atlantic dearly, and owe them so much, but formats were changing. Radio was changing, the business was changing. If I wanted to be a storyteller with song, I felt my future would be in country music and country radio.

When I started out, I considered myself a combination of folk and country. I listened to Dolly Parton and Loretta Lynn as often as I did Joni Mitchell and Rickie Lee Jones. I loved their strong perspectives and willingness to speak from the mind and heart. To be played on country radio I would need a label built for it.

I never saw it as the change that others did—I wrote all the songs.

The funny thing is, I felt radio had changed more than I had. When I started in the '90s, country was more pop than I was, I felt. Mutt Lange helped Shania Twain blow up with slick and polished cuts that exploded on the airwaves. They were pop brilliance with a country twang. Shania and Faith Hill were dressed in fashionable clothes with amazing glam teams. I was a fan of both, but my simpler approach was certainly not where country was at the time. I'd only been able to get a foothold in pop thanks to the alternative movement, which was a wide-open format where there were no rules. I think that if "You Were Meant for Me" came out today, it would never have been considered for pop radio and gone directly to country. Country also allowed me to keep instruments up in the mix that I naturally favored, like steel guitar and banjo, which I'd had to turn down in my pop songs.

I had been around the western culture my entire life, yet knew I would have to start over as far as the business was concerned in order to pull it off. But the fans were my people. I knew the dignity of working the land, and the indignity of seeing the lifestyle made fun of on TV and in movies. I knew I would have to work hard to earn the trust of the gatekeepers and program directors at country radio. But I never had a doubt that the fans and I would get along just fine. That's something the industry sometimes forgets—a fan will buy a Johnny Cash record and a Bob Dylan record. My fans and Lady Gaga's fans are similar in the sense that they love to be encouraged to be themselves. We both built our fan base on a sense of inclusion rather than exclusion. I still feel labels miss big market shares by not understanding the core values of their artists and trying to market to fans who hold the same values in nontraditional ways. But the Internet of course changed that all. Artists and fans find one another because they have an intuitive sense of shared values.

Before the power of radio blew records up, bands toured a lot, and their music was the soundtrack to what they stood for. Fans bought into the culture of what a band was more than anything. They wanted to dress like them, talk like them, and walk like them, and they blasted their music proudly so that others might know who they were and what they stood for. Records were complete projects, and every track was good. DJs were allowed to play what they wanted and songs became hits by word of mouth. Fans listened to entire records over and over, and they were not disappointed for parting with their hard-earned wages. Every track was good. Soon label heads realized that a band didn't have to have a good record, or even play well live—they just had to have one song that sounded good on the radio. As technology advanced, producers were able to make any singer sound good, and make a hit that would explode on the air-waves. Artists, labels, and managers all played along—everyone stopped thinking about longevity and started chasing the short dollar. Labels threw twelve different acts against the wall to see which one stuck. They could afford not to develop acts or invest big in unknowns, because when an act did pay off, it offset the costs of all the other failures. Artist development fell by the wayside. Bands who had never toured, and more important, hadn't established who they were and what they stood for as artists, were suddenly on the radio and playing huge venues. And making records with only one or two good songs. Fans would show up to hear artists that were not good live, or would buy twelve songs only to find out they really only liked the two they'd already heard. They were getting ripped off. The Internet put the power back in the hands of the fans. With the digital age, they could pick and choose the songs they wanted to buy. A new generation of fans had no idea what it was like to actually buy, much less expect to enjoy, a whole CD. Labels and acts saw an amazing shift as the money began to dry up. There were acts that were huge on the radio but wouldn't sell a single song or ticket. This is when the industry missed its mark and played songs that tested well for radio, but elicited no passionate response from fans when it came to separating them from their hard-earned money. I chalk this up to the fact that many bands had no authentic message. Pure ear candy, but stood for nothing. Fans don't spend money unless they are inspired. Labels quit tending to their roster like a farmer does, and I think this hurt them. There are short-term cash crops in farming—produce that grows quickly and sells quickly—but a good farmer will also be working on longer-term crops that will pay off down the road. The industry needs to look at flash-in-the-pan, popular, trending, and novelty singles, but for the health of the whole business, they also need to identify and champion the acts they think have the legs and the talent to sustain a long career. These artists need to be allowed to develop, write, grow, and change. They need to be supported over a long period of time, when there are ups and downs. There have to be artists who have a strong identity and specific set of discernible values, who are supported by managers and agents and labels so they can do so. They need to bet on a horse, not just a race.

In a few short generations we are at risk of having musicians, fans, and an industry that have forgotten that entire albums should be worth listening to, that musicians should stand for something other than a trend, that a fan can follow an act for an entire career and grow and change with them, and that the freedom to decide what makes great music should be between a band and a fan.

My advice to young musicians is to keep your power by staying independent as long as you can and touring a lot. There are no shortcuts even now. Tour, tour, tour and practice, practice, practice. Do as much as you can one-on-one with your fans, as it's the only leverage you have and really all you need. Labels want ownership over so much of your career now that you will have better negotiating power if you have already established a fan base.

I had been with Irving Azoff for quite a few years at this point, and when I told him of my plans to change directions from pop to country we knew I needed someone established in the day-to-day of the country business.

I began recording my country record before I was out of my Atlantic deal, before I had a country label, and before I had a manager in the new space. Once again I made what seemed like a hard left turn against everyone's advice, but it felt right to me and it was where my music wanted to go. I'd spent a lot of time in Nashville over my career. I loved the town and the people. Most of the musicians who'd reached out to me over the years were country—Brooks and Dunn, Crystal Gale, Merle Haggard. I'd mixed and mastered *Pieces of You* in Nashville.

A friend named John Rich from Big and Rich coproduced the new record. One night we went out and John had a few too many to drive me back to my hotel, and a woman from his label offered to take me. Her name was Virginia Davis and she ran the imprint label John had on Warner Bros. She was young, twenty-seven or so, bright, and we hit it off. On the ten-minute drive at midnight, I told her about my plans to go country, and that beyond that I felt my future was in going direct to consumer, and eventually getting off labels all together. She agreed, saying that artists had a lot of power and leverage they seldom used simply because of the status quo. We pulled up to the hotel and as I opened the door, I said, "So, what are you doing the rest of your life?" I knew in that ten minutes that she was a rare breed because she was bright but also seemed kind and ethical—and ethical is hard to come by in my business. Virginia is self-made, moved away from home young, and she liked to work. She knew nothing about being a manager, but that stuff could be learned. I went to Irving and told him I'd found someone I wanted him to hire for me. He asked to meet her, and said he would do it.

Virginia and I have worked well together. She likes blazing new trails and learned the business quickly. I am a very detail-oriented artist when it comes to launching records, and she quickly ran details tighter than I did, allowing me genuinely for the first time in my career to relax a little.

Ty and I had been together again for a few years and many people thought I was going country because of Ty, but that wasn't it at all. Besides, Ty listened to rock. But how I managed my business and how much I worked was beginning to change because of my relationship with Ty. Building a life with him became my priority. I had moved back to his ranch at this point and had babies and marriage on my mind. Ty was not there yet. The wall that had come down after we reunited and he helped me to recover from my mom's betrayal had begun to come back up. It seemed he was very much in love with me, and yet had no desire to take it further. I was pretty exasperated by this time, and wrote three songs that summed up my confusion about the situation: "Stronger Woman" was about the part of him that pushed me. "No Good in Goodbye" was about that part of me that kept looking inside and feeling like it wasn't time to leave, as I loved him. A song called "I Do" was about the dance we did around marriage. It became a single and we made a video, which Ty was in. Despite his perplexing commitment-phobia, I worked a little less to accommodate my life in Texas. I was hopelessly in love.

As I geared up for the launch of my first country album, I approached it as though I never had a record or a hit in my life. I signed with Scott Borchetta's new imprint Valory. He believed in me and my ability to win over the country fans and he turned out to be the right partner for me.

I went in and introduced myself to every program director. They were a friendly and wonderful group. There were one or two skeptics. I remember one in particular crossed his arms when I sat down and said, "So, what the heck makes you think you're country?" I had flashbacks from childhood, eating squirrel soup, skinning cattle, field dressing a moose. My life was a country song. I sang my songs for him and told him stories and we ended up becoming good friends.

I loved working records at country radio. I loved the people. The DJs were respectful and they, along with the whole industry, had a reverence for songwriters and storytelling. They cared about lyrics and asked me about a song or a line every time I was on air. Country musicians are thankful for their fans, and they want them to know it. They sign autographs after shows and everyone in the whole genre just seems happier. Country stars are not divas—no fits like you see in the pop and rock side. The award shows are a whole other animal as well. I can't count the number of red carpets I have walked for pop shows and been ignored by someone I knew because I was not cool enough to be seen with. In country, the award shows are great big hangs. Everyone visits, everyone is friendly, whether there is a camera capturing it or not. Country does a great job helping up-and-coming artists to understand that their income depends on the fans they play for, and the proper way to behave. It goes a long way toward longevity, and why I think country fans are famous for sticking with artists for their whole careers.

My first single "Stronger Woman" had run its course, and "I Do" was my second single. In May we shot the video outside Nashville. Ty had been in almost all my videos since we'd met, starting with "Standing Still." It was an odd feeling to have such a personal issue that was still unresolved in my life turned into a video, with the guy I wrote it about in the video no less. As a kicker there's a scene where Ty slips a ring on my finger in a field. The video was fun to shoot, complete with a showdown as Ty and I play a game of chicken driving muscle cars. We wrapped the shoot on my birthday and Virginia threw me a party. The next day, May

24, Ty and I went home to the ranch and he gave me a present and our usual birthday letter. Since we'd met in 1999, he and I had exchanged letters on holidays and birthdays. We have a collection of Christmas, Valentine's, and birthday letters that talk about the year, our life, our love. They meant more to me than the presents ever did. This time I opened my letter and read, "Jewel, will you marry me and have my baby?" I was of course instantly in tears. And instantly said yes.

Ty is a methodical and calculated person. His mind is a steel trap. He takes time to look at something from every angle and make a decision, but once he has, that is that. It was forever. He had decided to retire from bull riding while he was still at the top of his field. He engaged in a deep and introspective battle, and when he came out he declared it was time. I knew he would never regret it or go back and change his mind. He had decided on it and he was done forever. I didn't doubt that marriage would be the same for him as well. He must have worked through whatever issues he'd had and decided to make a go of it.

We wanted to keep our engagement a secret, and so instead of wearing a ring, we fashioned a key to a band of leather and I wore it around my wrist. I was headed into an intense album launch and work period, but I was walking on clouds.

Perfectly Clear came out in June of 2008 and debuted at number one on the country charts. My single was top 10, and better yet, the community embraced me.

I toured with Brad Paisley on the days I wasn't filming a series for Great American Country and *Nashville Star*. And I planned a wedding secretly. No one knew: not my manager, not my dad, friends, or brothers. I made every phone call from backstage areas and buses. I arranged for the cake, the dress, the ring, and the venue myself in the few free moments I had.

We wanted to elope to the Bahamas, where we'd vacationed once a year. I was able to get a free week in August and told my manager I wanted it for a vacation in the Bahamas. I called the keyboard player Jason from my old band, whom Ty and I both loved, and asked him to come with his wife and marry us. He got himself ordained online, I figured out the legalities of international marriage and where to get our license and all the other details, and off we went.

I got my dress several days before I left Nashville for our secret ceremony. It was perfection, everything I hoped it would be. It was a lace mermaid dress with a halter top, casual yet elegant, perfect for a barefoot beach wedding. I found an antique Italian leather messenger bag from the 1600s and I wrote daily in a journal leading up to the wedding, and on the final day I wrote my vows in it, and placed it in the bag as Ty's wedding gift.

On August 7, 2008, we were married. The beach was lit with candles. Jason spoke, I read my own vows, and Ty read his. Mine of course were more verbose. I smiled ear to ear while he recited his. On the inside of his ring I had inscribed, *in you lives my hopes and dreams.* In mine he'd written, *I believe in you.* Jason said, "Now you may kiss the bride," just as the sun set behind us.

After the ceremony we sat down to dinner and began to call friends and family. Ty began drinking, I had a mojito or two, and we were both ecstatic. Our friends were shocked and happy for us. In the pictures from that night, I look the happiest I have ever seen myself. I belonged. I had my *forever.* I had a rock who vowed to love me and be tender and support me. I was so ready for peace and settling down and starting a family of my own.

The next morning Ty woke up hungover. He sat up and said, "I think I'm done drinking." "Oh yeah?" I said, laughing. "Yeah. I'm done," he said. And that was that. I knew he would never touch another drop, and he never did. He was going to do everything to be the best husband and dad in the world.

After our honeymoon I went back to work. It was a lot of fun touring the album and working hard to make it successful. Once that phase began to wind down, I started to think about what to do next. Despite our best efforts, I was not pregnant yet, so I focused on another project. It was time to do my first indie album, and with Virginia's help, to test my ability to take music directly to fans with no label and no radio.

Years earlier, during the height of *Pieces of You*, parents often told me that my music had a quieting effect on their babies. It gave me the idea to do a mood album, one that was soothing and tranquil the whole way through, based on the lullabies I'd written for myself when I was overcome with anxiety. The new album would be original lullabies for adults as much as for kids. And hopefully my own child would be soothed to sleep with them one day.

I produced it myself on the ranch. I wanted it to sound simple and organic. Virginia was aggressive, and we were making a good team. I made the record for a very small budget to keep the costs down. We found a company that had listening kiosks in Walmart and Target, in the baby and greeting card aisles, where they sold mostly generic instrumental records of public domain songs. I licensed my album to them for a short-term trial period. We then went to Fisher-Price and licensed their brand. We got the CD out of the music section and into the most trafficked areas. I did an HSN special, every major morning talk show, Leno, and a high-profile spot on *Dancing with the Stars*, where Ty was a contestant. Ty was not particularly thrilled to do a dancing show, but felt it would be good exposure for the Professional Bull Riders, cowboy athletes, and the western lifestyle in general, so he bucked up and did his best. America fell in love with his disarmingly earnest personality—much to the chagrin of the judges—and despite his being a self-proclaimed horrible dancer, viewers voted him into the finals.

We still were unable to get pregnant, and we began to engage in the highly romantic act of planned baby sex. Temperatures and calendars got involved. It was hilarious. Somewhere about six months into the marriage though, it began to show signs of stress. There are many stories here, but suffice it to say that once again my need for love and for a fantasy outpaced my ability to see the truth. However, we were both very determined and dedicated.

twenty-eight

a child of my own

Lullaby was wildly successful. It surpassed our expectations, and with no radio play and no traditional distribution sold an astounding half million copies. In the current market that was like having a platinum record. I was able to make a simple folk record I loved, for practically nothing, and found a way to get it directly to fans. It was a very rewarding experience.

I began to formulate the songs for my next country album with Scott Borchetta, once again drawing on old and new songs, and went into the studio with Nathan Chapman to record *Sweet and Wild*.

The complexities of life and relationships don't fit neatly into one song—it takes many to get at all the issues. "Ten" was about how often Ty and I had begun fighting. Since we'd gotten married, I felt Ty was growing increasingly critical and uncomfortable with me. I wrote the song in an optimistic effort to believe arguments could be healthy as long as we could pause and count to ten when tempers flared, allowing cooler heads to prevail rather than jumping in and tearing tender things apart. I really love this song.

jewel

Whoever said love is easy, must've never been in love;
Sometimes it's a land mine, one wrong step and it blows up;
A word, a look, lights a hidden fuse.

It's hard to see just what you have, when you're seeing red;
And easy to do something you know you both will regret;
Better stop, think, count to ten before I leave.

One, I still wanna hate you;
Two, three, I still wanna leave;
Four, searching for that door;
Five, then I look into your eyes;
Six, take a deep breath;
Seven, take a step back;
Eight, nine, I don't know why, we even started this fight;
By the time I get to ten, I'm right back in your arms again.

"No Good in Goodbye" was about my feeling that I had been around the block enough times to know that Ty was the person I wanted to spend my life with, even when times got hard. That's what marriage was.

Once upon a time used to feel so fine
I really made you shine
We laughed like we were drunk on wine
but not anymore

Used to feel so good
used to laugh like we should
we did what we could

Come on baby, I'm sorry
Would you open the door

Baby, don't say the stars have fallen from your eyes
Baby just say, say you need me one more time
For you and I
there is no good in goodbye

You know I used to love to leave
always had something up my sleeve
I guess I mistook being alone for being free
But no never again

We were still trying to get pregnant, and my mind often drifted to all the things I wanted to tell my future child, should I get to be so lucky. I wanted him or her to know that personal satisfaction and fulfillment are always simple and we often pass them by without even knowing. That happiness is delicate and gauzy, and flourishes in quiet moments and time with loved ones and in nature. It takes simplifying. I was taking this to heart myself. I wanted to work less. I wanted to build a family. I wanted to pour my soul and creativity into it. I wanted my child to know and benefit from the knowledge that was so hard won in my life.

Satisfied

If you love somebody
You better let it out
Don't hold it back

While you're trying to figure it out
Don't be timid
Don't be afraid to hurt
Run toward the flame
Run toward the fire
Hold on for all you're worth
'Cause the only real pain a heart can ever know
Is the sorrow of regret
When you don't let your feelings show

So did you say it
Did you mean it
Did you lay it on the line
Did you make it count
Did you look 'em in the eye
Did they feel it
Did you say it in time
Did you say it out loud
'Cause if you did hun
Then you lived some
That feeling inside
That's called satisfied

I have always felt I had to try so hard to be loved, as if being alive were not enough. I had to be perfect, had to make myself small, unfalteringly kind, without needs. Even though I knew better rationally, I felt that who I already was wasn't enough to be loved by a parent or a partner. In "What You Are" I was trying to speak to this part of myself, and to the part of everyone who still is unable to deeply know their own beauty, strength, and inherent nobility.

Gravity is gravity
It doesn't try to pull you down
Stone is stone
It can't help but hold its ground

The wind just blows though you can't see
It's everywhere, just like I'll always be
You already are what you are
And what you are is strong enough

Look in the mirror
Now that's another story to tell
I give love to others
But I give myself hell

I have to tell myself
"In every seed there's a perfect plan"
Everything I hoped to be
I already am

A flower is a flower
It doesn't have to try to bloom
Light is light
It just knows how to fill a room

And dark is dark
So the stars have a place to shine
The tide goes out
So it can come back another time

Goodbye makes hello so sweet
And love is love so it can teach us
That we already are what we are
And what we are is beautiful

And strong enough
And good enough
And bright enough

With pregnancy still eluding me, I was consulting fertility doctors and naturopaths and medical practitioners of all sorts. I'd felt a lack of energy for several years now, and in general just felt "off." I researched and talked to dozens of people on topics from how bell curve averages are set for analyzing blood work panels to how thyroid function affects fertility, from the debate of synthetic versus bioidentical hormones to all the nuances of in vitro fertilization should I have to go down that road. A dynamic doctor named Kim Balas, in Wyoming of all places, finally detected a hormone imbalance and an underachieving thyroid, although she felt these were not the underlying cause of the problem, but instead the result of long-term stress and exhaustion. All the stress in my life, the sleepless nights, and the touring had tapped my adrenal glands and caused a cascade of hormonal reactions. I called Virginia and said, "I don't think I am going to be able to do the work necessary to make this record a success. I need to take time off to get pregnant." We called Scott together to tell him and said that he could pull the album if he wanted.

Scott understood and said he still wanted to put the album out. This was new for me. I had never released a product knowing in all likelihood it would not thrive because of my unwillingness to support it. But I wanted a family more than I wanted more record sales.

I did a two-week tour, and then Ty and I headed for some rest and relaxation—just the two of us. We spent three months riding our motorcycles from Texas to Canada by way of the Rockies. My love affair with motorcycles had begun several years earlier when Ty called me up while I was working in L.A. "Hey hon, you'd never guess what I'm doing. I'm headed to go buy a Rebel motorcycle. Tony talked me into it." To which I responded flatly, "Well, get me one too." Ty was shocked, but I knew he would fall in love with motorcycles and they would be his new thing—I could either join him or be left behind. When he had dedicated himself to learning natural horsemanship in Northern California, I went with him and we lived in a trailer for three months while we both learned how to ride horses "at liberty," without saddle, head stall, or reins.

Our first ride was through Marfa, Big Bend, around the Panhandle, down by the ocean, then up through the Hill Country, in blistering heat and subzero temperatures. That's one thing about doing anything with a bull rider—you better be ready to go big and go extreme.

Riding motorcycles reignited my love for traveling. I had gotten so burned out by touring, but seeing the country from a bike made traveling feel free and fun again, like riding a horse—you could smell the rain coming and the hay fields freshly cut. The singular focus it takes to ride a bike safely is similar to meditating. You can think of nothing but the road unfolding before you.

Each morning we looked at the map and made the day's plan. It was spontaneous. If we liked a town, we stayed a few days so Ty could fish and I could write. I began to write poetry again, something I'd stopped doing when grieving over the separation from my mom. I had been so busy after that, getting out of debt and saving a nest egg, that words just never came, and it felt good to see them coming back, and to write about the land I was seeing around me. Nature was again the best medicine. I also wrote about Ty. I was madly in love with him, and while I sensed he was dealing with an inner war of emotion, I had no doubt we would make it through. We took our time exploring rivers and canyons and mountains. One stunning, sunny morning we rode into a box canyon in Telluride, Colorado, the snowcapped peaks keeping watch over the tiny hamlet nestled with Rockwellian charm in its valley. I knew instantly I would have this town in my life for a long time. We stayed several weeks before heading north. We saw wolves, bears, and buffalo in Yellowstone, and rode into Montana before turning around and slowly heading home. By the time we made it back to Texas it was fall. We moved into my large studio to begin a remodel of Ty's ranch house. The relaxing effects of the trip soon gave way to some of the recurring strains since we'd gotten married. But I did get pregnant.

Being pregnant was the best time of my life in so many ways. It felt like the opportunity of a lifetime. I studied which foods build great healthy babies, and being able to apply what I knew about nutrition and herbs to pregnancy made it feel so worthwhile. It was an honor and a privilege to create and house and give birth to a baby. Every day I spoke to him, wrote for him, and sang for him. After about six months I had doctor's orders to take it easy because I was having overactive Braxton Hicks contractions and quit traveling and playing gigs at all. As I was homebound in my studio, I decided to do my second indie release and make a children's record for my future son. It was fun to think of little fables and stories that would teach morals and lessons to him when he was old enough to understand. I wanted to make it a CD that the parents would enjoy as much as the kids. There were songs about loving him forever, about the magic of stories and books, about not being afraid of the dark, about celebrating the differences in each of us rather than condemning them. The record was called *The Merry Goes 'Round*.

One of the first things I did when I found out I was pregnant was call

Lee. He had stopped working for me in 2001 and gone back to Louisiana, where he was raised, to care for his dad, who was suffering from lung cancer. When he left, he told me that if I ever had a baby to call him and that he would come help. We had lost touch over the ten years that had passed, but I found him in Louisiana. It was so good to hear his voice and to share my news with him. I asked if he still wanted to help, and he said he was coming. I was so excited to see my dear friend, and knew it would be so helpful to have that support as a new mom—I still did not have many real friends in my life and was a bit isolated. Plus he was an amazing cook, so I would be the luckiest girl in the world. Lee packed his belongings (including six chickens!) into a U-Haul and arrived a few days later. He moved into a small house on the ranch and we spent hours catching up. He had no idea what all had happened in the aftermath with my mom, and when I told him, he held me and we cried together. It felt so comforting to have him by my side again.

My pregnancy was uneventful except for one moment when I was six months pregnant. I was driving my car from town back to the ranch when out of nowhere a heavy metal brushfire truck T-boned me. The fire truck had blown through a stop sign while responding to a meadow fire and without looking absolutely smashed into us. I barely had time to brace as I saw the bright green truck out of the corner of my eye. The next thing I knew, I was coming to, my air bags deployed all around me. I felt my tummy immediately. It felt okay. I was confused, unsure what had happened exactly. My car was so mangled the door would not open. The firemen in the truck that had hit me used a crowbar to pry me out. I was not bleeding. I knew my name and where I was. I was visibly pregnant and they kindly gave me a coat and sat me down. The firemen said they'd called an ambulance and asked whether there was someone I wanted to call. Oh. Yes. I should call Ty. I needed to keep my blood pressure down and focus on whether I could feel the baby move inside me. I kept one hand on my tummy while I dialed Ty. When he picked up, I said hello in the eerily calm voice I use when I'm under extreme duress. "I got in a car crash. I am fine. A fire truck hit me. I'm waiting for the ambulance. I am fine though." "Goddamnit Jewel, you have that ultra-calm voice—how bad is it really?" He was at my side within minutes. I was sitting leaned against the cab of the truck, and when I saw him, my tough exterior cracked slightly. I whimpered in half-shock. "I don't know anyone here. I don't know any of these people," I told him, tearing up. I have always had fear and anxiety around strangers if no one I know is with me, especially in a vulnerable situation. I act calm and strong until someone safe is there and then I will quietly turn into a puddle of tears. Ty held me and kissed my forehead and asked if I felt okay. I still hadn't felt the baby move, but I felt like he was okay when I closed my eyes and focused on taking long, deep breaths. I didn't let myself get worked up or go there. I did not want the boost of adrenaline or the chemicals produced by shock to make it to the baby's bloodstream. The ambulance came, they loaded me up, and after they'd checked my pulse and blood pressure, I remember one medic saying, "God, your vitals are not elevated. It's like your body doesn't believe you were in a crash that bad." I was looking at the roof, doing my meditation. That's one thing about abuse or trauma—small things will trigger you, but in an actual crisis you often stay quite calm.

At my ob-gyn they took a sonogram. I was so eager to see his face and see his little heart beating. The nurse spread the gel neatly on my belly while I wanted to scream, "Just hurry already!" I kept my mouth shut and my eyes on the screen. Out of the gray static appeared the beautiful face of my baby, sucking his thumb. He was all right, the doctor said. Ty and I were both so happy. On the drive home I got a call from my frantic publicist, who explained there were photos of the wreck already on TMZ. Thankfully the story had a happy ending.

. . .

I GAVE BIRTH TO KASE TOWNES MURRAY on July 11, 2011, in Stephenville. I was a week past due, which is quite common with a first baby, and had gone in for a routine checkup. The doctor checked his vital signs in her office and the next thing I knew I was being rushed to the hospital for an emergency C-section. I went right into my super-calm breathing mode. My blood pressure remained even. I listened to the doctors and made all the decisions necessary. Ty, however, was a nervous wreck. He was weaving back and forth on his feet, like he did when he was competing. I was given anesthesia and could feel the knife cutting into me, and tugging and pulling deep into my body, but felt no pain. I could hear the wet sound of them taking my intestines out and setting them on a table next to the doctor. I could hear the doctor's voice intensify as it came time to pull Kase out. It was surreal and strange. I just kept waiting to hear my son's cry. Ty could see everything, and when they pulled Kase out, they handed our son to his father. It was the first time I had ever seen him cry. He showed Kase to me and I could see his little mouth pursed and making sucking sounds. He was not crying. He was hungry. He was healthy and hungry and absolutely the most beautiful thing I had ever seen. The doctor sewed me up and put me in a recovery suite, where my vitals would be monitored for an hour. It was the longest hour of my life. Kase stayed with Ty. I asked if they could bring my son in, and the nurse watching over me said no. I wanted to stab her with the pencil she was fiddling with as she read her book and go running in to see my baby. Instead I focused on the ceiling and tried to stay calm. I was so excited to meet my son I nearly jumped out of my own skin.

Finally I was rolled in and saw Kase all bundled up. His hair had been washed and Ty was sitting in a rocking chair holding and talking to him. Finally I got to hold him and smell him and see his cloudy gray newborn eyes. I was eager and determined to breastfeed but had been warned it was actually a learned skill and took practice. The umbilical cord had been wrapped around his neck, but despite this, Kase was a strong and healthy baby and he was just as determined. Breastfeeding him in those first hours was heaven. It was the best of everything that nature and nurture had to offer. It felt like what I was made for. I stared down at his little kitten hands. He was impossibly small. His ears were as thin and soft as rose petals. I wept with joy to have my very own baby. I can't help but weep now as I write this. I loved him impossibly more than I could have ever known. He slept on my chest for the three days I was in the hospital, and I stayed awake to make sure he was breathing. His small panting breaths rose and fell with my own. All was well with the world.

Ty was so nervous driving the car home that his knuckles were white on the wheel. I could tell how much he loved this baby. Both our hearts forever changed.

After the pain meds they gave me post-surgery the first day, I didn't take so much as an Advil. I didn't want anything to get into my breast milk and contaminate Kase's little system. I ate like an athlete competing in the breastfeeding Olympics. Lots of avocado and fatty acids to help his brain develop. Herbal concoctions for colic and upset tummies and black walnut extract full of rich minerals to help his teeth and bones to form. As my milk came in, I could not believe how many hours in a day would be dedicated to feeding him and me. I was a human milking machine. I slept and ate and fed Kase. There had been times I worried and wondered how on earth I would know how to be a mom when I'd never had a good example. But when it happened, I felt my heart swell with love and ability. I knew my son. My instincts were intact and my curiosity would let me learn what I did not know.

MILK AND LAVENDER

you fell asleep
in my arms
this evening

you had your
evening feeding
in your usual
fashion

looking at the
burlap lamp shade
as it swayed
rocked by the unseen hand
of the air conditioner

you fidget
with your left hand
the more tired you get
it starts with a curious exploration
feeling my face
playing with the tassel
on my sweater
but as sleep overtakes you

the herky-jerky motions
increase until
you flop your whole arm wildly

I grab your tiny hand
wrap your finger
to make a fist
around my thumb
then fold my fingers
over yours
let the weight of my arms
hold your own firmly
against your belly
this quiets you
and you relax
and begin to
eat in earnest
looking at me
your eyes grow
so heavy
you shake your head
as if to wake yourself
fighting sleep

but the warm milk
and holding you close
lull you into
such a sweet
serene state
until the nipple
pops
out of your mouth

I straighten my blouse
lean back into my chair
cradle you close
and kiss your cheek
repeatedly
while you sleep

I can't stop staring
you are completely relaxed
your mouth
puckers and pooches
your cheeks droop heavily

your eyebrows like
bows empty of an arrow

I stand with you
still nestled in my arms
turn the light out
hover over your crib
but cannot bear
to put you down
and so I stand there
in the dark
straining to see
your shape
in the dwindling light
swaying back and forth
bending over your
sleeping form
to kiss your temples
that smell like
milk and lavender

twenty-nine

family tree

I took more time off after the birth of my son. I had friends who went right back to work after having a baby, and they really regretted it. I thought, *You know what? I've made money. I built and rebuilt a career so that I could have this.* So I gave myself time to find my sea legs. Once again, I switched genres from country artist to mom. I poured all of my creativity and energy into my exciting new job. As he grew I began to make art inspired by my new muse, writing several children's books. I did not make a new record and would not for six years.

That's a lifetime in rock and roll years. But I wanted to figure out how to be a mom without having to figure out how to be a professional on top of it. As ever, my greatest highs are simultaneously my greatest lows. My relationship with Ty began crumbling. It was a great time and also a sad time all at once. I loved getting to know Kase. There were a lot of things I was fascinated by. There were some I was a little terrified by. I remember holding him on the couch, watching TV while I fed him. It's funny that the natural world has always been what's educated me and given me the greatest insights into living. I was watching an orangutan cuddle her baby. She snuggled it and licked it and watched it play and touched it and kept it from wandering away as it playfully explored. And I thought, *Oh, yeah. That's all it is.* I remember feeling completely calm after that. I just have to lick my cub and get to know him. I just have to be here and engage.

New mothers have this misconception that they're going to immediately have a very storybook, specific type of love for their child. And you do in many ways—you would die for them instantly and you do all kinds of crazy things that you normally wouldn't because it's your child. You're bonded at birth—but you also fall in love over time, and I didn't know that. You discover each other. And you can't beat yourself up that you're not in love yet. And your baby isn't in love with you yet. They don't know enough to be in love with you yet. But as a mom, I can't help thinking you have an advantage. They know your voice, they lived in your tummy. You know them in a certain way, but still it's an unfolding and it really is a relationship that develops. There's a billion chemicals helping you do it, but it really is a slow falling in love and I enjoyed that once I realized it.

Having Kase was the first time in my life that I had unconditional love. I'd never had that. And surprisingly, everything I'd experienced in my crazy life along with my natural creativity actually made me a great mom. It wasn't the opposite. Being willing to look at something I don't know and lean into it and get excited about it, cultivating my listening skills, my intuition, my ability to look inward and feel for something, feel for somebody, feel for an audience—that sixth sense would make me a good mom. I was surprised. And I also began to see that my artistic approach would help in my childrearing. Artists are very comfortable having nothing and knowing that soon something would be coming from that nothing. As an artist you really learn to get comfortable with that idea: "I don't have a song right now but by tomorrow I will." Whether you're male or female, there is fertile possibility within you. That unformed dark matter is the fabric of the universe that art is made from, and our job as artists is to physically manifest and put matter around thought. All artists give birth. It's alchemy and it's really an amazing process. As a creative person you get a tremendous sense of security over time with the concept of having nothing and trusting something will come. It terrifies everyone else. In the music industry there are a lot of executives who will say, "We have a fourth-quarter budget, and we have no music—where is it going to come from?" They try to rely on statistics and math to contrive a sense of security, but if you impose that on art, then the real dysfunction happens. Parenting is the same way. You have nothing, you're just terrified. But if you can get comfortable with the concept that from nothing something will come, if you can learn to let go of control, you can start to engage and be part of the otherworldly creation in front of you. You have to have faith.

Before you have a baby, you have an ego, an image of yourself that's been built up over time. You have an identity forged in the ways you define beauty, sexuality, romance, success, the who and how and why of your self-worth. And when you have a child, you literally just take a hammer to it. The center of the universe is changed, and you have to redefine who you are relative to this new addition in your life. Sex and what's sexy to you are no longer the same. What's romantic to you is no longer the same. Everything is redefined. I saw all my new mom friends go through a sadness other than postpartum depression: it is grieving the loss of your old self, of who you used to be. It's very real and nobody talks about it. We mourn the loss of freedom and identity, and we must discover and redefine what makes us feel beautiful, sexy, supported, romanced, successful. We really lose who we were and that ego is dead to us forever—and that's okay, we wouldn't change it for the world, but to not talk about it and not acknowledge it makes you feel crazy and it makes you feel sad. Knowing this makes things easier and less scary. Before I had Kase, I sat down and made a list of the things that up to that point had defined me. I then started a new list with a blank space next to each one. I didn't know what all the answers were yet, but I knew I would discover them with time.

BEAUTY IS _____
SUCCESS IS _____
SEXY IS _____
SUPPORT IS _____
A PARTNER IS _____
A MOM IS _____

You have to give yourself space to learn what the new definitions are—you don't know overnight. I was a new piece of art. I was a work in progress. I wrote about all this before Kase arrived, and it really prepared me to have a baby. I was able to engage creatively, I was able to grieve the loss without wondering what it all meant or if I was depressed. I was just grieving a part of me and getting to know a new one. I had to let myself go through a process. In the past my sense of self-worth had come from accomplishing career goals, but I knew it would have to come from different places now. My goals were different. What I didn't realize was that men have a death of the ego all their own. I didn't realize it for quite a while and then I watched Ty deal with it and I watched other wives' husbands struggle after childbirth. Men don't have great role models for what true masculinity is. Neither sex does, really. Not pumped-up machismo, but a yielding and supportive partner and provider who lifts a family rather than lives at the center of it. In general, men start as boys who are idolized by their moms and they're the center of their universe. They're little kings. They grow up and when they meet a woman who falls in love with them, who makes them feel like a king, they generally fall in love. A woman in a new relationship with no kids has time and energy to dedicate to making her man feel like a king, and they think, "I want to get married."

When a woman has a baby, however, her time and energy are redirected, as they must be, and the man can feel suddenly insignificant and emasculated. And this is where grown-up boys are invited to become full-grown men. To redefine themselves. Both parents have to redefine and share their new self-images with each other so that they can adjust to new information and continue to know who their partner is and what they need.

Women who aren't aware of this will try to build up their flailing sense of self-worth by looking for imperfections in their partner. The man who is not in touch with this process feels demoted, and it can create a really horrible dynamic as they look for other ways to reclaim their throne. It can slowly burn like this until love gets used up. The successful parents I saw were able to redefine who they were and renegotiate their needs and roles as humans, parents, and partners.

I spent a lot of time thinking about this concept, about redefining myself and communicating my new needs, as well as what kind of parent I wanted to be. And what kind of family I came from. I was worried I'd carry on some legacies I did not cherish. That I might be impatient, for instance, like my dad had been. I hoped I'd done enough work on my own Emotional English, but had to take a long hard look at my patterns.

I had to admit that in my professional life I could be irritable and lean toward perfectionism. I wondered whether it would come into my parenting. I've worked hard to make sure it hasn't. I am patient and have learned to embrace the process, and see so many similarities between Kase and me—I would never criticize my son for not knowing how to do something he has yet to learn. I teach him, and in the process I am able to be kinder and more generous with myself. Loving my son has helped me to love myself more.

Boundaries were another issue. My parents didn't have many, and I've done enough work to understand how important firm, healthy, and clear boundaries are for my child. It's a very loving act to give your child consistent boundaries. And just when you figure one thing out, it changes altogether. Parenting is constant readjustment. When I am comfortable with that, it makes parenting more fun. We learn together. Nobody is perfect, nobody knows what they're doing. If you have too much ego and brittleness and perfectionism, you struggle more as a parent. I need to be willing to be uncomfortable and yet excited and energized to figure it out. I have had no plan for being a mom and career woman, no magic formula for balancing work and motherhood, but I know that I am a mom, and I am a singer and a writer who loves her child, and that's all I need to guide my decisions each day. I feel my way through it as I go. My growth and evolution as a human matters to me, and so does my art, but I know it's unacceptable for my son to feel like he loses out so that I can be more famous. He is my priority, I have not quit being creative for my son, but how I go about my job has definitely changed. I know there are many ways of succeeding and meeting everyone's needs.

Already there are striking differences between my current lifestyle and how I was raised. I was raised poor in a far corner of the remote north. My son will be raised by two parents with money and stability, right smack-dab in the middle of pop culture. I learned my values from nature, and from having nothing that I was entitled to—I had to earn it all. There was no backup plan, no allowance, no safety net. How will I teach my son those values when I have money, when all his needs will be met, when he will be around affluence and other kids who may feel entitled? How can I teach him that hard work is not just an option? That fame is not reason enough to be liked? That you have to treat everyone equally, to respect their inherent dignity and worth, and to judge people on their actions not their accolades. I know the answer is by setting a good example. The greatest responsibility parenting brings is in living my life as the kind of human I want him to know.

I'm learning that if I set Kase up to win, in the sense that if I tell him what's expected of him ahead of time and break those expectations down into small steps, he does really well. Kids don't know the definition of large concepts like sharing. They hear the word and don't know what the rules to sharing are, yet we expect them to know. I learned to tell my son that when a friend is coming over to play, we will share our toys. Sharing means that if you have a toy in your hand, you may keep it. When you set it down, someone else can play with it and we may not take it from him. We will take turns. When we go out to eat, I will tell him about the good manners I expect from him. Nice manners mean looking a waitress in the eye and saying "hi" when she walks up. It means telling her what kind of juice you want. It means saying "please." In a restaurant I will say, "Okay, we get to practice our first good manner! Let's look her in the eye and say 'hello!'" Kase will be so excited and prepared for each manner that he swells with pride as he tries each one. I am learning to build confidence in my child from the inside out. A gift I was never given but learned through the privilege of being his mom.

Kase recently went to his first show of mine, and so I was careful to explain the manners that would be expected of him. Being quiet was the first one. No loud talking, I explained, we use our best listening. And so he wouldn't get startled, I told him to expect everyone to clap at the end of songs. The show was in Vegas. I was singing at a convention at 10 a.m., a perfect non-nap, non-bedtime showtime! He sat with Lee the whole time and was so quiet and well behaved. The one thing I didn't anticipate was how closely he would listen to the anecdotes I tell between songs. I told my stories about hitchhiking and Mexico and shoplifting and after the show he asked, "What do you mean, mommy stole? What's hitchhiking?" I had a lot of explaining to do.

I talk to him a lot about choices and about how each day is full of choices. We don't always make the right choices but we always have another chance to make a better choice. Choices don't make you a good or bad person, I tell him; there are just good and bad choices. Hard thing to explain to a three-year-old why I stole, but I love that being a great parent doesn't mean being perfect. Being human is okay. We will all make mistakes and it's how we adjust the attitude we have toward them that measures success. I'm learning to love my mistakes through a parent's eyes—I don't want Kase to be afraid to try things or to avoid opportunities. Life is about drawing and redrawing who we are and how we behave without shame or judgment.

Kase is aware that Daddy's a cowboy and Mommy's a singer, and he asks often about jobs, like, "What's a house's job?" I say, "A house's job is to shelter people." He says, "What's a cow's job?" I say, "To give us milk and food." "What's my job?" "Your job is to be loved and to learn how to be a happy person." "What's your job?" "My job is to love you and to help you be a fulfilled person with strong values and the courage to do what you love." "But you sing too." "Yes. I sing too. That's my other job." It's so much fun watching him develop and unfold every day.

I read a study by a group of psychologists who wanted to understand why some children who have faced hardship have such emotional resilience. The study revealed a surprising answer: the kids who were resilient knew their "oscillating family narrative." This meant they knew the good and the bad. Not only where grandma went to school or grandpa's favorite hobby, not just the accomplishments, but the darker moments as well. They came from families who did not keep secrets, and knowing that there are ups and downs that people face over time gave the children a sense of security. They would also have ups and downs, and that was okay. There was an overall arc that kept climbing onward. Honesty and transparency were key to emotional resilience.

As I write this, I am proud to say my dad and I have come a long way in healing our relationship. A lot of this is due to my dad's determination to find his own health and happiness. While I took my own path to find happiness and healing, my dad spent years dedicated to healing his own wounds and trauma. We have had moments where he was able to not only communicate his regret and ownership for his shortcomings as a father when I was younger, but he has shown me with his actions that he has made real changes. He comes to my house and stays with us for months, and he is easy to have around. There is no tension. When he needs something, he lets me know clearly. There is nothing passive-aggressive. If I hurt him, he will tell me. If he hurts me, I will tell him, and we know we are both responsible enough to sit and listen, and we make amends. He allows me to be myself and he is encouraging of me as a mom and a person. He tells me he is proud of me and articulates why. He thinks I am a thoughtful parent, and he is very proud of the changes I have made to ensure I don't repeat the patterns I was raised with. Often he puts a hand on my shoulder and with a tear in his eye says, "Jewel, I'm so amazed and so proud of who you have become despite what you had to work with. I admire you, honey." I can't tell you how good this feels.

He and I spend a lot of time talking about the past, about our journey and our healing. I was surprised to find out that when he married Nedra, she made him feel a lot like she made me feel—as if he didn't know very much and that she was an all-wise, all-spiritual person. He was so scared and empty from his childhood that he was thankful to meet someone like her and was happy to let her tell him what should be done.

I admire my father. While I wish he had been able to intervene earlier, I think it takes more courage to face these things after you have displayed years of abusive behavior. The shame and the hurt and the guilt make it nearly impossible to face up to. Making amends takes tremendous vulnerability, but it takes accountability to earn back a relationship that was lost. Words can be said easily, but one can't fake actions. My dad and I are a loving father and daughter. We may not be what other fathers and daughters are, but what we have is real and safe and he shows up with honesty and I am thankful for it. I thank my dad for letting me tell my story uninhibited. When I told him about the book I was going to write, he said, "Jewel, this was your life. The things I did affected you and you have a right to talk about them." He is willing to be seen on every step of his journey. This takes courage. I like to think of my dad as his true self now—I think as a child he was a gold statue covered in wounds and abuse, under layers of mud and crud. I feel I am getting to know who my dad really is and who he was meant to be.

One of the things my dad said he struggled the most with over the years in regard to my public life was learning that I was living in my car. People asked him how on earth he could let his child be homeless. I did not know this had been hard for him. At the time, I never did call family to tell them what was going on. When I moved out at fifteen, I just never looked back. It's not that I thought that if I went back to Alaska, my dad would not give me shelter. He would have. I just never thought about it or thought to call. My dad knew I had been living with my mom in San Diego. I think I called him to say I was going to live in my car, but other than that I never called home when times got hard. He told me recently that his own feelings of inadequacy made him feel un-qualified to parent, especially from far away, and so he never called or checked in either.

I am thankful my dad has done the work it takes to live a different life. He has been sober for many years now and works hard at being honest with himself and others about his feelings and fears instead of lashing out to protect himself from them. I am astounded my son gets to have a rela-tionship with him, and it warms my heart to see Kase get to know my dad as a loving and patient grandparent.

I am proud and thankful my dad stopped the generational cycle of abuse while he was alive. He was able to find tenderness and honesty with his kids sooner than his own father did. My dad found it before he was on his deathbed. I'm proud to have looked at these things and broken the cycle before I had my child. I hope Kase will be able to live a life always knowing his own worth and that he will avoid the traps that took me until I was forty to find my way out of.

My life, so far, has been about examining what worked in my child-hood, keeping the good while being willing to see and let go of the bad. I wrote a song I call "The Family Tree." I sang it for my dad, and after-ward we both cried and hugged each other. We're both warriors of the loneliest battlefield—the one that is contained within our own flesh. Both seekers of truth. I am proud of my life. I am thankful for the gifts both my parents gave me. I was made into a curious, creative, thoughtful person. The rest I give back. It never belonged to me anyway.

The Family Tree

Mama, I see your face now
In the mirror, it's getting clearer

jewel

Daddy, all those things I said I wouldn't do
I've been drawn to, 'cause I looked up to you

And I've loved you through this tangled legacy
Tracing the twisted roots of our family tree

I stayed strong like you did
I moved on like you did
And I wound up tough as stone like you did
If I don't learn to bend, I know I'm going to break
Like you did

Lover, I must forgive you
I confused you with what I couldn't see
Inside of me dark things pulling
Not evolving, made a puppet out of me
And you came with your own history
Both caught in the branches of our family tree

I stayed strong like you did
I moved on like you did
I wound up all alone like you did
If I don't learn to bend, I know I'm gonna break
Just like you did

I love you but I need to look at who we've been
Take the fruit but choose the seeds I scatter on the wind
That's the job of the kid, to do better than our parents did

So I'll stay strong like you did
And I'll move on like you did
But I won't hide from the truth like you did
I'm learning to bend so I don't break
And you can bet I'll teach my kid that love will always find its way
just like you did

TO MY SON

long night of the dark soul
what once nurtured me
I must turn from now
yet leave the most tender part of me
behind
half of the time

child

I know you will read this one day
I know you will have questions
I know you will love that which I
    turn from
dearly as he is a part of you
and so I fear my turning from him
will make you feel as if I turned
    from
a part of you
as well

this drops me to my knees
even now as I write this
tears sting my eyes

and my lungs turn to iron
too full of sadness to breathe

it breaks my heart
to think you may ever
feel rejected in any part
by my decision
to separate from your father

I want you to love him
as he loves you
so deeply
so undeniably

but what he and I have created
aside from you
has turned from growth
to not merely stagnation
but the opposite of growth
we are reverting
and it is damaging to us both
and compromises us each
to the point I fear it may

compromise you
and so it is with love
that we turn from each other
it is with love for each other
and love for you
though it is hard for me
at this time to feel anything
but sadness for the pain
I fear I inflict on you

I have a hard time forgiving myself
for not seeing things sooner
for not being more perfect
as to figure this out
without leaving
but I suppose
I need to look at myself with
    the same
kindness I will look at you
when you are older
and you are learning
to form and reform yourself
I must be gentle with myself
    here for
I never knew love before you
how could I be touched
by something I knew not of in
    the past?
but loving you has showed me
how to love myself

and in this way your gift is twofold
in my life
loving you has echoed back
and bathes my own love
over me

I love myself enough to leave
I love myself enough to make sure
I am the kind of woman I want you
    to know

this has set a healing process
    in motion
it is literally as if
the future washed over the past
to change it forever
and then ripples into the more
    distant
future
of our family legacy to heal it
    as well
in ways I cannot foresee yet
but sense
the way an animal senses shelter
is near

it is not about perfection
it's not about withholding love until
we feel we have earned it
and arrived at perfection

it's about loving ourselves
in the process of becoming
what we want ourselves to be

it is a work in progress
it is a sculpture
that is not wrestled from stone
immaculately overnight
but the labor of a lifetime
and with hope
we are given a pencil to draw
scratchy lines
and with confidence our family
    gives us
we find courage to make bold ones
and with self-love
we are given the eraser needed
to scratch out and redraw a more
    accurate shape

we should not be so bound
    by shame
that we cannot renegotiate
or reimagine
our selves
we cannot be so bound
by the vision of others
that our own true shape
becomes obscured
. . .

I want to imagine myself boldly
I always wanted to
but you inspire me
even now
at two and a half
to be the best version
of myself I can be
to have the courage to
see myself
so that you may learn to see
yourself also
to imagine yourself
to create yourself in your
    own image

for you to do that
you need to see it modeled for you
and though it frightens me
I am dedicated to
offering that so you may see
the willingness
to be a work in progress

your father and I came together
in love
and we clung to each other
because each of us
had a puzzle piece
we needed to solve
to the puzzle of ourselves

you were born from love
from longing
desire and purpose birthed you
and our arms
once empty
our hearts
once vacant
now are filled with the song
of your laughter

I know this:
you are with me
but you are not my own
you belong to yourself
you are the arrow
shooting forward into your own life
and I am the bow that must bend
true
that must be steady enough
for you to go straight into
your own future
without detours through fractures
of my unknowing
you must be free of my past
and supported enough
so that you may hear
your own voice calling

for me to be steady for you
I must heal what is

raging in me
so it does not consume you as well

I go now into my own life
to find the steadiness
so that my past does not become
    yours
so that our futures have a separate-
    selfness
so that you can see your own
beautiful shape
not defined by your parents
but sprung forth from us
with love
unconditional

I don't know
at what age
you will read this

I don't know what form you will
    be in
nor do I know the shape
I will be in

I do know
my love for you
will grow
impossibly
. . .

I do know my love for myself
will grow also

I do know I am excited
to watch you unfold the rose petals
of your soul
and blossom

and that though I live with
    sorrow now
a quiet sense of excitement
is growing in me
to see who I will become
and to discover who you become
and help you on your journey
as steward and vessel
of unconditional love

. . .

for as I am your parent
I am learning to be my own as well
and to provide myself
the space to define and redefine
and if I can believe in myself
the same way I believe in you
I know we will both make
great works of art
of ourselves
and we can laugh and reimagine
and redefine
as we share this journey
together

thirty

i choose love

Ty and I were both kids when we met years ago. We were lucky enough to have a beautiful child. We worked hard on our relationship. But it became evident to me that while we loved each other dearly, we were hurting our love, not building it, and we did not want that to be what our son grew up to see. Ty loves that child more than anything on earth. For me, having a child opened a window into my heart and showed me the kind of woman I wanted to be. Kase inspired me to examine every corner of my heart and soul, and to have more courage than I ever knew I would need.

The failure of my marriage was a loss of a dream I felt incapable of grieving. It was heartbreaking to see the patterns I thought I could escape reemerge in my marriage. When I began to face the fact that our relationship needed to change, I looked deeply inward with all the self-love I could muster. There was still a little broken piece of me that had never seen the light of healing. This part of me continued to look for approval on the outside. It gave another person power over my own sense of self-worth. This wound wreaked havoc on my life until I committed to seeing it and healing it.

Ty and I filed for divorce in April 2014. The shock was staggering. We went for long walks and rode around in his truck, and it was as if the act of saying we would let each other go had immediately soothed many of our struggles. We both wanted a family more than anything in the world, and we both felt so sure we would be married forever. It has been a heartbreak to lose the picture of the family I had so wanted. But something could be salvaged. Ty and I needed to rebuild the friendship that had suffered, and we still got to be a team—Kase deserves two parents who are kind and respectful to each other. Anger and bitterness are not an option when you have a child who loves both his parents more than anything in the world. It has not been easy to do, but nothing worthwhile is.

I found myself in a place I never imagined I would be. A forty-year-old divorcée with a three-year-old. Starting over. Again. My companion of sixteen years was gone. I had few friends and no real place I belonged. I had to move and find a new place to settle down. Suddenly I had three new jobs.

To grieve the death of my marriage,

To examine the dark corners of myself that had yet to be healed,

To be a steady, emotionally available, and grounded mom for my son in this precarious period of transition.

Looking back, I realize that I was so busy surviving and recovering and problem solving since being a toddler that my development as an emotional human stopped at certain times in my life when a crisis stunted it. It's true for all of us and that's what inner-child work is—going through the divorce has actually been a lot like engaging in time travel within myself, because for the first time I'm really able to integrate all these parts of myself that didn't get a chance to grow up. I'm not surviving anything. I'm safe. Parts of us evolve while other parts remain frozen, until our attention allows them to thaw, and our dedication lets them catch up with the rest of us at our current age. I can watch myself now, witness my thoughts, and I can see the historic fears, doubts, and grief that were waiting for the right time to come to the surface.

I was driving the other day, feeling a lot of anxiety. I took a moment to check in with myself and ask what it was rather than just living with it. And suddenly I thought, *I really miss having a husband. I really miss having a mom today. I feel small and scared and I wish I had a mom to hold me or to call.* A tremendous sadness came over me and I cried as I drove. But I was self-aware too. With the divorce, there is a new layer of grief and a feeling of being so alone in the world. I can allow myself to feel deeply while at the same time witnessing myself. I'm not worried about holding it together anymore. I know how to do that. I've held it together, and worked and showed up and been a soldier and a professional pretty much my whole life. Now I'm learning how to let it go when I can, so that the grief doesn't build up and spill over into the rest of my life. I can tell my grief is escalating when my anxiety surges. Anxiety makes me feel I'm vacant, and so this time I have been actively dealing with my grief and feelings of betrayal in healthy and adult ways, like writing, meditating, taking walks in nature by myself, and therapy. And being still. I want to be a present, happy, and engaged parent for my son, to keep what I am going through from spilling onto him. To do this I make moments to be alone to let myself unload. My mind does not have all the answers. But I don't need answers to feel safe. I just need to feel my heart beating inside my chest and the beating heart of my son. No one has all the answers. I am learning finally to trust my own ability to know them when I need them. And to know all is well right now. In this second.

I still make sure to dedicate time after I wake and just before I go to bed for my prayers of gratitude. There is always so much to be grateful for, and pain causes us to lose sight of that. It's important to see how much good there is in the day, and that it always outweighs the pain. My son is such a beautiful miracle. Ty and I are both committed to being great parents and finding our way with love. I am healthy. I have a job I love.

And I have Lee. When I was sixteen, I told him I was headed to the Talkeetna Bluegrass Festival five hundred miles away to sing. He asked how I would get there, and I said I'd hitchhike. When he asked who I was singing with, I said I would just find a band onstage and ask if I could sit in with them. He was there when I returned a week later and told him that I did indeed get up and get to sing. He was by my side as I wrote my first songs. I wrote him letters when I was lonely at school, and told him first when I got signed. He was by my side as I toured the world. He has been through the turmoil with my mom, my romances, the birth of my son, and my divorce. All the major events in my life. He lives with me still, and helps me with Kase, and nourishes us in so many ways. He plays never-ending games of dragons, and reads the same book to Kase a thousand times in a row, and gives hundreds of horse rides on his knee to my little boy. Kase loves him. Lee sticks by my side in whatever is next in my life. If love and partnership mean being a witness to someone's life, and loving and supporting them the whole way through no matter what, then Lee is my surprising love story. We create our own families in life, and he and Kase are mine. Having Lee's support during my divorce has made a stressful time manageable. I feel so blessed to have him as a friend. He is the embodiment of an Every Day Angel.

Life is simple right now. Simplicity is where happiness is for me and where I can heal from. I get up and get my son up. I feed him and brush his teeth and we play before I take him to a few hours of preschool. While he is there I work half the time on my job and half the time on myself. I employ all the skills I have learned with time, and the first one is being here now and asking, What do I need today? What does that part of me that is sad need? Often it just needs witnessing, some room to be seen and known and experienced. Unfelt feelings don't cease to exist; they stay bottled up in our minds and our bodies. They dissipate when given expression. A heart can break only if it is closed—if it remains open there is nothing to break. I am learning to be a whole human who has the internal permission to allow myself to find expression without editing.

The divorce is teaching me to be impossibly supple and open. I know I am strong enough to see the truth and handle it now. I feel energized. This is life. Happiness is not a perpetual state. It's not like saying, "I found Europe. I'm living in Europe now." You have to get happy with the process. To me, there's a real peace in accepting that, and being able to say life is never one thing. It's all things. The whole universe is expanding, stretching, tearing down, and creating, and we are made of the same stuff. We expand, contract, decay, and grow all at once. We are mirrors of the universe and the natural world and what created us. We are made like trees, with our roots firmly planted in the ground, and if we can see we are built to bend and give, then the winds of life will pass through our branches without breaking us. Some days it passes through with fury. Some days with a gentle caress. Each morning I wake with gratitude that I can have the confidence to meet these ups and downs without being uprooted. The faith to step into pain when it comes and the courage to let it ravage me and pass through instead of hanging on to it and letting it tear me down. Life is ever-changing. What is consistent is knowing I am up for anything. That I am never broken.

MY STORYBOOK ENDING isn't one written in Hollywood. I didn't get to ride off into the sunset with a cowboy. But I do get to ride off into the sunset with my son, myself intact, full of optimism for what I might experience and accomplish in my future and for what I will be able to teach my son. My innocence is not lost—it has been converted into wisdom.

The sensation we call "breaking" is the pain that comes from resisting truth. Life broke parts of me that needed to fall away for me to live an open and truthful life. But the only things that broke away were the things that did not serve me anymore. Life demanded that I get rid of my ego, my facade, my contrived safety nets, until I was reduced to my true nature, so it could shine unhindered. I needed to know great darkness to know my light. I needed to understand extreme constraint to know my freedom. I needed to face shame to know my own worth.

When angered I ask myself, "If I removed my anger or hurt from this situation and acted out of love and unity—if I acted from my highest self—what would I do now?" Hatred is hurt masquerading—it is an energy used to fool someone into thinking they are frightening when in truth they are frightened. It is used to defend a wound, and when we see it, we can see it is a neon sign advertising not the strength it boasts but pointing directly to a wound.

It's important to recognize when we feel hurt. Brendon Burchard, author of *The Motivation Manifesto*, says, "Integrity is learning to feel hurt but not integrate its darkness into our soul or cast it into another." Doing this for me means sitting with the hurt until I can transmute it into self-love. He also writes, "When loyalty is chosen over truth, corruption is near." When the need for someone else's love or approval outweighs one's own, self-betrayal is near. The world offers many opportunities to be small—it is our discipline and actions that lead to character and help us stand tall when faced with the temptation of being reactionary rather than self-empowered.

Love is the spring eternal. It is the healer of all wounds. It can be administered by yourself to yourself and be most effective. We do not need to wait for permission to be granted love and no one can deny us love. When we are in the eternal flowing river of love, our hurt feels small and can be washed away. We can experience the generosity and abundance we all inherit. Do not drown in hurt when you can swim in a sea of love. Pain is a thorn of truth waiting to be witnessed and then released. The spirit can no more hold on to pain than a branch the wind. Let it pass through you and then turn your mind once again to the bounty of love that exists exquisitely for us at all times. We can never be separate from love except in our forgetfulness.

I have been hurt but I am not hurt personified.

I have felt betrayed but I am not betraying.

I have simplified all feelings into two categories: one that expresses love and one that doesn't. The one that doesn't betrays my belief in and love for myself. Pettiness shows me I do not believe I can provide for myself. Jealousy shows I don't believe I am enough. Greed shows I feel I have to cheat and that I can't come by abundance honestly. Obsession is a lack of ability to release and feel the generosity love provides. It is never about the other person. It is always about my faith, love, and belief in myself and I look at the clues of self-hatred as miraculous teachers—I thank them for showing me the places I still need healing. I look for them with excitement. I welcome them in and ask them to come closer. All of me is welcome here, I say, even the imperfect parts. They hold the key to my growth. I thank them and I eagerly give them a seat at the table so I may know them better. These parts of us will not show up if we hold a hammer in our hands, if we beat ourselves up the second an imperfection rears its head. Next time you feel small say, Ah, there you are friend! Tell me about yourself! Where did you come from? The next time you feel jealous say, Hello! What part of you feels you alone are not enough? I am here to tell you that you are, and to bless that person and let it go and transmute the energy of jealousy for someone else into love for yourself, where it may serve you better. If we feel shame, be most tender, most kind. Say, come into the light so I might see you better—what, dear friend, makes you think you are somehow separate from love? What illusion are you suffering under? You are love! Always! Give me your worst secret and I will still show you a human deserving of kindness and together we can do better in our actions once we operate from a belief in our goodness rather than of our shame and unworthiness.

I love you and I want to see and know all of you, even the worst parts—especially those. All of you gets to be here, seen and loved.

It is a great fallacy to operate under the illusion that there is not enough love and so we must hoard, hang on, or somehow administer it like a limited resource. Giving love is not about the worthiness of the receiver. It's about the truth you wish to live by. Love knows not how you deem another worthy or not—it is not even yours to declare such things. It is impossible, in fact, and to deny another because you deem them unworthy is simply starving your own soul and creating a smallness inside you. It does not punish another to deny them love—it punishes you. Stop this self-abuse. Once and for all declare there is enough and that you will let love flow through you rather than cut your own self off from the source. If another is hurtful, give them the love that they so desperately thirst for, not knowing how to ask. Keep yourself safe, and create a distance if needed, but in your mind do not let smallness or obsessive or hurtful thoughts consume you. Give them love and flow on with your life.

There is love for us that exists at all times if we will but open ourselves to feel it. No one can deny us of it any more than they can deny us air to breathe or our thoughts to think. When we move away from love we become shells walking through a life that should be rich and fertile. I choose love. I choose an open heart.

Mercy

Simplicity does not come easy
When you're dreaming of being someone else
And grace you see is fleeting
When you're bleeding your inner self

Give mercy to me please
Have mercy I'm on my knees
I'm being broken again and again
I'll keep being broken until I remain
Open

When you're locked away, fighting shadows
A contstant battle trying to feel safe
When your armor starts killing you
'Cause it's causing you to sink beneath its weight

Call for mercy, won't you please
Call for mercy, drop to your knees
You're being broken, again and again
You'll keep being broken, till you remain
Open

Feel the pain, give in to it
Cry till you crack, that's how the light gets in
Set your weapons on the ground
Until you're naked and trembling now
And when you think you can't stand anymore

jewel

Give mercy, to someone in need
Give mercy, don't you see
Life will break our hearts again and again
And we'll keep being broken until we remain
Open

Don't you see, don't you see
Life will break your heart again and again
Lest you let yourself be broken until open
Let yourself be broken until open
I have broken
I am open

epilogue

July 2015. Greetings from Telluride. The weather is glorious. I hiked the Jud Wiebe Trail this morning and then sat in a café working on my book and album.

Kase is with Ty today, and I have enjoyed these rare luxurious hours of doing nothing but turning inward with no definition beating me to the draw. In this moment I am not mother, nor child, nor musician. I am the culmination of a million variances of light that swirl in here, within this flesh cathedral. This is my *I am*.

I am looking deep inside—not daughter, writer, nor woman, even. I am merely dancing inside here, enjoying the view from behind my eyes . . .

I'd like to share one of my earliest memories. I was at the bottom of the stairs in the unfinished basement of a home my parents were building in Anchorage. I was very small, because I remember holding on to the bottom stair for balance. I was down there by myself, looking up the dimly lit stairs, at the bright square of light that shown through the open door, the dark silhouette of my mother standing there, like a cookie cutter of a woman's form—long skirt, hair flipping just so at the shoulder.

She was calling, "Jewel . . . Jewel . . . are you down there? Jewel?"

In that moment, I was being entertained by the most vibrant frenzy of colors swirling inside myself. I had a sense of great space inside me, a living, breathing darkness lit by these colors, almost like living stained glass shining within the walls of a great cathedral. Like curtains of northern lights shimmering and undulating in this vast space within myself.

"Jewel." My mother's voice came calling again. I looked from behind my eyes and up at her long shadow, unfolding like an accordion across the geometric zig and zag of the stairs. I knew that was my mother's voice—but her voice was not her. I knew that was my mother's shadow, but that shadow was not her. I heard the echo of her voice bounce against the wall.

"Jewel, how did you get down here?" she said, her eyes seeing me now, but her eyes were not her. Just like my body was no more me than the echo of her voice was her.

I looked inside myself, at the colors dancing. I remember thinking, *Am I Jewel?* I remember consciously connecting my name to the colors. I was the colors. For years I would have these strange experiences, aware of myself, alive in here, like the operator of a magnificent machine that was growing miraculously around me.

Another vivid memory like this was during a play at our church. I was sitting on the hard bench with my mother, father, and younger brother. My older brother was in a play with other nine-year-olds. Every child onstage was nine. To distinguish roles, they dressed the part. The nine-year-old boss wore a tie and suit and sat behind a cardboard desk they had made. The nine-year-old mom wore a dress and a wig and comforted a nine-year-old baby who sucked on a pacifier and wore comical diapers.

Other nine-year-olds "drove" to work, walking behind a cardboard cut-out of a car window. I was so stricken by the moment I almost became ill. I looked over at my mother and father, and all I could think was, *We are all playing roles.* We were all the same, deciding who we were and playing dress up and playing our roles. I suddenly could see no difference between any of us, and I became so frightened that it was like all the life had been sucked out of life. We left the church and drove in our car (it was much more clever than a cardboard one, but it felt just as silly all of a sudden, just as self-made and unreal) and went to see my brother play soccer. I remember all the kids running across the field, and the bright sun of the summer day, but it felt like none of it was real. We were all in the same play, pretending.

It took me a long time to make peace with this one. In time I found it creative, even, in its truth. We are playing roles.

And here I am again. I am forty-one. My feet quit growing farther from my face quite a while ago, but my body continues its wise evolution, and I am awake in here. Like Plato's theory of forms and the allegory of the cave, we witness shadows cast on the wall and strive to know the shadows are not reality, and that like those prisoners chained within the walls of the cave, we are constantly tasked to know reality beyond the shadows cast forth upon our world. Plato's *Phaedo* contains similar imagery to the allegory of the cave; a philosopher recognizes that before philosophy (what I call self-reflection), his soul was "a veritable prisoner fast bound within his body . . . and that instead of investigating reality by itself and in itself it is compelled to peer through the bars of its prison." Descartes said, "I think, therefore I am." But for me perhaps it is more accurately described as "I perceive what I think, therefore I am." If I am able to witness my thoughts, I am not my thoughts. I am something other. And this Otherness is far wiser than my mind or my experience. It has a greater sense of intelligence and is the voice that speaks to me in my quiet moments when my mind is still. It has been with me since I was a child and remained even when I turned my ear away. It is in each of us.

This has been a long and imperfect journey. It is a journey I am still on. I will always be on. And it is one I would like to share with you. I want company along my road. This is an invitation to question your life and, should you desire, to find the courage to erase the lines that imprison you and to reimagine a better you. And if you do not get it just right (none of us do), you are invited to keep redrawing and redrawing until you feel your outer world matches your inner life.

If falling short of our goals is truly what terrifies us, then we should do away with half measures. The notion that dipping a toe in the water somehow protects us is nothing short of fear propagation—and in fact guarantees the hurt we fear. Be bold. Name what you want. Give it voice and then give it action. Success is not guaranteed but commitment and courage are the only insurance we have.

This is serious. Every day that passes is another day closer to looking back on your life and seeing whether you have done something meaningful. Don't let the days pass without doing something great. Be the architect of your dreams.

WHOLE HUMAN

part of me dies
while part of me comes alive
both equally slow
an eclipse of self
in same body
one going
one coming
and me in here
somehow
watching the self I built
all these years
deconstruct
while at once
I build a new self

grim reaper
and creator

I am in the dark
it seems
the certainty of my old life
gone
my old beliefs

conspicuously absent
my old loved ones
starkly missing

but it is not just darkness
I am in
it is potent in here
womblike
my ears ring
dark matter making crystalline
    sounds
as if in outer space
I drift lost
but not lost
watching the ego I had built shatter
drift away
grief filling every cell
as I mourn the loss of her
tears bending what light
finds its way to me
but in the lunar distance
I see a horizon
faint as a fingerprint

quiet as a sigh not yet exhaled
I see the blueprint
the seed
being sown
of my new self
and I like her

at once I grieve and rejoice
as I give body to this seed
as I lend flesh and bone and belief
to rebuild myself

this rebirth is painful
as all birth is

true creation is not all zen
once an idea is dreamed the
    wrestling
must begin of embodying it
drawing it out of spirit
and into the physical world

artist:
part dreamer
part sculptor
part executioner

things must be carved away
to create the shape that resonates
and expresses outwardly

the inward dream
and
I don't want to be
just an artist
of art
I want to be an artist
of self
and so the emptiness I bear
to create song and poem
is turned on myself
and the art becomes
not just song
not just life
but me

most importantly
the art
is me

I could no longer sit
like a counterfeit
in the shape a child dreamed
simply from fear

I dream a new dream
I dream it well, sometimes
sometimes it is clumsy
I am learning but
I see it
and I am willing to walk

through the fire
of creation
to embody it

but such sadness
comes in waves
as I grieve the girl
I lovingly built
as I say goodbye

kiss her forehead
smooth and shining
kiss her armor
a little dinged-up
a little war-torn
kiss her mouth
half starved most of her life
and I thank her
from the bottom of my soul

thank you thank you thank you
girl for carrying me all this way
(such a distance!)
through shit and muck
and spittle and
and for being brave enough
and soft enough during it
to allow me to remain whole
inside

so that I may now
stand above the burial
of my dead ego

oh the sorrow!
how I cry!

before I lose myself
in the sorrow of her cooling outline
I force my head
back to the horizon
to the task at hand
and get about the work
of rewriting
redrafting
rebuilding

no editing
no shame
no apologies

permission granted
as I create myself
with every color
this time
I need not be just one

whole.
human.

afterword

What is in this book took me forty years to learn. My hope is that anyone in need who reads this might be helped by witnessing what I have gone through. Looking back, I can see the lessons that have been critical to my success and resilience, and if they can help you to get where you are going in less time and with less pain than it took me, then this book will have been worth writing.

Hard wood grows slowly. Be thoughtful about the shape you want to grow into, and be mindful that there is no shortcut to strength and character. Have the patience to allow yourself and your goals to develop.

You can't outrun your pain. You are strong enough to face whatever is in front of you. Medicating your pain will only bring more pain. The only genuine shortcut life offers is facing your feelings. They won't kill you. Feelings are your soul's way of communicating. Pain is trying to teach you something, and if you don't listen now, it will speak louder and louder until it is heard.

afterword

Emotional English. What emotional language were you raised with in your home? Volatile? Avoidant? Passive? Abusive? Loving? If there were dynamics you feel did not serve you, identify what new language you wish to speak in the family of your making, with your own husband, wife, child, or friend. Make a plan to learn it that you can execute. Spend time with those whose Emotional English you admire, or talk with a life coach or therapist to help learn to avoid repeating the cycles that have been handed down through generations. It can end and begin with you.

Spend time in silence. Take time to get to know yourself and your genius in stillness. This also lets your soul speak. Its voice is quiet and you must choose to turn an ear to it. Any endeavor in your life, be it creative, business, or personal, will benefit from spending time alone and exploring your own thoughts, ideas, and dreams.

Access your Greater Intelligence. Your mind is a wonderful tool, but it is not all that we are. Get out from under your critical thoughts. Practice meditation or prolonged prayer. Sit in nature or write. Do things that help quiet the circular thoughts of your mind and that allow you to gain the greater understanding and acceptance that is available beyond what your mind offers. This can foster inspiration. A eureka moment. A flash of insight that comes from beyond what your education or experience make you capable of. You are experiencing your whole self when your body has a calm feeling, rather than an anxious energy.

Establish a gratitude practice. Gratitude is incredibly healing because our reality becomes what we perceive. See not just what is going wrong in your life, but actively engage in and acknowledge what is right. Let it wash over your being and fill your heart with the calming peace of gratitude.

Flip the switch and retrain your brain. Identify negative thought patterns and learn to starve them. Don't indulge in fear, worry, jealousy, anger, resentment, lies, or inferiority. I have found it best to start with just one idea you want to replace at a time. Establish and feed positive thought patterns. Joy, peace, love, hope, humility, kindness, empathy, and truth. Create a light switch in your mind. When you have a disruptive or damaging thought, intervene by flipping the switch and replace it with a thought that is in line with your true goals and values. Repeat the thoughts you wish to have often enough until the habit creates its own momentum, forming new neural pathways. With time the habitual effect becomes second nature, and you become a much more positive person who is able to create change in the moment.

Find the antidote. If you are consumed by self-doubting or self-loathing internal voices, ask yourself what the opposite of those thoughts are. If you are afraid you are not capable of something, intervene each time you think that, and replace it with the new thought: I am capable. Do it again and again until you feel your anxiety lessen. With time and practice, the anxiety will subside altogether.

Create a home for happiness. Happiness is not a perpetual state. It has an ebb and flow, but it can be encouraged. Do things that lend themselves to the happiness you desire. Exercise. Eat well. Do something that makes you feel joy, even when you don't feel like it. Surround yourself with people you admire and who add substance to your life. Soon peace and satisfaction come as your life creates a discipline that is the reward for living thoughtfully.

Practice being present. "Being here now" is the only chance we have to make new choices. Fear-based thoughts cause us to live in a past that we project onto the future, robbing us of being awake in the only moment that exists for us to create change within. Observation causes us to suspend judgment so we can use our senses fully. It forces us to be present. Begin with small steps, like noticing each time your feet hit the ground in the morning. Extend your mindfulness to noticing the feel of each footstep as you walk up a flight of stairs. Watch your hands. They are the servants of your thoughts. Count how many times they greet someone or wave hello.

afterword

Being a witness to your behavior is the first step in meaningful change.
This allows us to be present without judgment. This is critical because I
have learned that when I judge myself harshly, I am not able to see the
truth about myself. But when I witness myself with love, without
judgment, it allows me to identify patterns that might be less than
desirable. We cannot change what we are unwilling to see. If you can
witness your behavior, that means you are something *other* than your
behavior. In seeing your behavior, there is hope of change in the future.

Brilliant resilience. Identify the natural gifts or beliefs that served you as
a child but that may now be creating limits to experiencing intimacy
and joy. Does the loyalty that once served you now keep you beholden
to others? Does the competitive spirit that helped you rise to great
heights now keep you from connecting? Has the natural independence
that once helped you to leave a bad situation now caused a stumbling
block when it comes to true intimacy and trusting someone to help you?
Look for areas you feel blocked and meditate on them. Ask yourself
whether they started out as instincts that worked for your well-being or
survival but now may feel stiff and hold you back. Learn to let them go.

Believe in the law of enough. Don't accept the fear that that scarcity
exists in any corner of your life. There is enough love, enough time,
enough healing to go around. Give what you wish to receive.

Let go of what does not serve you. Make a commitment to choose
happiness over anger, love over pain. Let go of hurt and resentment.
Let go of what weighs you down and keeps you from ascending to the
height you choose. The cup is half full and half empty simultaneously.
Your reality will be defined by which you choose.

A soul cannot be broken. It is not a teacup. If you have suffered abuse of
any kind, know that perfection exists untarnished within you. You need
not fix yourself so much as exhume it. Engage in a loving archaeological
dig back to yourself. Let all that is not yours within you fall away until
only your real nature remains. You are trusting. You are loving. You are

worthy. Your innocence is not lost when you are hurt, but converted into wisdom.

Be an Every Day Angel. Nothing saves us from our own misery like community service or helping a friend. Be less self-centered by thinking. Give to charity, donate time, learn about how other people live. Your self-esteem will be genuinely bolstered as you give to others, and it will also help bring gratitude to your heart, as it will inevitably remind you of how much you have to be grateful for.

Embrace imperfection. Life is a journey and there is no destination. There is nothing static to life. Employing rigid standards inhibits growth and makes you unhappy. Remove the armor that weighs you down and cuts you off from your joy. Instead, learn where safety exists for you, in the process of accepting yourself and others as they are right now. Be brave—be more open, more yielding, more transparent.

Give internal permission. To be the kind of person you want to be and live the kind of life you want, the only person you need permission from is you. No one is standing in your way but you. Give yourself permission to be as radical as you need to live the life you want. Be bold in all the parts of your being. Be as silly, serious, seductive, or spiritual as you want in any given moment—or all at once! Invite your whole self to the table. The hurt child, the brave, the shy. Don't let shame, fear, or doubt cause you to self-edit in an effort to find approval in any other person. When you give yourself permission to be the sum of all your parts, you will be amazed to find that others do as well. You don't need anyone's permission to be exactly who you want to be.

Stay sensitive. By numbing pain you also numb your ability to experience joy. If someone or something has hurt you, don't be hurt twice by choosing to limit your ability to ever experience trust or joy again. Being vulnerable in the world may cause you to feel pain, but you are strong and can let it pass. It will not defeat you. Let your emotions do what they are best at: communicating how safe, happy, and fulfilled you are in your life. If you cut yourself off from your feelings, your soul has no feedback system, and you will be deprived of that deeper sense of satisfaction and purpose every day.

Let go of shame. Shame does nothing but drown us in that which we wish to be free from. Communication is the antithesis of shame. Give your worst fears a voice—speak out loud your deepest, most shameful thoughts. None of us have a secret shame that others don't share in the world. Find out that you are deserving of love despite your flaws. Find a notebook or a loving friend to be truly seen by. We cannot change what we are unwilling to bring into the light of day.

What's simple is true. We are so busy looking for and working toward the things that will make us happy that we blow right by our actual happiness, thinking surely it must be more complicated. But often the things that make us truly happy are much simpler: sitting quietly under a tree. Being present with your child while you read a book to them. Living in a smaller home, perhaps, so you can work less and have more quality time with your family. Doing fewer "enrichment" activities so that you and your children can experience the joy of play. Peace and patience are learned by practicing.

Choose love. You can boil down all interactions to two categories: ones that grow love and ones that diminish it. Choose love. Do not choose how to behave based on who is in front of you. Choose because it is a value you hold in high esteem and because it is how you want to experience your own life. Choose love.

If you want to be a warrior for change and mindfulness, visit my website, Jeweljk.com, where I break down each of my guiding principles into simple challenges you can apply to your own life. We are never broken. Join the community.

acknowledgments

I'd like to thank my editor, Sarah Hochman, for her patience and un-flagging help while I learned the ropes of long-form writing. Thank you to Virginia Davis, Lee Greene, Alan Bershaw, West Kennerly, and Eric Greenspan for your support over the years. Thank you to everyone at Blue Rider Press and Penguin Random House who had a hand in publishing this book. I thank all those who have helped me on my path, and also those who stood in my way. I know my strength and worth through you all. I thank my son for inspiring me to be the kind of woman I want him to know.

credits

credits

"Life Uncommon": Written by Jewel. © Wiggly Tooth Music (ASCAP) administered by Downtown Music Publishing LLC.

"Little Sister": Written by Jewel. © Wiggly Tooth Music (ASCAP) administered by Downtown Music Publishing LLC.

"Mercy": Written by Jewel Kilcher. © Wiggly Tooth Music (ASCAP) administered by Downtown Music Publishing LLC.

"My Father's Daughter": Words and music by Lisa Carver and Jewel Kilcher. © 2009 Stage Three Songs (ASCAP)/Carvee Tunes (ASCAP). All rights administered by BMG Rights Management (US) LLC. Used by permission. All rights reserved.

"Near You Always": Written by Jewel. © Wiggly Tooth Music (ASCAP) administered by Downtown Music Publishing LLC.

"No Good in Goodbye": © Wiggly Tooth Music (ASCAP) administered by Downtown Music Publishing LLC.

"No More Heartaches": Written by Jewel. © Wiggly Tooth Music (ASCAP) administered by Downtown Music Publishing LLC.

"Painter": © Wiggly Tooth Music (ASCAP) administered by Downtown Music Publishing LLC.

"Pieces of You": © Wiggly Tooth Music (ASCAP) administered by Downtown Music Publishing LLC.

"Satisfied": Written by Liz Rose and Jewel Kilcher. © Warner-Tamerlane Publishing Corp. / Orbison Music LLC (BMI). All rights reserved.

"Standing Still": Written by Rick Nowels and Jewel Kilcher. © 2001 Spirit Catalog Holdings, S.à.r.l., and Wiggly Tooth Music. All rights for Spirit Catalog Holdings, S.à.r.l. controlled and administered by Spirit Two Music, Inc. (ASCAP). International copyright secured. All rights reserved. Used by permission.

"Ten": Written by Dave Berg and Jewel Kilcher. © 2010 Spirit Catalog Holdings, S.à.r.l., Stupid Boy Music, and Wiggly Tooth Music. All rights for Spirit Catalog Holdings, S.à.r.l., and Stupid Boy Music controlled and administered by Spirit Two Nashville (ASCAP). International copyright secured. All rights reserved. Used by permission.

"Two Hearts Breaking": Written by Jewel. © Wiggly Tooth Music (ASCAP) administered by Downtown Music Publishing LLC.

"What You Are": Written by Dave Berg and Jewel Kilcher. © 2010 Spirit Catalog Holdings, S.à.r.l., Stupid Boy Music, and Wiggly Tooth Music. All rights for Spirit Catalog Holdings, S.à.r.l., and Stupid Boy Music controlled and administered by Spirit Two Nashville (ASCAP). International copyright secured. All rights reserved. Used by permission.

"Who Will Save Your Soul": © Wiggly Tooth Music (ASCAP) administered by Downtown Music Publishing LLC.

about the author

Jewel is an American singer, songwriter, poet, actress, philanthropist, and mother. She has received four Grammy Award nominations and has sold more than thirty million albums worldwide. She is the founder of Project Clean Water, and author of the *New York Times* bestseller *A Night Without Armor: Poems* as well as two books for children. Raised in Homer, Alaska, she currently lives in Tennessee and Colorado with her son.